CW00344777

99
ICONIC
MOMENTS IN
SCOTTISH
FOOTBALL

99

ICONIC
MOMENTS IN
SCOTTISH
FOOTBALL

Mark Poole

**From the Famous to the Obscure,
Scotland's Glorious, Unusual and
Cult Games, Players and Events**

First published by Pitch Publishing, 2023

Pitch Publishing
9 Donnington Park,
85 Birdham Road,
Chichester,
West Sussex,
PO20 7AJ
www.pitchpublishing.co.uk
info@pitchpublishing.co.uk

A CIP catalogue record is available for this book
from the British Library.

ISBN 978 1 80150 506 2

Typesetting and origination by Pitch Publishing
Printed and bound in Great Britain by TJ Books, Padstow

Contents

This book is dedicated to Susi, Vita, Cosmo, Mum, Dad and Mike. Thanks Dad for taking me to Hibs games (and that Celtic game at Tynecastle!) in the '80s!

Acknowledgements

Thanks to everyone at Pitch, to everyone at the National Library of Scotland, and to Dad for translating the verbose *France Football* article!

Introduction

Finding out about St Mirren winning the Barcelona Cup was my first step down the path to writing this book.

Led down a fascinating rabbit hole by a post from the National Library of Scotland, I stumbled across a picture of 1920s St Mirren dignitaries with the Barcelona Cup. What's the Barcelona Cup? And how come our very own Buddies won it?

Further down the hole, I found out that Motherwell had won the same Catalan trophy too – and a few days earlier they'd also won the Copa del Rey.

I love stories like that; the sort of ideas that I like to research and write for magazines.

I quickly compiled a list of my favourite moments in Scottish football and was soon approaching 100. There was a book in this – a curated list of assorted anecdotes from Scotland's unique football history.

The list eventually swelled to 117 moments. The 99 that I researched, wrote up and included here are chosen not just because they're the best ones, but for their variety too; I resisted the temptation to include too many classic cup finals or glorious European adventures.

So Kilmarnock thrashing Eintracht Frankfurt, Hibs finally winning the Scottish Cup again, and Rangers and Aberdeen's epic 1987 League Cup Final all narrowly missed out. But I had to draw the line somewhere. Maybe I'll write about them all later. And there are plenty more stories about Killie, Hibs, Rangers and Aberdeen in here.

As well as choosing as many different types of stories as possible – from the glorious to the obscure; from cult players to off-pitch intrigue and loads more between – I've included teams of all sizes, from across the country (first up, Royal Albert).

I found out things that I didn't previously know about famous stories and I stumbled across fascinating hidden gems that I couldn't believe I didn't already know about.

And although I have my own club – and assorted opinions on just about every other team in the country – I strived to choose stories fairly. Not by 'balancing out' East Fife winning the Scottish Cup, for example, by finding a story for their local rivals Cowdenbeath, but by treating every club fairly and without prejudice. And if it's balance that we're after, it helps that Celtic and Rangers both outclassed Leeds in the European Cup.

Apart from the final three, top, moments, there's no specific order to the rest of the book. It's not chronological; it's not a countdown. I took the same approach as how I imagine a band compiles an album, giving myself the freedom to mix it up in a flow that felt good, and with a few natural segues between pieces that sit nicely next to each other.

I've loved researching and writing this book – the subject matter is so far up my street that it's moved in next door. There aren't many experiences as satisfying as finding that extra bit of detail and colour that's been lying dormant for many decades, waiting for you, in an old newspaper in a library reading room, and breathing new life into it. I hope that you enjoy reading it just as much.

1

Saturday, 6 June 1891

James McLuggage Scores the World's First Penalty

The International Football Association Board's 1891 Annual General Meeting was particularly productive. In spite of their grand name, IFAB, the guardians of football's laws, only featured representatives from Scotland, England, Ireland and Wales. Even now, the UK FAs still hold half of the decision-making power on football rules.

At that busy meeting at Glasgow's Alexandra Hotel, four men – Messrs Snedden of Scotland, Crump of England, Reid of Ireland and Hunter of Wales – formalised multiple innovations that are still integral elements of the game.

They formalised pitch and goal dimensions, ball sizes and weights, and the latest pitch markings – including, for the first time, a centre spot with its now-so-familiar ten-yard circle.

They also revolutionised the referee's role and introduced linesmen. Previously, the referee operated from the side of the pitch, while two umpires were on it. Snedden, Crump, Reid and Hunter decreed that umpires should be removed and that the referee should be allowed on to the pitch, with wide-ranging powers, assisted by neutral linesmen. Basically the arrangement that continues to this day.

But probably the most controversial rule change ratified in Glasgow that evening was the introduction of penalties.

Previously, fouls or handballs right up to the goal line were rewarded just by free kicks, which were easy for defenders and goalkeepers to block, and which consequently rewarded deliberate rule-breaking. Penalties would change that, but, like any football innovation, the idea was treated with suspicion, particularly from 'gentlemen' footballers who couldn't tolerate the mere suggestion that a player would seek to gain advantage from foul play. Remarkable sporting all-rounder C.B. Fry reportedly said that the new rule was an insult to sportsmen and that it was based on the assumption that players behaved 'like cads of the most unscrupulous kidney'.

But the traditionalists would have to tolerate the insult. Penalties were introduced, initially to be taken from any point on a new penalty line, running across the pitch. The goalie could advance off his line, but no more than six yards, and all other players had to be at least six yards behind the penalty taker.

Just four days after the IFAB meeting, and only 12 miles to the east, at Mavisbank Park in Airdrie, Royal Albert player James McLuggage took – and scored – the world's first ever penalty, against Airdrie.

The *Coatbridge Express* reported that, about 15 minutes into the final of the Airdrie Charity Cup, the referee, James Robertson, 'pulled up Mitchell for throwing Lambie and granted a foul under the new law'.

The *Scottish Sport* reported that the players were initially confused by the new rule and tried to form a wall between McLuggage and veteran Airdrie goalkeeper James Connor, until Mr Robertson set them straight, and McLuggage made history by shooting past Connor.

McLuggage, who was born in Ireland and moved to Scotland as a child, had an otherwise modest football career. Royal Albert still exist, and now play towards the bottom end of the West of Scotland Football League. Mavisbank is now a neighbourhood park. The location and protagonists may be unremarkable, but they were central to a key event in global football history.

2

Tuesday, 3 October 2000

Claudio Caniggia Signs for Dundee

Claudio Caniggia was a global star: lightning-fast, skilful and with an eye for goal, he was one of Argentina's best players of his generation, and one of the most popular too. It helped, of course, that he scored the goal that knocked Brazil out of the 1990 World Cup. And, to make matters even better, he looked like he was in Bon Jovi, with his devilish good looks and long blond hair.

By 2000, he'd played 47 times for Argentina and his club career had taken in River Plate, Boca Juniors, Atalanta, Roma and various other top-flight European clubs. So it was quite the transfer coup when he signed for Dundee.

It was an era when – inspired by a generous Sky TV contract – the misguided buzz-phrase in Scottish football was 'speculate to accumulate'. Dundee's owners, the Marr brothers, possibly took this phrase to heart even more than anyone else.

The first piece of the Marrs' unlikely cosmopolitan jigsaw was the recruitment of Ivano Bonetti as player-manager. They'd clearly chosen him less for his managerial experience – he didn't have any – and more for his sexy, burgeoning contacts book. His assistant manager was his brother – and former Italy international – Dario, who'd played alongside Caniggia at Hellas Verona.

The Bonettis made a lot of eye-catching signings, including Julián Speroni, Temuri Ketsbaia, Fabián Caballero,

Georgi Nemsadze, Zurab Khizanishvili, Fan Zhiyi and Juan Sara. They were all talented; quite a few were very famous, but it was typically the less well-known ones, like Speroni and Sara, who were more successful at Dens.

The exception was Caniggia; the most famous was also a huge success. At 33 he may have been a few years past his prime, but he would almost certainly still have been playing for Argentina if he hadn't refused to comply with manager Daniel Passarella's infamous no-earrings-homosexuals-or-long-hair decree. And it soon became clear that the man who the Argentina fans called *El Pájaro* hadn't lost his talent or his pace.

Dundee fans snapped up blond wigs and Argentina shirts and flags in tribute to their new hero. The club shop apparently ran out of enough letters to put on shirts because so many fans wanted the global star's name writ large across their shoulders.

Season ticket sales broke the 4,000 barrier for the first time since the '80s. Two and a half thousand fans filled the away end at Pittodrie to see Caniggia's debut. *El Pájaro* came on as a sub, Philip McGuire was sent off for a bad foul on him, and he grabbed his first goal for the club, with a characteristic run and neat finish.

For his next trick, at home against Motherwell, he scored with a 20-yard lob. Unfortunately, Dundee lost that match, 2-1. That combination of individual brilliance and ultimate disappointment characterised Bonetti's period in charge, as the club – despite their international stars – finished sixth in the league in his first season in charge, then ninth in his second, which would be Bonetti's last.

Meanwhile, Caniggia continued to score regularly – including in victories against Dundee United and Rangers, both of which went down particularly well – and earn plaudits from opposition managers. He was also shortlisted for the player of the year prize.

He was even immortalised on the pages of the *Beano*, and some Dundee matches were broadcast across Latin America; it's fascinating to speculate about what Saturday-morning bar patrons by the Copacabana made of matches like Dunfermline 1 Dundee 0. Hopefully they're still talking about David Moss's towering header – the only goal of that game – to this day.

If the Bonettis' little black books were impressive, Caniggia's contained the holiest grail of all: he was best mates with Diego Maradona. Inevitably, Dundee soon reached the next level of frenzied speculation: when would *El Diez* turn up on Tayside? Even if just to watch his pal play from the Bobby Cox Stand, or to wave to fans from the centre circle at half-time? But it soon looked like it would be even better than that: in January 2001, the club announced that they'd been speaking to Maradona and that it was looking 'increasingly likely' that he would play for them in a friendly against Napoli at Dens Park.

But it never happened. Getting off a flight from Cuba to Rome, Diego was arrested for alleged tax fraud and Bonetti soon had to admit, 'I do not see the possibility of a game involving Diego going ahead during this season.'

And it wouldn't happen any other time either, because Caniggia had been so successful at Dens that Dundee couldn't realistically hold on to him. In May, he was sold to Rangers for £850,000.

Unfortunately, Dundee treating the Bonettis' contacts books like an all-you-can-eat-buffet had unsurprising results. In 2003, at about £20m in debt, the club went into administration and had to sell Dens Park to survive.

Although the overall Bonetti experiment had been wildly overambitious, the recruitment of Caniggia was a roaring success. He'd boosted the club's turnover and been sold for a profit. But, much more importantly, he brought joy and excitement to the fans.

3

Wednesday, 24 May 1972

Rangers Win the Cup Winners' Cup

In May 1972, victorious Rangers celebrated winning the European Cup Winners' Cup at the Camp Nou – not, as the players would have wanted, on the pitch, but in the dressing room. But seven months earlier, in another dressing room in another great Iberian city, they thought that they'd already been knocked out of the competition.

In the second round, the Gers had beaten Sporting Lisbon 3-2 at home, on – according to the *Press and Journal* – 'a night of brilliance and blundering', as Colin Stein and Willie Henderson put the Scots three up after half an hour but they ended up winning by just one goal.

There was more blundering – this time by a Dutchman – in Portugal, where Sporting won by the same score and the match went to extra time. Both teams scored once more. It was the first season that the away goals rule applied in the Cup Winners' Cup, a rule that included goals in extra time, but the referee – beer salesman Laurens van Ravens – clearly didn't know that detail, and ordered a penalty shoot-out.

Rangers missed three of their first four spot-kicks, while Sporting scored four on the trot. While the Portuguese players and fans celebrated, Rangers retreated, dejected, to their dressing room, until journalist John Fairgrieve came in to tell them that the away goals rule still applied in extra time, and manager Willie Waddell marched out to find a UEFA official.

The *Press and Journal* said, 'Then came the arguments and counter arguments by officials who waved rule books as they became heated over the entire situation. Eventually UEFA officials were called into the argument and the matter was resolved – Rangers were IN and Sporting were OUT.'

The Sporting fans must have been livid, but UEFA didn't seem too bothered by Van Ravens' mistake: they entrusted him with the second leg of the UEFA Cup Final in the same season, between Spurs and Wolves. Thankfully, it didn't go to extra time.

In the meantime, in their next two rounds, against Torino and then Bayern Munich, Rangers defended heroically in the first legs, both of which were away and both of which they drew 1-1. An Alex MacDonald goal from a Tommy McLean cross at home in front of 75,000 fans against Serie A leaders Torino was enough to send the Light Blues into the semis, where they were imperious in the second leg against the Bavarian giants, when Ibrox was packed again.

The *Press and Journal* judged Franz Beckenbauer 'too cool and cocky' in Glasgow and Gerd Müller 'seldom seen', and reported, 'The Germans had no excuses in defeat. They were up against a team their masters in every sense of the term after the sensational opening goal in 60 seconds by Sandy Jardine.'

The match's two goals were similar: Jardine and teenager Derek Parlane – on his European debut, deputising for crocked skipper John Greig – crashing unstoppable shots past Sepp Maier.

Rangers had overcome top-class opponents to reach their third Cup Winners' Cup Final, against Dynamo Moscow, and the good news was that Greig had recovered from injury.

The 16,000 Rangers fans who made their way to Barcelona were in high spirits, and initially had lots to celebrate. Halfway through the first half, Stein burst through the defence to collect a long pass, and blasted the ball into the roof of the net. Crowds of fans rushed on to the pitch waving huge Union Jacks and held up play for several minutes.

Then Willie Johnston scored twice, either side of half-time – first with a header from a great Dave Smith pass, and then with a low, hard shot from a long kick from keeper Peter McCloy – to make it 3-0.

But Dynamo brought on substitute Vladimir Eshtrekov, who pulled one back in the 59th minute, two minutes after coming on. The Russians threw everything at Rangers, narrowly missing several chances, and forcing McCloy into two great saves, while Jardine had to clear a shot off the line.

And with five minutes to go, Aleksandr Makhovikov reduced the deficit to just one. Shortly after Rangers kicked off, hundreds of fans ran on to the pitch, holding up play until they could be removed. Then there were just a few minutes left for Rangers to hold on.

And at the final whistle many more fans took to the pitch. The Guardia Civil drew their batons, some fans threw bottles, and Rangers' reward for several excellent performances had to be presented to Greig in a room under the stands.

Because of the pitch invasion before full time, Dynamo lodged an appeal with UEFA, but – three weeks later – the governing body upheld the result, while also banning Rangers from European competition for two years, which was later reduced to one on appeal.

But – alongside the fan pitch invasions – Willie Waddell and his players had deservedly triumphed against a succession of top-quality sides to lift European football's second-greatest trophy. And they eventually got to celebrate in front of their fans, in a cup parade on the back of a lorry at Ibrox. All after it had briefly looked like they wouldn't make it past the second round.

4

Tuesday, 28 March 2023

Great Goals 1: Scott McTominay Strikes Spain Again

Scotland boss Steve Clarke had an unusual 'problem'. He had two of the world's best left-backs in his squad: Arsenal's Kieran Tierney and Liverpool's Andy Robertson. To make his pleasing conundrum even trickier, they were very similar: they both loved to bomb forward.

Should he choose one and leave the other out, or could he somehow squeeze them both into the team?

Previous Scotland bosses had struggled to answer that question. But not Clarke.

He settled on a 3-5-2 formation with Robertson as the attacking wing-back and Tierney on the left of the back three. Tierney, after all, could also excel at centre-back, although it wasn't his preferred position.

So was this a demotion for Tierney? Not a bit of it. Clarke gave him licence to break forward, in central positions as well as on the wing, while his two defensive partners covered for him at the back. It worked a treat. Including – in March 2023 – against Spain.

Scotland's second Euro 2024 qualifying match was one of Hampden's greatest nights. And the party really started early in the second half, when Tierney popped up to seize on a loose Spanish pass in his own half. And he was off.

He burst down the left wing, with Dani Carvajal giving chase. The five-time Champions League winner was gaining on the former Celtic man, who started to slow down. Carvajal leaned in for the challenge, but with exquisite timing Tierney suddenly accelerated again, leaving his illustrious opponent far behind him.

That audacious piece of skill and bravado would have made anything that came after it seem average by comparison. So what came after? Tierney continued his run, his cross broke to the onrushing Scott McTominay – who had timed his run perfectly – and the Manchester United midfielder smacked it through defender David Garcia's legs, past €80m keeper Kepa Arrizabalaga, and into the net.

Scotland 2 Spain 0. Hampden went wild.

We'd known we were good; we knew we were in with an outside chance of a great result if we didn't give them time on the ball and if we played to our potential. We'd gone one up early in the first half, but that slender lead against such aristocrats comes with its own nerves. The second goal gave us confidence. We weren't home and dried yet – far from it, with 40 minutes to go against Spain – but this was looking good.

And 2-0 it remained, with both sides making some chances but not converting them – although John McGinn came close to making it three, with an in-swinging free kick. It was a great win, which left Scotland top of the group on six points from two games, three ahead of Spain and – crucially – five ahead of Norway. And then they won their next two games too, against Norway and Georgia, in a brilliant first half of the qualifying campaign. But the main thing on that night was the glory of a fantastic performance and a great result.

And the other goal on the night? McTominay had scored that too – set up by Scotland's other top-class attacking left-back, Andy Robertson. Sometimes international managers have to fit their tactics around the players that they have. Clarke was rewarded for doing just that, and for doing it brilliantly.

5

Thursday, 16 April 1964

East Stirling and Clydebank
(Briefly) Merge

In some countries it's not unusual for struggling football clubs to merge. In Scotland it's rare. Struggling clubs sometimes shut down and reappear in the lower leagues, but usually stumble onwards, belligerently but proudly tolerating the dwindling on-pitch fortunes and leaking ceilings that are the price for maintaining their individuality and identity, as part of the rich tapestry of Scotland's distinctive, detailed and often humble football culture.

The small number of exceptions proves the rule. The merger of Inverness Thistle and Caledonian was controversial but forward-thinking. Another of the small handful of notable examples was far stranger.

East Stirling weren't even really struggling when their directors, businessmen Jack and Charles Steedman, announced in April 1964 that they would be merging the club with Clydebank Juniors and moving then to Kilbowie Park in Clydebank.

East Stirling had just come bottom of Division One, but the very fact that they'd been rubbing shoulders with Rangers, Hibs, Kilmarnock, Hearts, Dunfermline, Dundee, Aberdeen and Celtic – for only their second season in the top flight – was something that a club of their size was rightly proud of. It was thanks largely to the ambition of the Steedmans, but there was no desperate need to gamble on engineering a situation to try and become an established top-tier club.

Nevertheless, the Steedmans announced, 'Insufficient spectators have been coming through the Firs Park turnstiles to pay the basic expenses of a First Division club.'

The merger came at a time when Scotland's incredible massive postwar attendances were starting to decline, as other leisure opportunities sprung up to rival football. For the same reason, Clyde had recently tried to merge with East Kilbride Juniors, without success.

East Stirling's fans were livid to have their club wrestled 30 miles away from them, and started to fight the merger and relocation in the courts. Meanwhile, journalist Raymond Jacobs predicted challenges ahead: 'A mere shift in location does not, of course, guarantee success. These days the local public, however large their numbers may be, will support only a team who achieve something.'

The Clydebank public, initially at least, seemed pretty keen to support the team, who, as part of their reinvention as ES Clydebank, started playing in a new all-white strip.

Their first home game, against East Stirling's erstwhile neighbours Stenhousemuir, attracted 6,000 fans. But – spoiler alert – their last home game of the season, against Alloa, attracted just 554, apparent proof of Mr Jacobs' prescience.

There were highlights in between. On a Monday night in February 1965 they played a friendly against Sunderland to celebrate the installation of their floodlights, in front of more than 10,000 fans (they lost 5-1).

Two days after that, between 11,500 and 14,900 fans turned up (accounts vary) for a Scottish Cup replay against Jock Stein's Hibs (the great man had agreed ten days earlier that he would soon move to Celtic). ES Clydebank lost that one 2-1.

Clearly enjoying their new floodlights, in the next week ES Clydebank hosted Ipswich Town, who were going well near the top of England's second tier, in another midweek friendly, and won that one 2-1, with the Scots' 18-year-old goalie John Arrol the hero, and Andy Roxburgh – yes, the same Andy Roxburgh who went on to become Scotland manager – getting the winner. Twenty-one-year-old Roxburgh was ES Clydebank's second-top scorer in their only season, with 12 league goals.

And, to be fair, ES Clydebank did push for promotion, until a terrible run in their last ten games, when they won just once, left them well adrift.

But it was in the courts that the Steedmans' plans came undone. The Court of Session upheld the fans' and shareholders' complaints about the Steedmans transferring shares to contacts in Clydebank ahead of the relocation vote, when East Stirling's articles of association stipulated that they should have first been offered to other club directors. So ES Clydebank were split back in half.

East Stirling returned for the next season – without the Steedman brothers. Clydebank – with the Steedman brothers – applied to join the league and were granted a position in 1966.

In August 1965 East Stirling played their first game back at Firs Park, in their traditional black and white stripes, and beat Alloa 1-0 in the League Cup. The healthy crowd of 2,000 were cheered by locals as they made their way to the ground, accompanied by bagpipers.

6

Saturday, 19 May 2012

The Salt 'n' Sauce Final

The 2012 Scottish Cup Final was the first Edinburgh derby in the final for 116 years, so, amid great pre-match excitement and anticipation, the rivalry, one-upmanship, banter and gloating stakes between the fierce capital city rivals were off the scale.

Rangers had gone into administration three months earlier, ushering in a period of more opportunity for more clubs in the cups. And Hearts and Hibs grabbed that opportunity, by knocking out Celtic and Aberdeen respectively in the semis.

The match was labelled the salt 'n' sauce final, in tribute to Edinburgh folks' favourite chip condiments, and Glasgow's chip shops prepared for the game by stocking up on the delicious sticky brown sauce. Angelo Catena, the owner of a chippie near Hampden, said, 'I'll definitely be buying in loads of sauce for the final, no question. When you have Edinburgh teams playing at Hampden you need to. I don't even have to ask whether the customers want it. I hear the Edinburgh accent and just put it on.'

But if Edinburgh councillors had had their way, those Glasgow restaurateurs wouldn't have needed the sauce. They asked for the final to be moved to Murrayfield but the Scottish Football Association (SFA) said no.

Meanwhile, Hibs striker Garry O'Connor was so excited that, for reasons best known to himself, he promised/

threatened to walk down Princes Street naked if Hibs won. Hundreds of Hibs fans pledged on Facebook to disrobe and join him.

One confident Hearts-supporting grandad from Dalkeith got a 'Scottish Cup Winners 2012' tattoo before the game, which was pretty brave for a fan of a team that had only won the trophy three times in the previous 100 years. But his confidence wasn't unjustified. Not only had Hibs won the trophy zero times in that century – their previous Scottish Cup victory parade was conducted on a horse and cart – but Hearts clearly had the stronger team.

Vladimir Romanov had funded an expensive squad (more on this later), but the debts that came with that had started to come back to haunt Hearts. Players had gone unpaid earlier in the season, and midfielder Ian Black had done some painting and decorating work at the time. The Hibs fans had ridiculed him for it but he got a dig back in at the New Year derby at Easter Road, when he marked Hearts' 3-1 win by revealing a T-shirt that said 'I'll paint this place maroon'. And he would get more revenge in the cup final.

It would be his last chance for that revenge. Black was one of several key players for whom the final would be their last game for Hearts, because of the financial difficulties. The same went for their manager, Paulo Sérgio. No matter how well the final went for Hearts, it would have that bittersweet element; but in the eyes of excited fans on cup final day, it could be a joyous climax to Romanov's turbulent reign.

Meanwhile, Hibs' relative financial caution was evident on the pitch. Outside of a core of quality players, including strikers O'Connor and Leigh Griffiths, who both scored against Aberdeen in the semi-final, and captain and defender James McPake, they were reliant on several underwhelming loan players, and had just narrowly avoided relegation.

As well as the rivalry between the finalists, the match, of course, provided an irresistible opportunity to hammer home the fact that the cultural differences between Scotland's biggest cities ran deeper than a Gulliver's Travels-style cold war about what condiment should go on chips. And the *Edinburgh Evening News* couldn't resist that opportunity, as they recorded and released an eccentric song, 'Go East', all about those cultural differences, including humorous references to pandas and trams and dubious lyrics about soap and Buckfast.

The match lived up to the anticipation, especially for Hearts fans, who swept up all the bragging rights. It was lively and dramatic. There were six goals (at one point it looked like there could have been considerably more), false hope, and a dodgy-penalty-and-not-dodgy-red-card combination.

Hearts fans' favourite Rudi Skácel was at his best, in a team who all rose to the occasion. The men in maroon earned a two-goal lead, through Darren Barr and Skácel, before Hibs managed to drag themselves back into it just before half-time, with McPake – who'd just cleared off his own line – turning home a low Tom Soares cross at the other end.

The Hibs fans celebrated wildly. Was the comeback on? No.

Five minutes into the second half, Hearts were 4-1 up and Hibs were down to ten men.

First, Hearts winger Suso Santana went on a great run down the wing to the byline and cut inside. A couple of yards outside the box, Hibs left-back Pa Kujabi (who'd compared himself to Roberto Carlos when he'd joined Hibs) grabbed the Hearts winger's shirt. Kujabi got a well-deserved second yellow card and Hearts got a dubious penalty, which Danny Grainger blasted home.

Then, just two minutes after that, Ryan McGowan nodded home a Skácel shot. Now the only question was how many Hearts would end up scoring. Some Hibs fans started to leave.

Slightly surprisingly, there was just one more goal. Unsurprisingly, it was Skácel again, from the edge of the box.

The Hearts fans and players didn't seem disappointed that they didn't humiliate their fierce rivals by even more than 5-1. Their celebrations and gloating were long and loud.

Coach Gary Locke had no need to gloat – and also no need for hyperbole – when he summed it up as, 'Brilliant. Best day ever. I certainly didn't think it was going to go as well as that.'

Like Black and Sérgio, Skácel left Tynecastle after the final. He moved to Dundee United, where – to continue the wind-up of Hibs fans – he asked for, and got, a particular shirt number: 51.

Saturday, 7 May 1881

Scotland Win the World's First Ever Women's Football Match

The world's first ever recorded women's football match took place at Hibernian Park, just off Easter Road, in 1881, when Scotland beat England 3-0, with Lily St Clair the first woman in the world to score in a recorded match.

The fixture was a bit of a novelty; an attempt by its organisers – now believed to be (male) theatre entrepreneurs – to cash in on football's sudden massive popularity. It was a far cry from the modern women's game.

Nevertheless, more than 1,000 curious fans paid to see it, although many of them left before full time, as, the *Glasgow Herald* reported, 'The game, judged from a player's point of view, was a failure, but some of the individual members of the teams showed that they had a fair idea of the game.' It seems that the players were mostly dancers or other theatre performers, and as footballing pioneers their inexperience was, by definition, inevitable.

Their skills were also surely hampered by their footwear: high-heeled boots. Their strips also included stockings, belts and hoods.

Nine days later, on a Monday evening, the teams met again at Shawfield in Glasgow, where 5,000 spectators turned up, but the match didn't end well. Again the players' skills and tactics were – according to the *Nottinghamshire Guardian* – 'sorry', and, early in the second half, with the match still goalless, hundreds of spectators invaded the pitch and roughly jostled the players, who ran to their horse-drawn omnibus, which had to be quickly driven away, as fans hurled wooden stakes at it. The police had to baton-charge the mob.

The tour then moved on to Blackburn, Manchester and Liverpool, but experienced similar problems, and soon petered out.

After this brief early flourish, it was a shamefully long time before women's football became properly established in Scotland. When it became popular during World War I – mainly in England – the SFA, like the FA, banned women from using the established men's clubs' grounds, and didn't relent until the 1970s.

But, despite the SFA's chauvinism, Scottish women can still lay claim to having won the first ever – albeit unconventional – women's football match.

Sunday 15 May 1927

Motherwell Win the (Sort of) Copa del Rey

In 1927, Motherwell received an intriguing invitation: to compete in a special edition of Spain's most illustrious cup competition.

On the morning of Wednesday, 11 May, the team – who'd just finished second in the league – started their long journey to Madrid, getting a rousing send-off at Motherwell station as they travelled to London by special saloon.

The *Motherwell Times* anticipated a tour 'brimful of interest' and asked R.M. Macandster, a Scottish player for Águilas CF, in Murcia, to characterise Spanish football for their readers.

Macandster stated, 'In the south, the sweltering sun leaves the pitch innocent of grass, resembling nothing so much as an asphalt tennis court. This, coupled with the vigorous play of the fiery Spaniard, makes hard going, for every fall, while it highly amuses the less-informed section of the spectators, leaves bruises and broken joints.' He also noted the 'tremendous ovation given to Spanish players who score for their team. Their colleagues kiss and hug and lift and pat them in a way that will bring the blush to a laconic undemonstrative Scot' and how he was initially horrified by 'these intensely embarrassing displays'.

On the Thursday the Motherwell party – 15 players, along with boss 'Sailor' Hunter, director James Taggart and trainer W. Walker – crossed the Channel to France. On the Friday they arrived in Madrid, where they soon won the special version of the Copa del Rey.

On Sunday, 15 May, Real Unión de Irún won the official Copa del Rey Final, in Zaragoza. But the man who was the impetus behind the competition and who it was named after, King Alfonso XIII, was watching Motherwell play Swansea instead.

The *Motherwell Times* reported that the teams had 'a most enthusiastic reception from the king as well as his subjects. Before the game, the Motherwell and Swansea players lined up in front of the king's box and gave him a hearty British cheer, which was, according to Motherwell director James Taggart, much appreciated.' The Scots promptly beat their Welsh opponents 4-3.

Two days later Motherwell reaffirmed their *galácticos* status when they beat Real Madrid 3-1, with goals from David Hutchison, Bobby Ferrier and David Thackeray. *The Scotsman* reported, 'The *Madrileños* played with much spirit and vigour against the high-class display of the Scottish team.'

As if all that wasn't impressive enough, five days after beating Real Madrid the Scots drew 2-2 with Barcelona, and then beat Swansea again, 1-0, four days after that, which meant they had to squeeze the Barcelona Cup into their luggage alongside their Copa del Rey trophy.

And they still weren't finished. They went west for more matches. A Bilbao select were the only team to beat Motherwell on the tour, before the men from Lanarkshire beat Celta Vigo twice.

In Vigo, the travelling party were invited to the British consulate to celebrate King George VI's birthday. Some of the players went out on a boat but, ironically, 'Sailor' Hunter turned down the opportunity, because the sea was rough.

And finally, on the way home, they beat Red Star Olympique 5-0 in Paris.

More than a month after setting off, they got home on 14 June. Despite what must have been a tiring tour, the *Motherwell Times* reported that they were all fit and well, and that the whole team reported to Fir Park that afternoon. It was payday, after all.

That great Motherwell team finished in the top three in the league for eight consecutive seasons, with their greatest ever achievement coming in 1931/32, when they were the only club to take the league title out of Glasgow between the wars. Their achievements in Spain were very different but similarly glorious.

9

Saturday, 19 October 1957

Celtic Thrash Rangers in the League Cup Final

In the quarter of a century between the start of World War II and Jock Stein returning to Parkhead in 1965, Celtic weren't great. They were very poor in the 1940s; a bit better in the '50s, but still usually also-rans behind Rangers and often behind Hearts and various other clubs too.

It wasn't for a lack of quality players, but team selections were confusing, the line-ups were rarely the sum of their parts and they hardly ever won key games, particularly against Rangers.

In 1956 they finished fifth in the league. In 1957 they finished fifth again. In the autumn of 1957 they started the league a bit better, and reached the final of the League Cup, against Rangers, but in their last game before the final they seemed to revert to disappointing form, in a poor draw with Raith Rovers.

Evening Times reporter Jimmy Dunbar said, 'Celtic will have to do much better at Hampden next Saturday if they mean to retain the League Cup. Against Raith Rovers at Parkhead today they were suspect in defence and scrappy in attack.' Both were familiar accusations.

This was the first cup final between the Glasgow giants since 1928. The journalists thought it would be close, while the bookies had Rangers as favourites. No one could have predicted what would happen after that game kicked off at 2.45pm in glorious sunshine – Gair Henderson in the *Evening Times* said the sky was Mediterranean blue and the turf as green as emerald.

For once Celtic's assortment of stars – Charlie Tully, Bobby Collins, Neilly Mochan, Bertie Peacock, Willie Fernie, Bobby Evans – played to their cumulative potential. For once, Rangers weren't immovable at the back. New boy John Valentine copped the flak and never played for Rangers again, but he was far from wholly responsible.

Celtic were on the front foot from the start. They hit the crossbar. They hit the post. *Sunday Mail* reporter 'Rex' said that Rangers' defenders were shaking 'as if they were operating pneumatic drills' and the *Glasgow Herald* said Celtic might have scored four in the first 20 minutes, but, after coming repeatedly close but not scoring, some pessimistic Celtic fans, given their recent experiences, might have been starting to think that it was going to be the familiar story of playing well but missing out.

But then, in the 23rd minute, Sammy Wilson got that first goal, turning the ball past three defenders on the line after Billy McPhail nodded a Collins cross down to him in the box.

Rangers goalie George Niven turned a Collins free kick against the bar and it was beginning to look like Celtic would be going in for the break with just one goal to show for their dominance until, on the stroke of half-time, Mochan set off on a brilliant run, swept past two defenders then smacked the ball between Niven and his post from a tight angle.

McPhail later said, 'We went into the dressing room at half-time knowing it just had to be our day now, but nobody could have guessed just how sensationally it all turned out.'

Rangers reshuffled their forward line for the second half but after a few minutes – 'before the taste of the half-time lemon had left Rangers' palate', according to the *Record* –

Celtic were three up. Following a corner, Collins chipped the ball to McPhail, who nodded it home despite the attention of three Rangers defenders.

Rangers pulled one back when Billy Simpson bulleted a header past Celtic goalie Dick Beattie. Then Ian McColl came close to halving the remaining deficit with a free kick. Was a comeback on the cards? No. Quite the opposite.

Celtic's wingers Tully and Mochan and man of the match Fernie were finding more and more space.

With 20 minutes to go, McPhail blasted home the rebound from a Wilson header. Six minutes after that, Mochan made it 5-1. Then McPhail latched on to a long ball from Beattie, raced forward and slotted past Niven to grab his hat-trick. Mochan's glee was clear as he embraced McPhail.

Fighting broke out between Rangers fans, bottles were thrown and fans ran on to the field to escape it, while police spent a couple of minutes quelling the trouble on the terrace.

And finally, in the last minute, Celtic won a penalty. McPhail declined the opportunity to turn his hat-trick into a four-goal haul, and Fernie instead made it 7-1.

It remains Rangers' joint-record defeat in a competitive match, and a record score in any major British cup final.

Newspaper reports stressed Celtic's ball-playing skill and also their discipline, in an era when 'power play' tactics often yielded results.

The *Daily Record*'s 'Waverley' singled out Tully for particular praise, saying that he 'had the Rangers from first to last in a state of puzzlement'.

Even the Rangers Supporters Association annual praised Celtic's 'true art of football' on that day.

Unfortunately, the BBC's match highlights only included two of the eight goals. In those days, a live feed from Hampden was sent to a screen in a studio in London, where a telerecording operator had to record the footage from that screen with another camera. The operator put a lens cap on that camera at half-time and forgot to take it off for the second half, and by such a mundane mistake the second-half footage was lost for ever.

And, more seriously for Celtic, the remarkable cup final was the brightest of brief highlights, rather than a new dawn. Their talented players were getting on a bit. The rest of the season was blighted by injuries, chopping and changing and inexperienced replacements. They finished 16 points behind goal-greedy Hearts (see iconic moment 23), and went out of the Scottish Cup to Clyde.

It wouldn't have been Celtic in the 1950s if their talent and huge potential wasn't accompanied by relentless inconsistency. And on that bright autumn day their mercurial stars all clicked at the same time and achieved even more than what they or their fans could have dreamed of.

A whole book – *Oh, Hampden in the Sun* by Pete Burns and Pat Woods – is dedicated to the match. It contains many fans' evocative memories, and one particular snapshot illustrates exactly how much that victory meant to Celtic's supporters. Delighted Celt Peter Sweeney left Hampden and boarded a packed trolleybus: 'We soon found we were leading a spontaneous victory parade with scarves at every window and everyone singing. The good news had gone ahead of us because as we reached the Gorbals people were lining the pavements, waving and cheering. From house windows appeared scarves, banners, tablecloths and towels, anything with green on it. What a sight it was! We had waited a long, long time for this day.'

And the Celtic fans now had another song to sing. Harry Belafonte had reached number four in the UK charts a couple of months earlier with calypso classic 'Island in the Sun', which was easily enough adapted to 'Oh Hampden in the sun; Celtic seven Rangers one'.

10

Monday, 28 April 1941

Hibs Sign Gordon Smith from Under Hearts' Noses

When Lochee Harp opened their new ground, Beechwood Park, in 1941, they invited a combined Hearts and Hibs side to play in a special opening match, against a select XI of players mainly picked from junior clubs in and around Dundee.

In front of 3,000 fans, the strong Edinburgh team lost an entertaining and keenly contested game 3-2 to the assortment of locals. The great Tommy Walker was characteristically classy for the men from the capital, but, said *The Courier*, 'He was much less deadly in the goal area than [Dundee] North End's 16-year-old Gordon Smith, who collected a hat-trick.' It was far from the first hat-trick that the teenage forward had grabbed that year. And he wouldn't have long to wait for his next.

The *Evening Telegraph* reported, 'It is quite on the cards that Smith will sign for Hearts in the near future.' And indeed, after the match, Tynecastle chairman Alex Irvine offered Smith a trial for the Jam Tarts 13 days later – in the derby against Hibs. That week's *Sunday Express* got a bit ahead of themselves and actually reported that Hearts had signed Smith. The Smith family were Hearts fans and were delighted enough about the trial. It all seemed very straightforward.

But charismatic Hibs boss Willie McCartney had other ideas. He was at the Beechwood Park game too, and he also loved the look of the youngster from Montrose. He convinced ambitious Hibs chairman Harry Swan that they had to sign him and that the best way to do that was to turn up, unannounced, in Montrose and convince him face to face. But the only day that they could make was Sunday, 27 April, the day before the derby – when, of course, he was supposed to be playing against them, for Hearts.

The full saga of the signing is brilliantly told in detail in Smith's biography, *Prince of Wingers*, but here are the main bits:

The Hibs delegation's train never reached Montrose; they were stopped at Arbroath by a Luftwaffe bombing raid further up the track. And they didn't have a phone number for the Smiths. So they phoned Montrose police station to see if they could help. The police were, understandably, busy with the aftermath of the bombing raid, but the officer on the line knew where the young North End star lived, and gave the Hibs men a number for a lemonade factory on the same street. They got lucky when they phoned it, and the factory owner managed to get hold of Gordon.

Although he was excited about the Hearts trial, Gordon agreed to go to Arbroath to hear McCartney out. So he borrowed the factory owner's car and drove down the coast. Crucially, McCartney told Gordon that there was no need for any trial – everyone could see how good Gordon was, and Hibs wanted to sign him straight away. But Gordon wanted to talk to his dad about it first, so they agreed to meet again in the North British Hotel in Edinburgh the next day – a few hours before the derby.

In Edinburgh, Swan and McCartney's vision for Hibs, plus a £10 signing-on fee and the grandeur of the North British, sealed the deal, and Gordon and his dad were whisked to Tynecastle for the game. Among the new team-mates who Gordon was meeting was a familiar face: another highly talented teenage striker, Bobby Combe, who he'd played alongside for Scottish Schoolboys. Hearts had wanted to sign him too, but a couple of hours before the North British rendezvous, McCartney had been down to Combe's family home in Leith to snap him up too.

Alex Irvine was livid when he found out that – not only was Smith not playing as a trialist for him – but Smith and Combe had both signed for McCartney. McCartney had been manager of Hearts when Irvine became chairman, and there was no love lost between the two men. But for all his ire, Irvine could do nothing about the fact that Hibs had signed his targets.

Gordon still faced one stumbling block ahead of kick-off though. He didn't have any boots with him, and the only pair that coach Jimmy McColl could offer him were two sizes too small.

But Gordon's performance was so good that McCartney and Swan joked to him afterwards that he should always squeeze himself into uncomfortably tight footwear.

Tommy Walker – Gordon's childhood hero, incidentally – scored a hat-trick for the Jam Tarts that night, but for the second time in a fortnight the Hearts legend was upstaged by 'crack shot trialist' Gordon (the complimentary prefix is the words of the *Courier*), who grabbed three too. Combe was also on the scoresheet as Hibs won 5-3.

As Swan and McCartney beamed with joy, and Gordon and his dad walked away from Tynecastle back towards the North British, a 12-year-old Hibs fan approached them to congratulate Gordon on his performance and invite him round to his mum and dad's for tea. Gordon politely declined but would later get to know him very well. That boy was Lawrie Reilly, who joined Hibs five years later, as another key part of Hibs' Famous Five forward line, alongside Gordon.

Gordon went on to have one of the best club careers of any Scottish footballer. More on that later.

Saturday, 8 December 1984

Stirling Albion 20 Selkirk 0

If you didn't know which club notched the record win in a senior British football match in the 20th century, it might be a while before you guessed the right answer: Stirling Albion.

And the goal-happy record holders weren't even going through a particularly good spell at the time. The Binos – managed by Alex Smith shortly before he moved on to bigger and more successful things at St Mirren – had won only three of their 16 games in the Second Division so far that season; they'd gone out of the previous year's Scottish Cup to Caledonian from the Highland League; and a few seasons earlier, in 1980/81, they'd scored just 19 goals in 39 league games – fewer than they managed in 90 minutes against Selkirk in the first round of the 1984/85 competition.

Selkirk would have desperately loved such peaceful mediocrity. The Borders' oldest football club were heavily in debt, they'd recently had to withdraw from the East of Scotland League for financial reasons and they were now playing in the second division of the Border Amateur League.

But they'd maintained their membership of the SFA, which gave them a route to the Scottish Cup, and they'd achieved some impressive results in the Qualifying Cup, including a 3-1 defeat of Annan Athletic from the South of Scotland League, which put them into the first round of the cup proper.

They arrived at Annfield, from rugby country, in a coach borrowed from a cricket club. They wouldn't in their wildest nightmares have expected the cricket score that they suffered that afternoon.

It was 5-0 at half-time. Selkirk player-manager Jackson Cockburn furiously ripped into his players, telling them that if they kept playing like that, it could end up 10-0. Some hope.

In the second half the floodgates really opened on the muddy Annfield pitch, as the visitors seemed to be trying to play an offside trap with an extremely high line. The 371 fans, who'd moved at half-time from behind one goal to behind the other, seemed too worn out to celebrate properly by the time goal number 20 went in.

Eight Binos players got on the scoresheet that day. Davie Thompson got seven, and Willie Irvine scored five.

With a wry smile, Cockburn admitted after the game that his team were 'obviously very disappointed' before adding, 'The score seems daft but if he [23-year-old goalie, Richard 'Midge' Taylor] hadn't been playing so well, it could have been 30.'

Cockburn was being kind; Taylor's team-mates had let him down but the young keeper was culpable too.

The simple ease with which the home side scored most of their goals bordered on the bizarre, as if there was something not quite right with the game of football itself that day; like a football match on the ZX Spectrum with a crude hack to render your opponents motionless.

So Stirling marched onwards imperiously while Selkirk regretted even turning up? Not exactly.

The Binos lost 2-1 against Cowdenbeath in the second round, while the money that Selkirk got from the SFA for reaching the first round kept the financial wolf from the door. Some say it was that money that saved them from oblivion – for a few more decades.

They started climbing back towards the East of Scotland Premier League, and, in 2013, they were founder members of the Lowland League. Unfortunately, in 2019, new financial woes drove them out of business. But they'll always have their bittersweet place in the record books.

12

Saturday, 22 June 1974

Scotland Unbeaten in the World Cup

The 1974 World Cup was Scotland's first for 16 years, their postwar record was poor, they weren't on a great run of form going into the finals, and they – as usual – came home too soon, straight after the first round. But they received a heroes' welcome at Glasgow Airport. Why?

It's a tale of classy performances on the main stage, but the team and nation's hopes and positivity started building earlier, throughout qualification.

Tommy Docherty had rejuvenated Scotland in his brief period as boss. He was brash, charismatic and successful, and led his men to two (expected but convincing and necessary) victories over Denmark in qualifying. But he was also firmly on Manchester United's radar, and left Hampden to take over at Old Trafford.

His replacement in the Scotland hotseat was very different. Willie Ormond – the left-winger in Hibs' Famous Five forward line – had managed St Johnstone with relative success but was quiet and very different to Docherty, and his appointment was underwhelming. And he didn't initially get great results on the pitch, in friendlies or in British Home Championship matches.

Ormond trusted and respected his players – he once said 'in talent, we rank with anywhere in the world' – sometimes to a fault, giving them generous levels of freedom, on the pitch as well as off it. And his light-touch management style started to pay dividends as the team grew to return his trust and respect.

And never more so than when they faced their main rivals for qualification, Czechoslovakia (who would win the Euros a couple of years later), on a nervous but noisy Hampden night. A win would render the result of the return match meaningless, as Czechoslovakia had drawn their away game against Denmark. Czechoslovakia scored first but Jim Holton got the equaliser before Joe Jordan sent the 95,000 fans in the stadium wild with his second-half winner. Scotland had qualified for West Germany.

Easy-going management may well have been the only style that came naturally to Ormond, but his players' ability merited his respect. He was right to praise their talent, from full-backs Danny McGrain and Sandy Jardine, through to Davie Hay and Billy Bremner in the heart of midfield and an array of attacking talent in Peter Lorimer, Joe Jordan, Kenny Dalglish and Jimmy Johnstone – although, surprisingly, he chose not to play Johnstone at all in West Germany. And then there was Denis Law, for whom the 1958 World Cup had come ever so slightly too early, but who now, at the age of 34, finally had his opportunity to make his World Cup debut.

It wasn't just Ormond who thought these were great players. Germany boss Helmut Schön said Scotland should be rated one of the favourites at the finals and added, 'It puzzles us that the Scots themselves do not regard themselves in the same way as the rest of the world sees them.'

Scotland's opponents in their group were Zaire, Brazil and Yugoslavia. Finishing in the top two looked tough but possible, and Ormond said that if they could get through, he firmly believed they could win the tournament. It was the same sort of optimism which brought ridicule to Ally MacLeod four years later, and it was a stretch, with such great West Germany and Netherlands sides in the mix, but Ormond's quiet optimism was respected.

An unfair retrospective narrative has built up around Scotland's opening game against Zaire: that Scotland were too cautious and should have gone for more goals against their inexperienced World Cup debutant opponents. But every single Scotland player was also making his World Cup debut, and the Leopards were a good side; in qualifying, they'd knocked out Cameroon and Ghana before winning all four of their games in the final group stage. Three months before the World Cup, they'd won the Africa Cup of Nations, with main man Ndaye 'Volvo' Mulamba scoring a record nine goals.

Scotland's 2-0 win was a fair result, as both sides created chances but the Scots played that bit better. Goal difference would eventually haunt Scotland, but the most important thing was winning. Zaire would crumble against Yugoslavia, but there were reasons for that.

Next up were world champions Brazil, whose boss, Mário Zagallo, complimented Scotland's 'many fine individual players' and singled out Bremner in particular for praise. The Leeds midfielder so very nearly proved him right beyond doubt when the two sides met.

This was a very different Brazil side from the celebrated free-flowing assembly of stars who wowed the world in Mexican technicolor four years earlier. There was no Pelé, no Carlos Alberto, no Gérson, and no Tostão. Only Jairzinho, Rivelino and Wilson Piazza remained from the great 1970 side, and they were much more pragmatic and physical now.

Thousands of Scotland fans headed out to Frankfurt for the match, while 22 million people watched on telly back in Britain. It was a tough game – Pelé expressed his surprise at how physical Rivelino was – which was also pretty even, with each side creating a few half chances. Martin Buchan was commanding in defence, while Bremner and Hay were influential in midfield.

The best chance of the game fell to Bremner in the second half when a poor clearance from the keeper broke to him just a couple of yards out but he didn't have enough time to react and it pinged off him and agonisingly narrowly wide.

The 0-0 result was better for Brazil than it was for Scotland. The *Seleção* now had the benefit of knowing the exact result that they needed in their final game against Zaire. Scotland had played well but knew that they now had to beat Yugoslavia to get through. It was a tough situation for the players to take, but their spirits were raised back at their mountainside hotel when Billy Connolly turned up to entertain them.

Meanwhile, Yugoslavia had beaten Zaire 9-0, so they knew that a draw against Scotland would put them through. That 9-0 was an incredible result, and opened up conspiracy theories about naivety and corruption (especially as the Zaire boss was Yugoslavian), but the truth was very different.

Zaire's national team was very much the vanity project of President Mobutu Sese Seko, and the players faced multiple restrictions, which they tolerated because of a large bonus that they'd been promised at the World Cup. But between the Scotland game and the Yugoslavia match, the official who was due to pay the bonuses absconded with the cash.

It was a kick in the teeth for the players, who consequently underperformed against Yugoslavia – and, to a lesser extent, against Brazil – through a combination of dismay and protest. The moment when it really went wrong for them was when Mulamba was sent off midway through the first half against Yugoslavia. And Brazil and Yugoslavia were the clear beneficiaries of the Zairean discord.

But Scotland's destiny was still in their own hands. A win against strong and technically gifted Yugoslavia – who'd knocked Spain out in qualifying – would put them through to a second-round group with West Germany, Poland and Sweden.

It was hot in Frankfurt, where Scotland, in white, played well and created good chances, with Leeds trio Bremner, Lorimer and Jordan all particularly influential. With ten minutes to go, at 0-0, Scotland were second in the table (which would have put them through to face the Netherlands, Argentina and East Germany), because Brazil hadn't yet scored the third goal they needed against Zaire.

But then Brazil did grab that key goal, thanks to a goalkeeping howler, and to make matters worse Yugoslavia took the lead against the Scots. But two minutes from full time Jordan equalised, and Scotland were on the attack again, on the hunt for the goal that would have put them top of the group, when the ref blew for full time, and Yugoslavia fans ran on to the pitch in celebration.

Scotland were out by the narrowest possible goal difference margin, after one win and two draws.

Despite his disappointment, Ormond went to the Yugoslavia dressing room to congratulate them. Yugoslavia gaffer Miljan Miljanić said, 'Nothing finer will happen in the tournament. You are the greatest sportsmen in the world – and good, good players.'

As the Scotland players left the stadium, they were surrounded by cheering fans. The German newspapers highlighted Scotland's bravery and bad luck.

Scotland were clearly unlucky to play Zaire first. Brazil definitely benefitted from knowing exactly what they had to do in their last game. The Zairean bonus scandal went against Scotland too – although clearly not as much as it went against the Leopards. Scotland got the respect that their impressive World Cup performances merited when 10,000 singing, cheering fans turned up at Glasgow Airport to welcome them home.

Billy Bremner said the welcome was fabulous and fantastic, 'You'd think we had won the cup.'

A civic reception was organised in the team's honour, and Tennent's voluntarily overpaid their sponsorship money, in tribute to their performance.

Quite right too. Of the 16 teams that took part in the 1974 World Cup, Scotland were the only ones who didn't lose any games.

13

Saturday, 28 January 1967

The Wee Rangers Knock the Big Rangers Out of the Cup

Jock Wallace was only 31 when he became Berwick Rangers player-manager near the end of 1966. One of his first results there was one of the most famous cup shocks in Scottish football history.

Just two months before Berwick Rangers met Glasgow Rangers, Jock was playing in the English FA Cup for Hereford. He'd also played for them in the Welsh Cup in the same season, so turning out in the Scottish Cup already gave him a rare trinity of national cup appearances in the same season. But that unique distinction pales in comparison to the fame and legacy of the Scottish Cup tie, and its longer-term impact on Berwick's illustrious opponents.

A record crowd of 13,365 fans turned up at Shielfield Park for the first-round tie. Cup holders Rangers had nine internationals in their team. But none of them would score the only goal of the game; that honour was claimed by Sammy Reid, who worked as a gear cutter in a local engineering yard, and who blasted the ball past Neil Martin after half an hour. The *Evening Telegraph* described Reid as a constant menace.

Rangers had dominated most of the early play, but the match was much more even after Reid's goal, with chances coming for both sides, as Berwick defended well and played on the break. Wallace was excellent in goal for the home side; former Aberdeen defender Doug Coutts was a rock at the back. The *Press and Journal* praised Berwick's 'triumph of teamwork'.

Rangers couldn't score, and at full time thousands of delirious home fans streamed on to the pitch to mob their heroes, while Gers captain John Greig shook hands with every Berwick player.

The win was also sweet revenge for the Wee Gers, who, three years earlier, were one of the five clubs that their colossal namesakes had hand-picked to be chucked out of the league as part of Rangers' proposed league reconstruction plan; plans that the clubs had had to fight in court.

After the game, Rangers manager Scot Symon visited the home dressing room to offer his congratulations. But he was angry and frank in his post-match comments, saying, 'I can hardly describe just how shocked and distressed I feel. I was appalled to see professional players failing to understand the consequences of what was happening. Defeat was staring them in the face and they did nothing about it ... the performances of certain players cannot be forgotten. The manner in which we lost the goal was shocking – typical of the slipshod work in our defence. But the forward line must shoulder most of the blame.'

Rangers fans booed and jeered and blamed the club directors for the result, but two days later chairman John Lawrence angrily claimed, 'It's a downright scandal that people should blame us for this defeat. The men to blame were not sitting in the directors' box, but were out on the field. The play of some members of the team made me sick.'

Within weeks, Rangers scapegoats Jim Forrest and George McLean were transferred to Preston and Dundee. Alex Ferguson was signed from Dunfermline as one of the replacements, for £65,000 – a record fee at the time.

Those Rangers players can't have been all that slipshod though. A few months later, they reached the Cup Winners' Cup Final against Bayern Munich. Unfortunately, without Forrest or McLean, they had to improvise, and played defender Roger Hynd as a stand-in striker (Ferguson didn't make his Rangers debut until the start of the next season). Hynd had a goal disallowed, before Bayern Munich won 1-0 after extra time.

Later that year, although they were top of the table, Rangers sacked Symon – who'd led the club to six league titles, five Scottish Cups, four League Cups and two European finals in his 13 years at Ibrox. He received the news from his accountant.

Meanwhile, back down in the less bombastic Border country, Berwick couldn't quite repeat their heroics in the second round of the cup. They got another big tie, away against Hibs, which they lost 1-0.

And they couldn't hold on to their inspirational manager for very long. The next year, Wallace became a coach at Hearts, and soon after that moved into the same role at Ibrox. And in 1972, the young man who'd masterminded one of Rangers' biggest ever embarrassments became the Glasgow giants' manager.

14

Saturday, 10 May 2003

East Stirling Use Four Goalies in One Match

Sometimes – not often, but sometimes – teams have to use three keepers in one match. Sometimes goalies get injured, sometimes they get sent off. It's very unusual for that sort of thing to happen twice in one match. What's extremely rare is lightning striking the same team three times in 90 minutes. But that's exactly what happened to East Stirling on the last day of the 2002/03 season.

Just seven minutes into their game against promotion-chasing Albion Rovers, keeper Chris Todd had to go off injured. Substitute goalie Scott Findlay took over, and lasted until after half-time. Long enough to concede a hat-trick to Rovers midfielder Jim Mercer.

Eight minutes after the restart, Findlay's day got even worse when he was sent off for fouling striker John Bradford, 40 yards from his goal. Midfielder Graham McLaren pulled on the gloves, but ten minutes later he was sent off too, when he hauled down striker Charles McLean and conceded a penalty.

Defender Kevin McCann took over between the sticks, and saved the penalty. The nine men of 'Shire lost by a respectable 3-1 scoreline, with neither of the outfield stand-ins having to pick the ball out of their net.

The events were dramatic but the result immaterial; East Stirling finished bottom of the league on 13 points, 15 behind Elgin, while the Wee Rovers missed out on promotion by one point to East Fife.

15

Monday, 7 June 1993

Ally McCoist Wins the Golden Boot – Again

Rangers hitman Ally McCoist was the first player ever to be Europe's top league scorer in two consecutive seasons, when he scored 34 league goals in 1991/92 and then repeated the exact same trick one year later – despite breaking his leg seven games before the end of that season.

His success came at a turbulent time for the Golden Boot award, with a spokesman for the sponsors, Adidas, saying, 'We were thinking of ending the award and then along came McCoist to spark it back to life.'

A year earlier, it had been unclear whether McCoist would even win his first award, with senior Adidas executive Peter Csanadi saying, 'In some leagues, such as Cyprus or Turkey, it's very difficult to monitor the actual scorers, just as it was behind the Iron Curtain. That undermines the whole purpose of the competition. Obviously this doesn't apply to Ally McCoist and it would be unfortunate if he lost out. This is a delicate matter, which we will have to work out.'

As well as waiting to get his award, McCoist first had to wait to see if his 34 goals were enough to top the charts, with his closest rival Ricky Owubokiri's season, in Portugal, finishing later than Scotland's. In late April, Owubokiri scored a hat-trick for Boavista in a 4-4 draw with Chaves, which left him just two goals behind the Rangers star.

But McCoist scored in the penultimate game of the season, against Hearts, and got two more on the last day, in Aberdeen, despite partying with students until about three o'clock the night before. That left Owubokiri needing six in his last game of the season, which was a bridge too far for the Nigerian goal-getter.

A delighted McCoist said, 'It is genuinely a great honour and I just hope the Golden Boot is, in fact, presented. I believe there's some doubt about this. You can bet your boots I'll be in Paris to get the boot if they want to present it to me.'

They eventually did, and he became only the second British winner, after Ian Rush. Scottish shooting stars Bobby Lennox, Joe Harper and Charlie Nicholas had all previously won the Bronze Boot.

McCoist's second Golden Boot victory was even more impressive than his first, since his 34 league goals in 1992/93 came in the first 37 games of the season, before he broke his leg playing for Scotland in a terrible 5-0 defeat in Portugal.

But another nervous wait for Ally finished happily when his nearest challenger, AEK Athens' Vasilis Dimitriadis, finished his season on 33. As the *Daily Record* reported, 'Now hit man supreme Ally McCoist has a Golden Boot for each foot.'

Four years later, the rules were changed, with goals counting double in Spain, England, Italy, Germany, Portugal and the Netherlands. There's only been one winner from outside those countries since then – Henrik Larsson won it in 2000/01 with his 35 league goals for Celtic, leaving him on 52 and a half goals after Scotland's 1.5 ratio had been applied.

And only two players have won it more often than McCoist. The Bellshill boy is rubbing shoulders with pretty impressive company: Cristiano Ronaldo and Lionel Messi.

16

Wednesday, 19 December 1962

Dunfermline 6 (Six) Valencia 2

For seven years in the 1960s, led by three formidable managers, Dunfermline were excellent in Europe. The list of sides they knocked out included Everton, West Bromwich Albion, VfB Stuttgart, Bordeaux and Olympiakos. They took two Spanish giants to replays and another to extra time, and recorded 8-1, 9-2 and 12-1 aggregate victories against Irish, Danish and Cypriot opposition.

They also claimed the dubious honour – under the great Willie Cunningham – of being the first club to ever go out of the Inter-Cities Fairs Cup on away goals, to eventual winners Dinamo Zagreb; and played on a pitch surrounded by barbed wire and gun-toting policemen in Skopje.

Under George Farm they reached the Cup Winners' Cup semi-final, but their most dramatic European night of all came under a better-known manager.

Jock Stein was just 37 years old when he pulled up at dilapidated East End Park in his rusty Vauxhall in 1960 to start his first managerial job. Dunfermline were 16th in the 18-team top flight, without a league win in three months and looking destined for relegation, with six games left to play. Under Stein they won all six of those matches and came 12th; the highest they'd ever finished.

By the time Stein moved on to Hibs in 1964, he was driving a new Mercedes, the stadium had been fixed up, they'd won the Scottish Cup, they'd consistently finished high in the league, and they'd played two impressive seasons in Europe, including a remarkable Fairs Cup match on a freezing December night in Fife.

Valencia were the Fairs Cup holders. They'd hammered Barcelona 7-3 in the previous season's two-legged final. Six British sides – including Celtic, Rangers and Manchester United – had previously faced Valencia; none had beaten them. Dunfermline's prospects didn't look any better when they lost the first leg 4-0 at the Mestalla.

Match commentator Bob Crampsey later said, 'I remember thinking it [the second leg] was a bit of a waste of time: four-nothing down against the holders ... and when the side was announced and two young fellows called Edwards and Sinclair were in the side, it seemed more than ever a waste of time.'

Sixteen-year-old winger Alex Edwards was Dunfermline's youngest ever player that night. On the other flank, his fellow debutant Jackie Sinclair was 19. It seemed to many – Crampsey included – a sign that Stein didn't think he could win; but it was quite the opposite – the big man was playing a remarkable trick card.

On a frozen pitch that was only just playable, the Pars were 3-0 up against their aristocratic opponents after just 17 minutes. Edwards set up the first two and Sinclair scored the second and third.

The Scotsman reported that, when the third went in, the huge crowd's roar 'must have shaken the Forth Bridge'.

Dunfermline were moving the ball forwards with pace, as the 'sliding señors' struggled to turn on the treacherous surface. But then Valencia pulled one back. Stein twisted again, sending centre-half Jim MacLean into attack. MacLean fired home the fourth.

Ten minutes before half-time they led 5-1, as veteran striker George Peebles – who'd scored four in one match against FK Vardar of Skopje the season before – strolled through the middle and levelled the tie on aggregate.

'For the last ten minutes of the first half I could not hear myself in my headphones. East End Park was absolute bedlam,' said Crampsey. 'Dunfermline were magnificent, led from the front by the two youngsters.'

After that remarkable first-half performance, the Pars may have been disappointed to 'just' beat Valencia 6-2 in the end, to send the tie to a replay in Lisbon, which the Scots were unlucky to lose, 1-0. But they'd recorded an incredible result against one of the world's top clubs at the time.

No one else came as close as the Pars did to knocking Valencia out of the Fairs Cup that season, as they reached the final again, and defended their title, with a 4-1 aggregate victory over Dinamo Zagreb.

And Dunfermline are still the only club to score six against Valencia in Europe in one game.

17

Wednesday, 19 September 1923

Dundee Hibs Almost Become Dundee City

Dundee United haven't always been Dundee United. In 1909 they were created as Dundee Hibernian, following in the footsteps of the defunct Dundee Harp as a sporting focal point for the city's large Irish community.

Dundee Hibs did well on the pitch but by 1923 were struggling financially, and decided – in order to save the club – to try to appeal to a wider potential fanbase, by making their identity less specific. So they changed their strip from green to white and black, and decided to change their name. But not to Dundee United. At least, not at first.

The directors favoured Dundee City, so they transferred the club's assets to a new company under that name, and had it recognised by the government's Board of Trade – and so were briefly, in official government correspondence at least, known as Dundee City. The final piece of admin would be to get the SFA to sign off on the name change. Simple?

But – as you'll have worked out by now – that was easier said than done. Dundee objected to their neighbours' choice of moniker, claiming that it would lead to too much confusion with their own name.

So the name change went to a vote at the SFA board in September. And it seems that it was purely by chance that it wasn't passed. The business of the name change was late on the agenda, and the representatives of Alloa and Raith Rovers, who were both believed to be sympathetic to the Tannadice club's wishes, both had to leave before the vote, which was subsequently drawn 8-8.

The SFA chairman – Celtic's Tom White – was given the casting vote and he said that the club should not be called Dundee City but that other names would be acceptable. One of his suggestions was Dundee Shamrock.

So the club that came so close to becoming known as Dundee City had to come up with an alternative name.

At the next SFA meeting, on 17 October, they agreed with Dundee that they would change their name to Dundee United, which the Dens Park club apparently thought would – for reasons best known to themselves – lead to significantly less confusion than Dundee City.

And so it's only by the slenderest of margins that one of Scotland's most famous football clubs isn't called Dundee City.

18

Monday, 1 January 1973

Tornadoes Blow Away Jam Tarts

What's better than winning your derby? Winning your derby on New Year's Day, away, against your historically dominant neighbours, by a scoreline of – let's say – 7-0? Oh, and going top of the league in the process. That's exactly what Hibs did as 1973 came in the door.

The Edinburgh derby was almost 100 years old by the time this game was played, and Hearts had won it almost twice as often as Hibs had.

But this was no run-of-the-mill Hibs side. Since he returned to Easter Road in 1971, manager Eddie Turnbull had assembled, drilled and inspired a wonderfully talented team.

Turnbull's Tornadoes were Herriot, Brownlie, Black, Blackley, Schaedler, Stanton, Edwards, Cropley, O'Rourke, Gordon and Duncan. They were all quality players, combining skill, strength and swagger, but three of them stood out in particular: 20-year-old flying full-back John 'Onion' Brownlie (he liked pickled onions) who was excellent in attack as well as defence, ultra-elegant captain and central midfielder Pat Stanton, and immensely talented right-sided midfielder Alex Edwards – the same Alex Edwards who'd starred for Dunfermline against Valencia, and who was one of the best Scottish players to never play for Scotland.

The Tornadoes played with four defenders and six attackers, or, when Brownlie and left-back Erich 'Shades'

Schaedler got forward – as they often did – two defenders and eight attackers. They played with the confidence, talent, positivity and swagger that Turnbull had epitomised when he was one of Hibs' best ever players two decades earlier.

Just three weeks before the New Year derby, the Tornadoes had beaten Jock Stein's all-conquering Celtic side in the League Cup Final. Turnbull had the same leadership strengths as Stein (who was a known admirer of Stanton) and the same attacking positivity – demonstrated in particular by their attacking full-backs.

Stein respected Turnbull's team so much that, at the end of the League Cup Final, he shook every Hibs player's hand and told Turnbull and Edwards that they deserved the cup more than Celtic did.

Everything else was going well for Hibs in the first half of that season, too.

They'd qualified for the quarter-finals of the Cup Winners' Cup, with aggregate scores of 7-3 against Sporting Lisbon and 8-2 against Albanians KS Besa.

Halfway through the season, they'd scored more than 100 goals in all competitions. Alan Gordon and Jimmy O'Rourke were competing with the likes of Eusébio for the Golden Boot; O'Rourke had already grabbed six hat-tricks.

Between the League Cup Final and the new year derby, they demolished Ayr United 8-1, and Ayr boss Ally McLeod said they were the best football team he'd ever seen.

Most importantly of all, Hibs were second to Celtic in the league, and if they could beat Hearts by six they would go top. Hibs fans in the 36,000 crowd at Tynecastle were only half-joking when they said they reckoned they could do it.

But Hearts weren't bad themselves, and sat just four points behind Hibs. In fact, the home team created the game's first two half-chances, with Donald Park snatching at their best opportunity and dragging it wide. Then everything changed.

After just 15 minutes Hibs were 2-0 up. First O'Rourke slammed home a shot from a characteristic long Schaedler throw-in, then Gordon controlled Edwards' brilliant long pass on his chest and slotted it past the keeper.

Both teams had lined up with 4-3-3 formations and it was Hibs who were dominating the open spaces in midfield. Stanton was imperious in the middle; Schaedler and Alex 'Sodjer' Cropley were getting forward on the left, and Brownlie and Edwards in particular were having the time of their lives on the right, where Hearts were playing without a winger. Everything was clicking for Hibs. Their passing and attacking were crisp and exemplary, and the back-heels and flicks were coming out.

It was 5-0 at half-time. Arthur 'Nijinsky' Duncan – named after the racehorse rather than the ballet dancer – got number three when he strode forward and cracked a simple shot under the keeper and into the net

Cropley made it four. Hearts tried to clear a Hibs attack, the ball looped up and out to Cropley on the edge of the box, and he slammed a perfect 20-yard volley home.

Just two minutes later, Duncan got his second, placing a header just inside the post.

John Brownlie's wife Jean had arrived at the match during the first half and later said that, when she got there, she thought that it had been abandoned, because so many Hearts fans were leaving.

The Hibs players were cock-a-hoop at half-time. Alex Edwards stripped off and got in the bath for a laugh, because he'd already completed a great day's work, but Turnbull left him in no doubt that he wasn't yet ready to celebrate. The boss made it very clear to his players that they had to go out and do exactly the same again.

Slightly half-hearted debate bubbles away to this day about whether Hibs went easy on Hearts in the second half, as they only scored twice.

First, Stanton won the ball on the halfway line and strode forward with typical great unharried purpose. With Hearts players desperately trailing behind him, he steered the ball towards goal, and just before it crossed the line, O'Rourke got a touch on it and stole the skipper's glory. To this day, Stanton insists that he forgives his best mate for nicking the goal that his imperious performance so richly deserved.

Then with 15 minutes left, Schaedler won the ball with characteristic strength and bravery, it broke to Duncan, Duncan crossed to Gordon, and Gordon headed home number seven, into the bottom corner.

The newspaper subeditors dusted off their seventh heaven and magnificent seven headlines, while *Daily Record* reporter Hugh Taylor went one better with his appropriately hyperbolic report, 'Hibs sprinkled the stardust of super soccer all over Tynecastle. With magic touches reminiscent of Real Madrid, Brazil and the unforgettable Hungarians, they climbed to the top of the First Division. Hearts were humiliated, baffled and run into the ground ... This was football with speed, artistry and arrogance. This was glamorous, glittering football ... Hibs are now playing with all the flair, polish and venom of a top team and by a top team I mean one of the top teams in the world.'

The Scotsman spared a thought for Hearts' busy goalie, Kenny Garland, saying that he made three excellent saves from Stanton, Gordon and O'Rourke to prevent it becoming a 'double-figure tale of woe'.

Hibs were flying high. In the capital's factories, offices, pubs and schools, their fans had the boldest derby bragging rights ever. And they were top of the league. They'd also won the League Cup. They were going strong in Europe too. They had some of the best players in Scotland.

But their seventh heaven only lasted for five days. In their next match, against East Fife, an accidental collision broke Brownlie's leg in two places. He missed the next 11 months.

In the same game, Edwards was booked for throwing the ball away, which put him over a disciplinary points threshold, and the SFA Disciplinary Committee banned him for eight weeks. That was the last time all 11 Tornadoes ever played together.

Their immense potential wasn't rewarded with as many trophies as their talent deserved. They finished third in the league, went out of the cup, 2-1 in a replay against Rangers, and lost their Cup Winners' Cup quarter-final 5-4 on aggregate, against Hajduk Split.

But it's not the disappointment that stands the test of time; it's the glory of one of the greatest derby victories of all time, or, in the words of Turnbull, 'a prize beyond compare: footballing immortality, at least anywhere where the fortunes of Hibs and Hearts are followed'.

19

Saturday, 24 June 1989

Scotland Almost Win the Under-16 World Cup

At 4pm on 24 June 1989, Scotland were leading 2-0 in the World Cup Final, at half-time. Admittedly, it was the Under-16 World Cup, but it was still a remarkable position to be in. Just 45 minutes away from glory, unless anything went wrong.

And to make it even more exciting, this final was at Hampden. And the old place was rocking, stuffed to its (temporarily reduced) 57,000 capacity.

The tournament was a big success, both on the pitch and off it. Future top-level players including Luís Figo, Abel Xavier, Victor Ikpeba, Claudio Reyna, Mark Schwarzer and Roberto Abbondanzieri all featured heavily, but they were outshone by two players in particular – Scotland goalie James Will and 14-year-old Ghana midfielder Nii Lamptey – who both featured in the opening match, a 0-0 draw in front of just 6,500 fans in the rain at Hampden. Scotland seemed nervy. Kevin Bain had a penalty saved and somehow skied the rebound with the goal wide open ('about three miles over the bar', Bain would later admit). Ghana played with skill and grace but couldn't find their shooting boots.

The weather improved greatly after that soggy opener, and so did Scotland. In their next game, they seemed more

65

relaxed in front of a large crowd in Motherwell, as they beat Cuba 3-0, with first-half goals from Dundee United's John Lindsay and Morton's Kevin McGoldrick, with Arsenal's Paul Dickov pulling the strings. After that, the Fir Park crowd's good evening continued in the same vein as they were treated to the skills of Ghana and surprise package Bahrain straight after, with the boys from the Persian Gulf – who'd also beaten Cuba 3-0, in their first game – winning 1-0.

The final matches in Scotland's group also took place at Fir Park, as the Motherwell locals struck up special relationships with Ghana and Bahrain, thanks in no small part to both sides' flair and skill.

Scotland needed just a point against Bahrain to guarantee a place in the quarter-finals. In front of 13,000 fans, Celtic's Jim Beattie scored in the second minute, from a Dickov cross after a great run. Then the Scots seemed to sit back, and skilful striker Mohamed Abdulaziz latched on to a diagonal through ball and fired home the equaliser on 34 minutes. It was all a bit nervy but Scotland hung on to set up a quarter-final tie with East Germany.

The Fir Park crowd gave Ghana a rousing reception after their last group game, a 2-2 draw with Cuba. Most teams' squads were almost all 16 years old – but more on that in a minute; Ghana's 18-man squad included eight 14-year-olds and five 15-year-olds. The *Glasgow Herald* praised their 'balletic brilliance', said they 'dazzled and sparkled all over the field' and singled out Nii Lamptey's 'exquisite skills' for particular praise. As the group stages ended, FIFA sent Portugal goalie Paulo Santos home for dropping his shorts after their match against Guinea.

East Germany were formidable quarter-final opposition for Scotland; they'd put five past the USA in the group stage, and had finished as runners-up in the Under-16 Euros in Denmark the month before; a tournament at which they'd earlier drawn 2-2 with Scotland.

This quarter-final, at Pittodrie, was a tight match in front of 10,000 fans, and the only goal came ten minutes from the end, when Lindsay picked up a pass in the centre circle, tried a one-two with Dickov, the ball broke back to him off a defender, and he fired it home to put Scotland into the semis.

Meanwhile, back at Fir Park, the locals' beloved Bahrain took on Brazil in the quarter-final. FIFA were so impressed with the fans that they asked Motherwell to pass on their thanks for their support, and handed out free FIFA pens and hats to children at the game. Bahrain won the game on penalties. FIFA moved their semi-final from Hampden to Fir Park.

FIFA were even more impressed by the turnout at Tynecastle for Scotland's semi against Portugal – Craig Brown v Carlos Queiroz – than they were with the Fir Park crowds. Thousands of fans were locked out as the sunny Gorgie ground reached its 28,500 capacity, and kick-off had to be delayed by 40 minutes. With the players and the referee out, warming up and awaiting the delayed start, fans had to be led around the edge of the pitch to areas where there was enough space.

FIFA officials were reportedly visibly astonished by the size of the crowd, when they had apparently been expecting average crowds of about 2,000. FIFA spokesman Guido Tognoni said the attendance was more than they could have imagined.

If East Germany had been formidable opponents, Portugal were more so. They were the team who'd beaten East Germany in the final of the Euros the month before. Figo was already more than a bit good.

Scotland definitely rode their luck in that game. Portugal should have had a penalty, and they had a goal disallowed after the ball had hit a striker's hand – a nerve-jangling moment for the Scottish players and all those fans. But an open, tense and exciting game, in which Scotland had their fair share of chances and Will, Dickov and Gary Bollan were all hugely influential, was settled by a solitary goal: a brilliant towering header from Celtic's Brian O'Neil.

Scotland had qualified for the final, against Saudi Arabia. Which is where the tournament gets controversial and infamous. The Saudis had knocked out tournament favourites Nigeria in the quarter-finals, and – at Fir Park, of course – beaten Bahrain in the semis. The large Motherwell crowd had naturally given their new Bahraini mates a rousing reception after that game.

The Saudi authorities registered all their players as being 16 years old. But they didn't look it. Portugal and Nigeria both raised their suspicions with FIFA, but there was nothing FIFA could do about it. They couldn't prove that the Saudi players weren't 16.

The day before the final, Bordeaux, on a pre-season training trip to Scotland, offered the young Scots a practice match but Craig Brown decided not to risk his players' fitness in a game where they would have faced players including Jean Tigana, Jesper Olsen and Alain Giresse.

Irrespective of the age rumours, Scotland started the final brilliantly, with Bollan and Dickov again at the heart of things. Dickov, who had created so many goals throughout the tournament, was provider yet again when he set up Aberdeen's Ian Downie to open the scoring. The huge Hampden crowd went wild. And then Dickov got the goal that he thoroughly deserved, a brilliant chip from a very narrow angle; 2-0.

But Scotland seemed to tire in the second half. The Saudi players were bigger and stronger than them. Sulaiman Al Reshoudi pulled one back with a fierce strike from a free kick. But then Bollan made a great run into the box and was tripped. Penalty to Scotland – just what they needed. Unfortunately, the goalie saved semi-final hero O'Neil's spot-kick. And 13 minutes from full time, Waleed Al Terair equalised. There was still time for the Saudis to have a man sent off, but there were no more goals, and the game went to penalties, which the Saudis won 5-4. The Scottish dream was over, but the unheralded lads had still massively over-achieved.

There were no stars like Figo, Ipkeba or Lamptey in the Scotland team, but they achieved so much, based largely on teamwork, hard work, passionate home support and good goalkeeping. FIFA made James Will the player of the tournament – a rare accolade for a goalie. Players like Dickov and Bollan also played well throughout, but most of the Scotland team wouldn't go on to realise their potential again, mainly due to subsequent injury problems – including to Will. Such is the unpredictability and insecurity of young footballing stars' futures. Dickov, Bollan, O'Neil and Andy McLaren had good careers; most of their World Cup teammates drifted away from the game.

The rumours about overage players refused to go away. SFA chief Ernie Walker later said that a coach from Germany, who'd worked in Saudi Arabia, told him that one Saudi player had previously played for him at club level, and was an army captain and a married father of three.

Despite the controversy, the tournament, and Scotland's performances in it, were excellent. Ian Paul wrote in the *Glasgow Herald*, 'We have all been gloriously reminded of why we took to football in the first place,' and he praised the feinting, flicking and dribbling of the 'kids from Africa in particular, but other far-flung centres of the great fitba' brotherhood too'. And he said the young Scots all 'deserve our gratitude for the way they have played and conducted themselves'.

20

Thursday, 17 March 1988

Scotland (Schoolboys) Thrash Brazil

No one who was at Pittodrie on 17 March 1988 would have been surprised by Scotland's impressive performance in the Under-16 World Cup a year later.

On that cold Aberdeen night, several of the players who would reach the 1989 final – including goalie James Will, captain Gary Bollan, Kevin Bain, John Lindsay, Brian O'Neil and Paul Dickov – were instrumental as the Scottish under-15s thrashed their counterparts from the world's most famous national side, 5-0, although Will didn't have much to do and Dickov only appeared as a late substitute.

Five thousand fans – including Scotland boss Andy Roxburgh and Aberdeen stars Willie Miller and Jim Bett – witnessed the young Scots' utterly dominant performance, where they could easily have scored even more.

With Dundee United's Bollan repeatedly bursting forward from defence – which was typical of the Scots' positive, purposeful play – the lads in dark blue created several chances before another United youngster, Tom McMillan, opened the scoring from close range, from one of many great crosses that – you've guessed it – young Dundee United player Lindsay made in the match.

Brazil had one chance to equalise but Russell McKeever and Scott Kinross combined to clear it off the line. The only other thing of note that the young men in the hallowed yellow shirts achieved in the first half was their captain getting booked for bizarrely repeatedly encroaching on a free kick. And, just before half-time, Bollan doubled Scotland's lead with an impressive flying header.

Ten minutes into the second half, Scotland were four up, thanks to young Morton winger Kevin McGoldrick's header from another Lindsay cross, and a goalkeeping howler: the Brazilian keeper completely missed a simple catch from a Kinross long ball, and Craig McNaughton (yep, United) turned it home.

Barry Davidson's neat chip, Kevin Bain's lovely overhead kick and Bollan's fierce shot all came close to extending Scotland's lead. And then Dickov came on and stepped it up another gear, shooting narrowly wide and then drawing a good save from the keeper.

At the other end, Brazil could muster just one second-half chance, which substitute keeper Guy Arbuckle saved easily.

And then, four minutes from the end, Bollan pounced on a loose ball from a corner and blasted it into the far corner from 20 yards, to make it 5-0.

Under the headline 'Youths Run Riot', the *Glasgow Herald* reported, 'On the evidence of last night at Pittodrie there is a bright football future for Scotland.' Sadly, most of this talented team didn't make a huge impression on senior football, but in this match they showed what they would be capable of in their impressive campaign a year later.

21

Sunday, 24 May 1936

Queen of the South Win the Algiers Invitational Tournament

Queen of the South have got a unique, exotic trophy in their club museum. In 1936 they were invited, alongside Spanish side Racing Santander and Floriana from Malta, to compete against Racing Universitaire d'Alger (RUA) in the Algiers Invitational Tournament.

RUA won the North African Cup twice in the 1930s; Racing Santander had just finished fourth in La Liga. It's not immediately clear why the 15th-placed team in the Scottish Division One or a Maltese side were invited to face them.

Perhaps the organisers got the Doonhamers mixed up with Queen's Park; maybe they liked their name. Or maybe they were expecting both Racings to breeze through against inferior opposition and meet in the final, although they were kind enough to describe the Doonhamers on the tournament programme as *La Belle Equipe Ecossaise* – the beautiful Scottish team.

From *La Belle Equipe*'s point of view, there was a logic to their exotic trip; their manager, George McLachlan (a former Manchester United captain), had previously managed French side Le Havre, so was familiar with Francophone footie.

As well as the two tournament games in Algiers, the Scots built in nine more games in France and Luxembourg to their month-long tour, on their way to Algeria and back.

Highlights in France included being presented with a trophy by FC Sète, who'd recently become the first club to win the French double, for beating them 2-1; beating OFC Charleville – whose captain was future Inter boss Helenio Herrera – 5-0; and, on the way home, edging a cracking game against Stade de Reims 5-4.

But the real glory came in the heat of the African spring, as goals from Willie Thomson and English winger Joe Tulip condemned the hosts to a 2-1 semi-final defeat.

Norrie Haywood got the only goal of a bad-tempered final against the Spaniards. Two years later he would score a whopping 45 goals in one season at Raith Rovers, as they set a British record of 142 league goals in a season.

The Spanish tackling was fierce, with Jackie Gordon sustaining a broken collarbone. Tulip said afterwards that about 50 bottles were thrown at him from the crowd, and at one point a policeman chased a Queen of the South coach along the touchline. But none of that mattered; the men from Dumfries had won the tournament.

Boss McLachlan left Palmerston Park less than a year later and never became a manager anywhere else. But his legacy includes the unique achievement of leading a team from Dumfries to intercontinental triumph.

22

Sunday, 26 August 1984

Rose Reilly Wins the World Cup

Several Scottish footballers have carved out successful careers overseas, but one stands head and shoulders above all others, winning eight Scudetti, four Coppa Italias, two golden boots, the French league and a de facto World Cup, where she also scored in the final.

All in the face of deliberate institutional discrimination and adversity. Women's football was effectively banned in Scotland until the early 1970s, by which time Rose Reilly had expanded her horizons in pursuit of her dream.

Rose gave her love to football from the age of three, playing keepie-uppie on her way to the shops and back. Every day at primary school, she got the belt for going into the boys' playground to play football.

When she was seven, she took herself down to the barbers without telling her mum, and got a short back and sides so that she could play in the boys' team, under the pseudonym Ross Reilly. A Celtic scout wanted to sign 'the wee boy who scores all the goals' until he was told, 'You can't, she's a wee lassie.'

When she was 16, Rose was invited to a training camp for the Scottish pentathlon team for the Commonwealth Games, and her athletics coach advised her to quit football. It was the watershed moment when she realised which sport she loved the most and decided to follow her heart. A year later, Rose played in Scotland's first official women's game, but there wasn't yet any prospect of a football career in Scotland for women, so Rose – and her friend Edna Neillis, who'd played alongside her in that international – walked into the *Daily Record* offices to seek the advice of their sports editor, Jack Adams.

He looked into it and arranged a trial with French side Stade de Reims, who immediately signed them both. They won the league, then Milan bought both of the young Scots, who won two league titles at the San Siro. Reilly started out as a striker then moved into the classic number ten position.

Then came surprising news; the Scottish Women's FA gave them both lifetime bans, for reasons that remain unclear but seem connected to their continent-crossing ambition. Neither Reilly nor Neillis ever played for Scotland again.

But Rose had moved on. She played semi-professional football at a variety of clubs, including Napoli and Fiorentina, and won two golden boots, scoring 43 goals for Catania in one season, and 45 for Lecce – where she won three consecutive league titles – in another. In one season she played in Italy on Saturdays and back in France for Stade de Reims on Sundays.

But her greatest moment came in 1984. By now she was considered Italian enough to play for the national team, and she turned out for her adopted homeland in the Mundialito, the 1980s precursor to the FIFA Women's World Cup.

Italy beat West Germany 3-1 in the final, with goals from Carolina Morace, Elisabetta Vignotto and Reilly, their captain. The Ayrshire lass was carried shoulder-high by her jubilant *Azzurre* team-mates.

And to put the mascarpone on the tiramisu, two months later, Reilly was top scorer at the Xi'an international tournament in China, with ten goals in five games, and was promptly named as the world's best female footballer.

Scottish football's loss was very much Italy's gain. And thanks to Rose's love affair with *calcio*, she's – for now, at least – the only Scot to win a World Cup.

23

Saturday, 29 March 1958

Hearts' Incredible Goal-Hungry Season

Hearts' answer to Hibs' Famous Five was the Terrible Trio: forwards Jimmy Wardaugh, Alfie Conn and Willie Bauld. Conn was renowned for his movement and passing; Bauld brought the footballing brains, and Wardaugh was a finisher *par excellence*. Conn and Bauld could score too. In ten years together at Hearts, the trio scored more than 900 goals between them in all competitions, including 500 in the league.

Ironically, Hearts' greatest season of that golden era came when Conn was injured and could only play five league games (he still managed to score four times). The men from Tynecastle romped to the 1957/58 title and set a British top-flight scoring record of an incredible 132 goals in just 34 games.

Hearts started the season as they meant to go on: in their first game they hammered Dundee 6-0, then they beat Airdrie 7-2 away, before taking a brief breather to win the Edinburgh derby by a mere 3-1, and then thrashing East Fife 9-0.

In November they put eight past Queen's Park and nine past Falkirk. In January they beat Third Lanark 7-2.

It wasn't just the Terrible Trio who were responsible for Hearts' scintillating form. Forward Jimmy Murray was knocking them in too – he finished joint-top scorer in the league that season, alongside Wardaugh, on 28 goals each.

That summer, in Sweden, Murray scored Scotland's first ever goal at a World Cup. Young winger Alex Young got 24 goals, and was on such good form that he was actually keeping club legend Bauld out of the team, near the start of an excellent career, first at Tynecastle and later with Everton.

And the Tynecastle men also had by far the league's meanest defence, conceding just 29 goals all season, which was unsurprising with the hugely talented and formidable Dave Mackay still in their ranks, before he went down the road to Spurs.

And masterminding it all was the great Tommy Walker – the classy, elegant, popular, handsome player-turned-manager leading his club through possibly the greatest ever period in their history.

Alongside their remarkable league exploits, they even found time to beat Scotland – despite resting Wardaugh – in a trial match for Scotland players hoping to be chosen for the World Cup. Nine of the Scotland players who faced Hearts in a dramatic match in front of 30,000 fans at Tynecastle made the cut, but they still lost out to the men in maroon, who went two up before Scotland got back on level terms and Mackay grabbed the last-minute winner.

It was in a 4-1 win over Raith Rovers on 29 March, with four league games left to play, that the men from Tynecastle broke Motherwell's top-flight record of 119 goals in one season.

The *Glasgow Herald* reported that 'Rangers and Celtic, who have won many league championships because of their consistency, have never possessed that quality in greater degree' than that Hearts side.

At that point, the Jam Tarts were 18 points ahead of Rangers – who'd pipped Hearts in a dramatic title race the year before – but still couldn't quite celebrate winning their first league championship for more than 60 years, because Rangers had six games in hand.

Six became seven a week later when Rangers sat out the league fixtures again, to face Hibs in the Scottish Cup semi-final.

But a week after that Hearts could finally celebrate the league title that had been inevitable for so long, when they beat St Mirren 3-2 away. The *Evening Times* said, 'Although St Mirren fought them like ferrets to the last second, it was football skill – and the football brains of Jimmy Wardaugh – which brought the great and final rejoicing.'

There was still time for another comprehensive win – 4-0 away to Aberdeen – before more great rejoicing in Hearts' final game of the season as they beat Rangers at a packed Tynecastle. They'd only lost one game all season.

And, once the men from Govan have played all their games in hand, Hearts finished 13 points ahead of them – and with an astonishing goal average of 4.6, to Rangers' 1.8.

24

Sunday, 27 August 2000

Celtic 6 (Six) Rangers 2

The joy of most derby victories is intense but fleeting. At other times it's much more significant than that. Sometimes it's a sign of changing times, shifting sands, a changing of the guard. There can be false dawns, but some great derby wins are portentous. Strange as it seems, it probably wasn't being 3-0 up against Rangers after 11 minutes that convinced Celtic fans that Martin O'Neill's team really were the long-awaited long-term answer to their rivals' almost total dominance of more than a decade of Scottish football.

The signal that this was the real deal was fired early in the second half, with a moment of characteristic, exquisite skill from possibly the greatest footballer to ever play in Scotland. The crowning jewel in a match that was relentlessly captivating and spellbinding; a flawless diamond of a goal that Celtic fans will treasure for ever.

O'Neill had arrived at Celtic in June. This was his seventh game in charge – he'd won his first six – and his first match against Rangers. Rangers had won the previous season's league by 21 points, had subsequently spent more than £10m on Peter Løvenkrands, Kenny Miller and Dutch defenders Fernando Ricksen and Bert Konterman, and also had a 100 per cent record in the league going into the derby. They were unbeaten in their last seven games against Celtic. O'Neill's start had been impressive but this was the real test.

After 51 seconds of the Irish manager's first derby, Celtic were one up, when his fellow derby debutant Chris Sutton blasted a loose ball home from close range, and celebrated with a smile as wide as the Clyde, while the fans went wild.

In an all-action opening, Billy Dodds – who was superbly marshalled throughout by new Celtic defender Joos Valgaeren – and Neil McCann were both booked for bad fouls, and Dodds missed a great chance from a Giovanni van Bronckhorst free kick, before, in the eighth minute, Stiliyan Petrov raced into the six-yard box past the oblivious Ricksen, leapt to meet a Lubo Moravčík corner and planted a brilliant header across Stefan Klos, straight into the bottom corner.

And just three minutes after that, Celtic winger Bobby Petta evaded several desperate Ricksen lunges, and found Moravčík in the box. Paul Lambert raced on to Moravčík's cut-back and blasted the ball into the net; 3-0.

In the commentary box, Ian Crocker exclaimed, 'In Paradise, this is the stuff that Celtic dreams are made of.' His assessment was as accurate as it was evocative. Those 11 minutes were a magical realist dream or a twisted, sickening nightmare, depending on your persuasion.

Parkhead was rocking – the referee Stuart Dougal later said that he was sure that the stadium was literally moving with the fans – and the home players were clearly as jubilant as the supporters (and ball boys). But with 80 minutes still to go, stubborn memories of recent Celtic heroic defeats weren't banished yet.

Petta had been giving new boy Ricksen such a torrid time that, after just 21 minutes, Rangers boss Dick Advocaat replaced his defender with midfielder Tugay, matching Celtic's 3-5-2 formation, and his side started to improve. Then Lambert had to go off injured, Claudio Reyna pulled a goal back, and Rod Wallace had another ruled out for a very tight offside.

At half-time it was merely 3-1; had Celtic's dream start been a glorious aberration? No. Five minutes into the second half, Henrik Larsson – in just his sixth Celtic match since returning from a sickening leg break – scored possibly the greatest goal in the club's history.

Sutton chested a long ball back to the Swede just inside the Rangers half. With Tugay chasing close behind him, Larsson raced forward, calmly poked the ball past a stumbling Konterman and then – apparently effortlessly – produced the most perfect chip you'll see anywhere, to lift the ball well over Klos and comfortably back down under the bar.

In the summer, Advocaat had considered buying Valgaeren but opted for Konterman instead. If he had time to stop and catch his thoughts, he was probably regretting that.

It was the moment that proved that this was no false dawn; the goal that declared O'Neill's Celtic's arrival, providing the evidence to back up Sutton's braggadocio (the big Englishman had talked of 'putting Rangers in their place' when he arrived in Glasgow the month before).

There was still time for three more goals – a Dodds penalty before Larsson and Sutton each made theirs a double, turning a comprehensive 4-2 into a beyond-the-fans'-wildest-dreams 6-2 – but the real significance was longer-term.

Rangers reacted with an almost immediate spending spree, but Celtic went on to win that season's treble, with a 15-point lead at the top of the league.

This was the match when their turnaround to replace Rangers as Scotland's dominant club in the 21st century really started; the key test that they passed with flying colours. They'd comprehensively drubbed a strong Rangers team, ruthlessly exploiting their opponents' few weaknesses, and revelling in their own strengths.

It was an incredible transformation for a club that had been so under the cosh of their big rivals for so long. A transformation that all started with an incredible rapid-fire three-goal blitz and an amazing, beautiful moment from a ludicrously talented player.

25

Saturday, 13 August 1994

Highland Clubs Finally Join the League

On 13 August 1994, a Scottish Third Division match kicked off at Telford Street Park in Inverness. It sounds unremarkable, but this was the first time that clubs from north-west of Aberdeen, Perth or, indeed, Dunbartonshire had played in the Scottish Football League.

And there were two of these Highland newcomers. While Caledonian Thistle were comprehensively beating Arbroath 5-2 at home, Ross County were defeating Cowdenbeath 2-0 down in Fife.

Highland clubs had to wait far too long for their chance to prove themselves in the league, and for Caledonian Thistle it was a difficult and often painful journey to achieve their membership; an almost certainly unnecessarily difficult and painful one. Teams could only join the league when vacancies arose, and they were chosen based on a vote of league members. Clubs voted in their own self-interest, but the main problem was the rarity of vacancies.

One of the three Inverness teams, Clachnacuddin, had made a speculative application to join the league in 1960 but lost out by 32 votes to five.

In 1973, when a vacancy arose, another Inverness side, Thistle, who'd just won back-to-back Highland Leagues, applied alongside three other Highland League clubs – Ross County, Elgin City and Forres Mechanics – as well

as Hawick Royal Albert and also, unusually, English side
Gateshead United, who'd also tried to join the Scottish league
in 1960. Inverness Thistle drew the first round of voting with
Edinburgh team Ferranti Thistle, on 13 votes each. The
other Scottish sides got just one vote each, while Gateshead
got seven.

But Ferranti won the second ballot, and joined the league
under the name Meadowbank Thistle.

Some clubs almost certainly voted for Ferranti because
they didn't want to travel up to the Highlands for games –
this was shortly before the A9 was significantly improved –
and some clubs fancied an opponent who they thought they'd
easily be able to beat rather than one who would enhance the
quality of the league; although Meadowbank did do better
than expected. Whatever the reasons for it, Inverness Thistle
were unlucky to miss out.

It was two decades before any more vacancies arose,
but when they did there were two spots, because of league
reorganisation, and from the start it was virtually guaranteed
that at least one of them would have to go to a Highland club.
Three of the five applicants were from the Highlands, and one
of the others was Gretna, and although their manager Mike
McCartney got his paintbrush out, no one really took them
seriously at that point.

Ross County had only won the Highland League once
before the 1990s, but they were coming good at precisely the
right time for the vote, topping the table in 1991 and then
1992, and they'd just opened a new stand at Victoria Park.
And their manager Bobby Wilson – who, as a player, had
made over 400 appearances for Dundee – lobbied his many
contacts to secure votes for their bid.

County's Scottish Cup results that season helped their
cause too. They hammered St Cuthbert Wanderers 11-0
in December, five days before the hopeful clubs made their
presentations to the league in Glasgow, and then, even more

impressively, beat Second Division Forfar 4-0 three days before the league clubs voted in January.

Elgin City were historically bigger than Ross County. They came from a much bigger town, had won the Highland League 14 times and had once reached the quarter-finals of the Scottish Cup. But a grubby shadow hung over their application. They'd moved the date of their final match of the 1992/93 season so that suspended players could play, and that season's Highland League was consequently declared void.

Gala Fairydean were the one serious contender from outside of the Highlands.

The other Highland candidates, Caledonian Thistle, didn't even exist at that point. Inverness's power brokers were afraid of missing out again and believed that a merged club stood a better chance of being elected than either Caley or Thistle alone, although the league never officially said so, and despite the fact that Caley alone would have been overwhelming favourites in the vote, as the biggest team in the Highlands, playing in the best connected and biggest town in the Highlands.

But the merger of Caledonian and Inverness Thistle went ahead, and it was unsurprisingly complex and painful; these were, after all, clubs with over a century of fierce rivalry.

Much of the impetus for the merger came from the Inverness and Nairn Enterprise group (INE), which could help the new club with the new ground that was a key pillar of their league application. Not unreasonably, INE were more interested in what was good for the town, rather than what was best for Caley or Thistle.

Clachnacuddin were also involved in the initial merger talks but soon decided that it wasn't for them. Almost half of Caley members – who soon became known as the Caley rebels – were angrily opposed to the merger. A large minority of Thistle fans were very sad about it. This could never be a merger of equals; Caley were significantly bigger than Thistle

– the 'Rangers of the North' had won the Highland League a record 18 times and had significantly more members.

The merger proceedings were beset by fractious meetings of Caley members, very tight votes and legal challenges. Meetings were full of angry arguments and accusations; at one a rebel let off a firework. Following a pitch invasion protest by rebels at an away match, the club banned some of the protestors from matches, and – crucially – from future votes. In a rare humorous moment, some rebels parked a double-decker bus outside their ground so that they could watch the Inverness Cup semi-final against Clachnacuddin, and displayed a banner saying 'So you tried to ban us'.

In an attempt to placate the rebels, INE and the club promised that the new stadium, when it was built, would be called the Caledonian Stadium, and that the club's strip would be predominately blue, like Caley's, and, indeed, the initial strip bore no trace whatsoever of Thistle's red or black. At one of the last ever derbies, Caley fans taunted their rivals with chants of 'What's it like to play in blue?'

If the merger had fallen apart before the January vote – which often looked possible – Inverness would probably have missed out. But they just about held it together, and Caley Thistle got 68 votes while Ross County were second with 57. Gala Fairydean missed out, with 35 votes, while Elgin got just ten. Gretna got two.

The merger problems continued after the vote, while Gala Fairydean kept a particularly close eye on proceedings at the other end of the country.

But the merger held together, steering a narrow path through questions of each club's identity.

Before the new stadium was built, the new club initially played at Caley's Telford Street Park, and Caley fans painted it even bluer than it had ever been. The only place where they added any red and black paint was on the insides of the urinals – although that was quickly removed.

Eventually though, to recognise Thistle's identity, it was agreed that a quarter of the strip should be red and black and the word Inverness was added to the club's name. Those were the key compromises that were narrowly accepted by both clubs' members.

So Inverness Thistle mostly disappeared, while Caledonian sort of lived on, and a kind of new club rose and flourished in the league, alongside the unchanged Ross County. Both clubs had well-above-average attendances for their new division, with their new derby setting Third Division records, and Ross County finished third in their first league season.

Both clubs fairly quickly ascended to much better things, often playing in the top flight, and achieving cup success, surely overachieving on their own ambitions and timescales.

Supporters of the Inverness merger point to that success as justification for the massive changes that were made to Inverness's football identity. Although it's highly plausible that exactly the same success would have happened, with Caledonian in the league, instead of Inverness Caley Thistle – and with all clubs continuing with their own identities – if no merger had taken place.

26

Tuesday, 8 February 2000

Super Caley Go Ballistic Celtic Are Atrocious

'Super Caley Go Ballistic Celtic Are Atrocious'. It's one of the best headlines ever written, and – unusually for pun headlines – it was nicely uncontrived and incredibly accurate.

When Inverness Caledonian Thistle took on Celtic in the cold February sleet in the Scottish Cup, they played a blinder. Much has been made – rightly – of their famous opponents' underperformance, but to focus solely on that would be to discredit a talented bunch of Invernessians, who made a mockery of the bookies' pre-match 18/1 odds.

But first, a bit of background. The 1999/2000 season was Celtic boss John Barnes's first in management and six-year-old football club Caley Thistle's first year in the second tier.

Barnes may have been inexperienced but he knew how he wanted his team to play: in the same attacking formation with which Brazil got to the 1998 World Cup Final. And he wasn't for turning, including whenever it became clear that his players – especially the central defenders – didn't have the skills that they needed to make it work. When the formation succeeded, Celtic banged in the goals. But it often didn't succeed.

Meanwhile, under popular boss Steve Paterson, the Highland part-timers had a good combination of experience, through midfielder Charlie Christie – who, over a decade earlier, had been a prolific goalscorer for Celtic's reserves – and 39-year-old goalie Jim Calder, and players who would go on to have good careers both in Inverness and elsewhere, like Barry Wilson, Paul Sheerin, Bobby Mann, Stuart Golabek, Ross Tokely and Dennis Wyness.

Celtic were missing Henrik Larsson, who'd suffered a horrendous leg break in a UEFA Cup match in Lyon, but still had strikers Mark Viduka – who'd been banging them in – Mark Burchill and Ian Wright.

Defender Olivier Tébily, meanwhile, was playing his first game after being detained at a military camp with his international team-mates following the Africa Cup of Nations.

Inverness were also missing their main man up front, Canadian international Davide Xausa. Winger Barry Wilson deputised for him, and opened the scoring after just 16 minutes, with a simple header from a Paul Sheerin cross.

Burchill equalised two minutes later. That was as good as it would get for the Bhoys. Eight minutes after that, Celtic's classy Slovakian midfielder Ľubomír Moravčík made a rare mistake when he deflected a Bobby Mann header past goalie Jonathan Gould.

Moravčík epitomised the untapped skill and potential in Barnes's Celtic squad. Other Barnes players who looked desperate that season, like Bobby Petta, would be revelations the next year, under Martin O'Neill. But on this night not even the likes of Moravčík or Tom Boyd could steady the ship.

The Celtic fans whistled their team off at half-time. And then there was a terrible row in the home dressing room. Assistant boss Eric Black had a go at Mark Viduka, who squared up to him. 'Fortunately Olivier Tébily and the fitness coach jumped in and hauled him away, otherwise he'd have killed me,' Black later said.

Viduka stripped off and got in the bath. Meanwhile, Gould questioned Eyal Berkovic's contribution in no uncertain terms. Ian Wright – who played the second half instead of Viduka – later said that he'd never seen a dressing-room dust-up quite like it. And he'd had quite a lot of experience by that point.

Barnes didn't seem to have any way of bringing his warring players together. Meanwhile, whereas some First Division managers would send their teams out to defend a half-time lead against Glasgow behemoths, Paterson told his men to keep attacking; he thought they had more goals in them.

Celtic forced some good saves from Calder in the second half, but Paterson's prediction about his men scoring again was accurate.

Twelve minutes after the break, Celtic winger Regi Blinker needlessly conceded a penalty and spot-kick expert Sheerin sent Gould the wrong way.

Subeditors started sharpening their headlines, while Celtic supporters started to leave early, and the 4,000 delighted travelling fans chanted 'We want four!'

It finished 3-1 to the men from Inverness. Paterson said, 'I think this is the moment Inverness arrived in Scottish football.' Once again, he was spot-on.

Hundreds of Celtic fans gathered outside to call for Barnes to be sacked. The players were advised not to leave the stadium until the angry supporters had dispersed but at one o'clock in the morning they were still there – while the Inverness players celebrated on their coach heading up the A9 – and security guards escorted the Celtic squad to their cars.

Director of football Kenny Dalglish flew home early from a trip to Spain, and Barnes – and both his assistants, Black and Terry McDermott – were sacked two days after the game.

Despite Barnes's Celtic's unpredictability, it was still a shock result. It did, as Paterson said, mark a significant step on ICT's swift upward trajectory, and it also ushered in decisive managerial change and a consequent long-term upturn in fortunes at Parkhead, with O'Neill arriving that summer.

Sometimes Celtic fans thank some of the Inverness players for providing the spark that led to that change.

But the headline which *The Sun* used to pithily summarise the game has probably become even more famous than either Caley Thistle's performance or Celtic's bust-up.

It was written by subeditor Paul Hickson, when his colleague, Steve Wolstencroft, recalled a similar one that commemorated Liverpool midfielder Ian Callaghan's performance against QPR decades earlier.

Shortly afterwards, Hickson modestly described his headline as 'good, but I don't think it's that good – a nice pun'. Wolstencroft admitted that it was largely a remake of someone else's work. But it achieved fame, and with good reason.

But the night should mostly be remembered for being another big step in Inverness Caledonian Thistle's inexorable upwards rise, towards both Premiership football and – in 2015 – winning the Scottish Cup. They beat Celtic in the semi-final that year, after extra time, but had been so successful in the meantime that by then they certainly weren't 18/1 outsiders.

27

Sunday, 8 January 2006

Clyde Outclass Celtic in the Cup

The Caley Thistle defeat may well be Celtic's most infamous cup collapse, but another part-time side delivered an equally humbling lesson to the Glasgow giants six years later.

Clyde's 2-1 Scottish Cup defeat of Celtic was especially notable for three reasons: the – very young – First Division side played like a Premier League club while the Bhoys looked like the team who were showing their opponents too much respect; the Bully Wee were so dominant that they actually had the ball in the net *five* times and also had a penalty saved; and all this in spite of the fact that the former Manchester United captain, and also the future China captain, were both making their debuts for Celtic.

All the talk before the match was about Roy Keane's Celtic debut. He may have been 34 and recovering from injury, but he was one of the best players of his generation.

And it wasn't just Keane; this was mostly a strong Celtic side – Artur Boruc, Neil Lennon, Shunsuke Nakamura, Shaun Maloney and John Hartson all also took to the Broadwood pitch for the SPL leaders, in their all-green away strip.

But another Celtic debutant had a huge, negative influence on the outcome: Du Wei. Although the tall Chinese defender was far from the only ineffective Celt on the day.

The green half of the sold-out Broadwood stands chanted 'Keano, Keano' early on, but it was Clyde who shot out of the traps like a greyhound with unfinished business. While Celtic tried to probe gently for openings, the young players in white headed straight towards Boruc's goal. The first decent chance was created by teenage midfielder Craig Bryson, who strode forward and blasted a shot narrowly over the bar.

This Clyde team looked like they would struggle to buy a carry-out. The oldest player in the starting 11 was 22.

Bryson created the next good chance too, clipping the ball forward to Tom Brighton, who got to it before Du and placed it past Boruc, but referee Kenny Clark pulled it back for a foul – that no one else saw – on the Chinese defender.

As the Clyde onslaught continued, Boruc made a good save from a long-distance Steve Masterton shot.

Then after more dominant attacking play, including a lovely back-heel on the edge of the box, striker Alex Williams got the ball in the net, but it was chalked off for offside against Brighton and Stephen O'Donnell, who probably weren't interfering with play.

The first goal finally came after half an hour. Eddie Malone made a great run down the left wing, and Bryson headed home from the cross; 1-0.

Five minutes later, Celtic showed their only moment of top quality of the first half, and it was all down to Maloney, who made a great run, but his shot from a tight angle was well blocked by Peter Cherrie, and Clyde broke straight up the other end, where Du hauled down Brighton in the box. The struggling defender might have welcomed a red card but none was forthcoming, and to compound the pain of that injustice for the home side, Boruc got down well to save O'Donnell's penalty.

But the holy goalie's efforts were in vain, as the resulting corner reached Malone, who blasted a fierce left-footed swivel kick into the net; 2-0 Clyde and the least they deserved. The home fans – including their former manager Craig Brown and *Sportscene* presenter Dougie Donnelly – were ecstatic.

Du didn't come out for the second half, as Celtic boss Gordon Strachan replaced him with Adam Virgo. But if anyone was expecting Celtic to take their turn to dominate, it didn't happen. Clyde were still knocking the ball around with confidence in midfield, giving their illustrious opponents no time in possession, and creating more chances.

Brighton fired just over the bar. Bryson set up O'Donnell, whose strong header smacked the base of the post. Then Bryson had the ball in the net again, but the flag was already up, for another debatable offside.

And with just seven minutes left, substitute Maciej Żurawski showed Celtic's second moment of quality in the match, cracking home a goal from the edge of the box. And, for all their dominance, suddenly Clyde were just one more Celtic goal away from missing out on the result of all their great work.

Nakamura whipped a late free kick into the box but Cherrie somehow claimed it. The last minutes were tense but when Clark blew for full time, Broadwood erupted in joy. Clyde had beaten the Premier Leaguer leaders 2-1, going on 5-1.

That first half in Cumbernauld was the only 45 minutes that Du ever played for Celtic. The *Daily Record* ran with the headline 'Show Him Du Wei to Go Home'. Although he can't have been all bad, because he played 71 times for China.

After the game, Clyde manager Graham Roberts said, 'Every player in our team today gave everything they had.' It was very true. But Bryson was the best of them all, while Brighton and Malone caught the eye too.

Later in his career, Bryson played 250 games for Derby County and got a couple of Scotland caps, but, 15 years after the Celtic game, he said that it was 'still one of the best days of my career ... we played brilliantly'.

And a Clyde fan interviewed on *Sportscene* outside the ground after full time summed up the irony of this particular giant-killing nicely when he quipped, 'Did you see Roy Keane trying to get Craig Bryson's shirt at the end there?'

28

Saturday, 13 May 2006

Gretna in the Cup Final

Gretna were only in the Scottish Football League for six seasons, but that was long enough for them to get promoted three times and reach the Scottish Cup Final. And they might have won it, if it wasn't for an unbelievably well-timed tackle by Robbie Neilson.

The village side, from a town of fewer than 3,000 people, took 12,000 joyous black-and-white-bedecked fans on a fairytale adventure to Hampden, made possible by the benevolence of one charismatic multi-millionaire, which brought the Borderers plenty of criticism from rival fans and also from some journalists.

One scribe accurately likened their adventure to a speeding train without a station. Gretna could never have the fanbase to support their ambitions of top-flight football and European competition, although they did – very briefly – achieve both of those goals too, right when they came off the rails and their journey ended in financial implosion and personal tragedy.

But first, happier times.

Following their failed application to join the league in 1994, Gretna returned with a better, successful application in 2002. At their league debut, at their Raydale Park home, against Morton, a self-made, ponytailed multi-millionaire, whose attempt to buy nearby Carlisle United had just fallen through – Brooks Mileson – was present for the first time. Soon afterwards, he was investing heavily in the club.

A year later, Gretna became the only full-time club in the Third Division, and started recruiting experienced players from higher divisions. They finished third and made a large loss. Mileson seemed nonplussed by questions around the financial situation. It was his money, he was giving something to the local community and it was fun; where was the harm in that?

The next year, his continued investment brought big results. The black and whites won the division with 98 points out of a possible 108, and scored 130 league goals. Young doctor Kenny Deuchar got 38 of them, including six hat-tricks, which perhaps wasn't surprising, as Mileson lent Deuchar his Aston Martin every time he got a hat-trick.

In the same year, the club got their first big taste of Scottish Cup excitement when they drew Premier League Dundee United at home. They built an extra temporary stand. Mileson bought all the tickets and handed them out for free, including to away fans. He also laid on brass bands, clowns and fire-eaters, as the home side lost, but just 4-3. It was a taste of the excitement that was to follow the next year. The finances may have been unsustainable, and Gretna were making no headway with plans to renovate their tiny dilapidated stadium, but this was still a fun ride. And it was about to get better.

The 2005/06 season was Gretna's greatest year. In the first two rounds of the Scottish Cup they thrashed two of the clubs who they'd beaten to election to the league just a few years earlier, winning 6-2 away against Preston Athletic and 6-1 at home against Cove.

Then they faced four First Division sides. A Steve Tosh goal was enough to beat St Johnstone away, before a tie against the Clyde team who'd just knocked out Celtic, and who'd knocked Gretna out of the cup in two of the previous three seasons.

That match was notable mainly for three red cards but was drawn 0-0 and went to a replay at Raydale on Valentine's Day. The temporary stand was up again, Mileson bought red roses for every female fan at the game, James Grady got a hat-trick and Gretna marched on to the quarter-final, where they beat First Division leaders St Mirren 1-0.

Gretna fans were in dreamland. Before their semi-final, they won the Second Division and a second successive promotion.

The semi-final, against Dundee, was on 1 April. That morning, the *Daily Record* reported that Gretna would be building an off-shore stadium so that Mileson could get around the smoking ban. It was, of course, an April fool, and also a mark of the impact that this tiny club was having on the national consciousness.

It was surprisingly easy for Gretna at Hampden, as they beat Dundee 3-0, with a Deuchar goal, a Ryan McGuffie penalty and a Barry Smith own goal, as the black and whites became the first third-tier team to reach the Scottish Cup Final.

But their opponents in the final were a different prospect: Hearts had just finished second in the Premier League and qualified for the Champions League. Vladimir Romanov was financially doping the Gorgie side in exactly the same way that Mileson was propping up Gretna, but on a far bigger scale.

While Mileson took his place in the stand with the thousands of Gretna fans, sporting his modest black-and-white rosette, Romanov conducted his own act of generosity, inviting a group of veteran Soviet submarine heroes – who'd averted a nuclear catastrophe in 1961 – to join him in the posh seats. Gretna boss Rowan Alexander – who'd been at the club throughout all of their adventures and before them, when they were still playing in England's Northern Premier League – led his team out in his kilt.

Unsurprisingly, Hearts dominated the first half. Alan Main pulled off a string of saves from Rudi Skácel, Edgaras Jankauskas and Roman Bednář, before Skácel opened the scoring five minutes before half-time.

But Alexander made an attacking substitution at half-time and the second half was much more even, with opportunities for both sides. Gretna sub David Graham created the best chance of all when he burst through the middle and rounded Craig Gordon but Neilson timed his incredible sliding tackle perfectly to somehow prevent Graham's tap-in.

Then Deividas Česnauskis tripped John O'Neill on the edge of the box, and McGuffie knocked home the rebound from his own penalty after Gordon initially saved the spot-kick; 1-1 with 15 minutes to go.

Neither side could find a winner, and Hearts' main penalty taker, Paul Hartley, got a second yellow card in the last minute of extra time, for retaliating to a clumsy foul.

But the Gretna dream ended in the penalty shoot-out, as Gordon saved from Derek Townsley, and then Gavin Skelton's effort came back off the bar (a couple of years later, Gavin's wee sister Helen became a *Blue Peter* presenter).

The Hearts fans gave the beaten finalists a standing ovation. The next week, Mileson took out a half-page advert in the *Edinburgh Evening News* to thank them for that. And despite losing the final, Gretna had qualified for the UEFA Cup.

Before their UEFA Cup tie though, Mileson was rushed to hospital for an emergency operation. Sadly, he was experiencing serious health problems. Meanwhile, the Gretna dream started to lose its sheen.

They had to play their UEFA Cup home leg, against Derry City, in Motherwell, 75 miles away, because Raydale wasn't up to scratch. A decent crowd of 6,000 were left to rue three Derry goals in nine second-half minutes, as Gretna's brief European diversion ended 7-3 on aggregate.

There was off-field turmoil, cost-cutting and player departures at the club in their First Division campaign but they still secured an unprecedented third consecutive promotion on a dramatic last day of the season.

They were still making huge losses, and owed millions to Mileson, whose health was getting worse.

Promotion to the Premier League was a double-edged sword. For the whole top-flight season, they had to play 'home' games in Motherwell. The results on the pitch were terrible and the financial problems led to the club being liquidated and leaving the league. Tragically, Mileson died, aged 60, a few months after that.

He'd pumped £8m into Gretna as he'd taken them on an incredibly dramatic and also controversial journey. He'd always said he was always doing it for the fun, and what can be more fun than taking a village side to a national cup final?

Remarkably, Gretna's Scottish Cup Final appearance wasn't the only iconic moment in Scottish football on that day.

29

Saturday, 13 May 2006

Scotland Win the Kirin Cup

On the Saturday morning before Gretna took on Hearts in the cup final, Scotland had an ersatz final of their own, almost 6,000 miles away. If they could avoid losing by a margin of at least three goals to Japan, at the Saitama Stadium, they would win the Kirin Cup: their first ever senior trophy. Unless you include the Rous Cup.

But because the Kirin Cup was squeezed between the domestic season and the World Cup, Walter Smith had to assemble a makeshift team for the competition, with precious little preparation time for a tournament on the other side of the world.

Smith had to do without cup finalists Craig Gordon, Paul Hartley and Steven Pressley – all of whom had played in Scotland's previous game. Kris Boyd, Chris Burke and Lee Miller all made their international debuts in the short tournament, goalie Neil Alexander got two of his three Scotland caps there, and Graeme Murty got two of his total of four.

The Scottish league season had finished on the Sunday before the tournament, and the players kicked off on the Thursday – in the early hours in Scottish time – in Kobe, against Bulgaria.

Bulgaria and Japan were also missing players for the tournament, but could still draw on top talent like Martin

Petrov and Shinji Ono, while Scotland did have their two most established stars of that era, Darren Fletcher and James McFadden.

Bulgaria and Japan were managed by playing legends Hristo Stoichkov and Zico and were both above Scotland in the FIFA rankings. So what the Scots did in front of a crowd of less than 6,000 – including a large contingent of Scottish fans – in the Kobe Wing Stadium was as surprising as it was impressive.

Either side of a Yordan Todorov equaliser, Boyd scored twice in his first 45 minutes in a dark blue shirt (a few months after moving from Kilmarnock to Rangers). But if the first half against Bulgaria was satisfying, the second was almost unbelievable.

McFadden replaced Boyd at half-time, hit the crossbar, and then flicked home a Gary Teale cross to make it 3-1. Teale, who'd been influential, made way for substitute Chris Burke with 15 minutes to go. Burke's first two touches in a Scotland shirt were phenomenal, as he scored the goal of the match, chesting the ball sublimely and cracking home a volley past the stretching keeper. And his short debut got even better when he made it 5-1 near the end.

It was a brilliant performance and a brilliant result for the patchwork team and – because Bulgaria had beaten the hosts on the Tuesday – it meant that, if Scotland could avoid a heavy defeat against Japan, they would win the strange, single-handled Kirin Cup.

But Scotland had just one day off before the Japan game, whereas their hosts had had a three-day break. So the Scots jumped on a bullet train for the 300-mile journey to the stadium that had hosted the Brazil v Turkey semi-final in the World Cup four years earlier.

Although it was chucking it down with rain, the big stadium was packed and rocking for the match. Japan were the better side, and created a good few chances, but Scotland, playing a 5-4-1, dug in and defended doggedly, forcing their hosts to mostly shoot from distance, and with Alexander making some good saves.

In the first half, Akira Kaji hit the post, then Ono skilfully created a good chance for himself but Alexander saved it well. At half-time the Scots – playing in yellow – could dare to dream, and they had a good chance of their own in the second half when a Boyd back-heel set up Gavin Rae, who fired the ball at the keeper.

But it didn't matter that Rae couldn't make it count. Scotland got the draw that their defending deserved, and captain David Weir was presented with the trophy and a novelty-size cheque for $100,000.

The players celebrated with a crate of beer that the sponsors had provided, before heading to a bar to watch the English FA Cup Final.

Several of them stayed out considerably later, and almost missed their early morning flight home, in a fitting finale to a whirlwind tournament.

30

Monday, 4 June 1979

Dundee United, Japan Cup Finalists

Early in Jim McLean's Tannadice reign, Dundee United reached the final of the Japan Cup – the precursor to the Kirin Cup – despite missing several key players.

Even though Dave Narey and Paul Hegarty were away on international duty, United topped their group, narrowly ahead of Argentinian *grandes* San Lorenzo, thanks in part to a Ray Stewart hat-trick in Hiroshima, where the Tangerines beat Burma 4-0.

By the time of their semi-final against Fiorentina, the Terrors were also missing goalie Hamish McAlpine, who'd been sent home after a disagreement with McLean. After the tournament, McAlpine was briefly suspended, and 37-year-old former England keeper Peter Bonetti was signed, although McLean unconvincingly denied that the signing was related to the suspension.

Twenty-two-year-old reserve Andy Graham played brilliantly against *I Viola*. He saved a penalty during the 2-2 draw, and two more in the penalty shoot-out, which the Scots won 4-2, to set up a final against Spurs.

The Japan Cup was the brief highlight of Graham's United career. After a few years as a largely unneeded reserve keeper, he moved to Stirling Albion, where he was hugely popular and made 222 appearances. As well as missing Hegarty, Narey and McAlpine for the final, United would also have to do without Stewart, who'd left to play for the Scotland under-21s. And as if all that wasn't bad enough, the remaining players went to a reception at a whisky company – and Davie Dodds was subsequently taken ill and also missed the final, while Graham and midfielder Derek Addison were also unwell but played, and John Holt played with an ankle injury.

Despite all that, United had a great chance to take the lead in the first half, when Paul Sturrock was brought down for a penalty. Walter Smith – by now, aged 31, only playing occasionally, following a pelvic injury two years earlier – took it but it was saved, and Gordon Smith and Ossie Ardiles scored in the second half to win the tournament for the Londoners.

United had gone toe-to-toe with three top clubs from across the world, and edged past all but one of them, despite being down to the bare bones.

Even McLean was impressed, saying, 'None of my players was outshone by the great Ardiles, and that speaks volumes for our performances ... They've proved a lot both to themselves and to me throughout the tournament.'

31

1934

The First Dugout in the World

The world's first ever football dugout was installed at Pittodrie in the summer of 1934. Before that, coaches sat on benches by the touchline. Aberdeen were pitchside perspective and precipitation protection pioneers, moving their coaching staff lower down, all the better to watch the players' feet, while also protecting them from the elements.

It was all Donald Colman's idea. The former Dons captain and Scotland international – who played well into his 40s, and was recent Scotland international Rachel Corsie's great granddad – was a great football thinker and innovator. He coached in Norway before being invited back to the Granite City as a trainer, by manager Paddy Travers.

Colman was big on fitness and technique. He rubbed players down with whisky before a cold Inverness cup tie, he encouraged players to drink cocktails of sherry, honey and raw eggs, and he loved boxing and dancing. He experimented with moulded boots and protective headgear for goalies, he had techniques to improve players' weaker feet, and he was ahead of his time tactically.

And, because he was convinced of the importance of good footwork, he wanted to be able to see players' feet as they played. So he invented the dugout. It quickly caught on. And the world's first ever dugout remained at Pittodrie, unchanged, until the main stand was redeveloped in 1968.

32

Saturday, 18 May 1991

The Greatest Scottish Cup Final of All Time

The 1991 Scottish Cup Final between Motherwell and Dundee United was billed as the Family Final, with the teams managed by famous McLean brothers Tommy and Jim, and that billing took on a bittersweet resonance when their father passed away shortly before the match.

The match, though, will be remembered mainly as probably the most thrilling and dramatic Scottish Cup Final ever, and should probably also be known as the Ally Maxwell Final, in tribute to Motherwell's brave keeper.

This was United's sixth cup final under Jim McLean, but they had never won it. Because of that, they'd stayed in a different hotel before each final, in case any of them were unlucky, and – after having stayed in Glasgow hotels for the first five, now stayed in one in St Andrews. Motherwell – who had beaten Aberdeen and Celtic to get to the final – had won the trophy once, almost 40 years earlier.

They may have only won the trophy once between them, but now both teams were going through good spells, and had some great players, including Tom Boyd – playing his last game for Motherwell, before transferring to Chelsea for £800,000, 19-year-old Phil O'Donnell, 35-year-old Davie Cooper; and for United, Maurice

Malpas, Jim McInally, 19-year-old Duncan Ferguson, and Darren Jackson.

The match was relentless and played at a frantic pace. Both ends of an almost-full Hampden were rocking throughout, with many fans waving large club flags on the open, uncovered, pre-redevelopment Hampden terraces, behind iconic Tennent's lager hoardings.

There was just one goal in the first half, but plenty of action and drama. United – the favourites, and playing in white – came close to opening the scoring twice in the first seven minutes. First, a fierce Hamish French strike was ruled out for an offside flag against Darren Jackson. And then Freddie van der Hoorn smacked a shot off the inside of the post, which ricocheted back across the face of the goal with so much power that it went out for a throw in.

Then Motherwell got the ball in the net, but it was ruled out for a foul on the keeper. United's Craig Paterson headed just over, before Ally Maxwell got a knock in the stomach when he went down to claim the ball in a penalty box scramble.

And then Motherwell opened the scoring. Iain Ferguson passed to Jim Griffin out wide, Griffin pinged in a lovely cross and Ferguson powered a great header into the net.

It was 1-0 at half-time. John O'Neil replaced Duncan Ferguson, who had been a pre-match injury doubt, for the second half, which was even more dramatic – significantly more dramatic – than the first.

First up, Maxwell got injured again when he leapt for a cross and clattered into John Clark – an injury that was far worse than his first-half knock. There was no replacement goalie on the bench, with the rules just permitting teams two substitutes each, and Maxwell played on for the rest of the game, clearly in constant pain, clutching his ribs throughout. It was later confirmed that he had a ruptured spleen and broken ribs.

And then four goals came in just 12 minutes.

First, Dave Bowman blasted a diagonal shot past Maxwell from the edge of the box; 1-1.

Then Motherwell scored twice: first with a brave header from Phil O'Donnell, to claim his first career goal, and then with a fierce, low, left-foot Ian Angus drive, from the edge of the box; 3-1.

Then Bowman crossed to substitute O'Neil, who headed home United's second.

With the 90 minutes almost up, United pushed for an equaliser. Maxwell came for a cross and claimed it well, under pressure, when he was clearly in a lot of pain.

In the 90th minute, with Motherwell fans whistling for full time, the Steelmen broke forward, but the ball broke to United keeper Alan Main. He launched it forward, it bounced once between Maxwell and Jackson, and Jackson bravely headed home the equaliser, sending the United fans wild.

Motherwell had come so close to winning, but now they – including their badly injured number one – would have to play another 30 minutes. The momentum could easily have shifted away from them, but they started extra time well. Main had to save well from substitute Steve Kirk. And then, from a Davie Cooper corner, just four minutes into extra time, Kirk headed in the winner.

The fact that it was the winner was thanks to Maxwell, who first had to throw himself to the ground to save a Jackson shot well, and, near the end, leapt to save from a fierce Malpas shot.

That was the last chance. Motherwell had finally won.

There was still time for more drama. The United players thought Chris McCart had fouled Main when Kirk scored the winner. In the Hampden tunnel, McInally threw his boot at referee David Syme. Syme sent him – and fellow protestors Jackson, Clark and Van der Hoorn – off.

Meanwhile, Motherwell's fans celebrated wildly, inside Hampden, and, shortly afterwards, on the pitch at Fir Park, where the players turned up with the trophy for a post-match celebration. Most of the players, that is. Ally Maxwell, the biggest hero of the day, was receiving treatment in hospital.

Maxwell later became only the second player to be inducted into Motherwell's Hall of Fame. O'Donnell was next, with Cooper, boss McLean and Kirk all following soon afterwards. Tragically, O'Donnell and Cooper's inductions were both posthumous, as they both died in their 30s.

After recovering from his injuries, Maxwell went on to play for other clubs, including Rangers – and Dundee United.

33

Saturday, 6 August 1960

Kilmarnock, Finalists in the International Soccer League

Kilmarnock's golden era was undoubtedly the early '60s, under manager Willie Waddell, but it was an era when they developed a bittersweet habit of finishing second.

In the spring of 1960 they were runners-up to Hearts in the league and Rangers in the Scottish Cup. But their form was good enough to earn them an invite to compete in the inaugural International Soccer League in the USA, and they would be playing in the first ever match in the new global tournament, against Bayern Munich.

The competition was the brainchild of Bill Cox, a US businessman and sports entrepreneur who wanted to make soccer huge in the States and so created an international competition with 12 clubs from around the world.

Cox was determined that his tournament would be massive, but it started with controversy that could have immediately stopped it in its tracks. Bayern wanted substitutions to be allowed. Killie, Burnley and Glenavon threatened to go straight back home rather than tolerate such modern indulgences. The UK clubs got their way: no subs.

So Killie and Bayern kicked off the big new tournament in front of a crowd of 10,000 at the Polo Grounds – a large stadium just across 110th Street, immediately north of

Central Park. Scottish journalist 'Rex' wrote that the venue's floodlights were so bright that you could tell if a player had forgotten to brush his teeth. The *Glasgow Herald* reported that the match was just what the organisers wanted: fast, entertaining and skilful.

Bayern were not yet the powerhouse that they would soon become; with West German top-flight football still regionalised following the war, they'd just finished fifth in the Oberliga Sud. But they were going places and had just signed Yugoslavian World Cup goalscoring striker Miloš Milutinović. Milutinović didn't find the net against Killie, but the Bavarian side did take an early lead against the Scots, through a Frank Beattie headed own goal.

The second half though, was all Killie. The *Herald* reported that the Ayrshiremen's bewildering ball control had the German defence in a tangle and the locals applauded Hungarian goalie Árpád Fazekas's every move, as he was the only Bayern man who kept the scoreline respectable. But Killie scored three late goals, through Jackie McInally (whose son Alan would play for Bayern), Tommy Bryceland, who was on loan from St Mirren for the duration of the tournament, and an 18-yard last-minute shot from centre-forward Andy Kerr.

After the match, Killie keeper Jimmy Brown said that, with his side so dominant in the last 20 minutes, he was so stationary that he could have stood in for the Statue of Liberty.

Unlike Bayern, Burnley were in the form of their lives in 1960. They met Killie at the Polo Grounds as English league champions, but the Scots won the physical contest 2-0, with goals from Kerr and a last-minute Vernon Wentzel free kick.

The physicality and entertainment continued against Nice. There was controversy when the referee accused the French coach, Jean Luciano, of spitting in his face and the faces of two Killie players, which Luciano denied.

McInally opened the scoring early in the second half, before Nice equalised shortly after from the penalty spot.

French international goalkeeper Georges Lamia made some fine saves late on as Killie pressed for a winner, and the game finished 1-1. Despite the spitting controversy and some tough tackling from the Scots, the French side later awarded Killie a huge silver trophy to credit them as the most accomplished and sporting team in the group.

Killie won their other two group matches, 2-0 against Glenavon, through goals from Billy Muir and Matt Watson, and 3-1 against the New York Americans.

When Rex had watched the New York Americans in their first match, he'd said that they looked like they'd learned football from a book. But the truth was that this very un-American team were still learning to play alongside each other, as a hastily assembled side to represent the home nation, including several players from Chelsea, Arsenal and QPR, and Wales international Alf Sherwood, all trained by former Liverpool centre-forward Albert Stubbins.

Killie's first goal against the very British Americans was an own goal that resulted from a fierce McInally shot, before McInally added the second without the need of any inadvertent intervention from the opposition, and then Muir dribbled past the adopted New Yorkers and fired past the keeper.

In the four weeks that they'd spent in North America, Killie had won four and drawn one of their five group matches. And they also found time to win two friendlies, each almost 400 miles from New York, 7-2 against a US and Canadian all-stars side in Ohio, with a hat-trick from Wentzel and a brace from McInally, and 4-1 against Montreal Concordia, with McInally and Wentzel again on the scoresheet and Kerr grabbing a double.

As well as the cup that Nice gave them, Killie returned home from the group stage with another trophy, for Brown, which he'd been awarded for being the best goalie in the group.

The players' flight arrived home at Prestwick at quarter to one in the morning, almost a month after they'd flown out to New York, and they were greeted off the plane by 600 jubilant fans.

They would have to wait another month and a half before playing in the final, with the second group stage taking place after the first. It was very hot and humid at the Polo Grounds when Killie took on Brazilian side Bangu in the final, in front of 25,000 fans. Bangu may be about as famous in Scotland these days as Kilmarnock are in Brazil, but they'd finished third in the 1959 Campeonato Carioca, the Rio de Janeiro state championship, and their captain was the talented Brazil international Zózimo.

And the boys from Brazil demonstrated their skills in the final, with good passing setting up diminutive forward Valter Lino dos Santos to sprint into the box and crack a low shot past Brown and into the net. Bangu didn't really let up after that, and only some good saves from Brown kept it at 1-0, but in the second last minute, Valter's speculative long shot span off Willie Toner and looped over Brown, who managed to claw the ball back, but it hit the bar and dropped in, while Brown ended up upside down in the back of his net.

At full time, the Killie players carried off Zózimo shoulder high. The Brazilians were awarded with a big trophy with a winged woman on top of it, while the Killie players made do with a third runners-up spot in a few months, before flying back to Scotland for the start of the League Cup – the fourth tournament in 1960 in which they would come second.

Bangu came to Rugby Park for a friendly in April 1961. Killie got some revenge, winning 1-0, in front of 18,000 fans, through a Kerr goal.

The International Soccer League continued for another five years, before succumbing to off-field political constraints. Kilmarnock represented Scotland three more times in the tournament – and lost to Bangu again, in 1961, 5-0 – and Dundee and Hearts each did so once, but none of them ever made it to the final again.

34

Tuesday, 8 May 1945

The Return of Bobby Combe

Hibs' outstanding success in the 1940s and '50s was consistently attributed to the Famous Five of Gordon Smith, Eddie Turnbull, Lawrie Reilly, Bobby Johnstone and Willie Ormond – probably Scotland's best ever forward line.

But as Reilly said, 'We knew we had great players behind us and we couldn't possibly have enjoyed the success we did without the tremendous support they gave us.'

Chief among those great players was Bobby Combe. Teenage Leither Bobby signed for his boyhood idols on the same day as Gordon Smith and made his debut alongside him, against Hearts. Starting out up front, he was joint-top scorer in his first season, with 29 goals.

Great things were expected of Bobby, and great things came – he starred up front in Hibs' first postwar title-winning season and, following the signing of Johnstone, was a key part of the half-back line for the other league titles.

But, near the end of the war, no one thought that promising young Bobby would ever play for the club again, or that they would even ever see him again.

Bobby was away fighting in the war, and in late 1944 the army reported him missing. No one knew if he was alive or dead.

On VE Day, the team were in chairman Harry Swan's restaurant on Leith Walk, celebrating the end of the war.

And you can probably guess who walked in, to their delighted surprise. Bobby had been imprisoned in the Sandbostel prisoner-of-war camp and was alive and well.

His team-mates were over the moon to see him. And to make his adventure even more like a *Boy's Own* comic strip, the next day he captained his team to victory against Hearts in front of the biggest ever crowd for a Roseberry Cup Final.

35

Saturday, 14 January 1928

Jimmy McGrory Scores Eight Goals in One Game

It wasn't unusual for Celtic striker Jimmy McGrory to score lots of goals in one game. He got more than 50 hat-tricks. But even by his remarkable standards, his achievements when Dunfermline came to Parkhead in January 1928 were incredible.

He notched a hat-trick in the first ten minutes, struck once more before half-time, and then repeated his four-goal trick in the second half, scoring eight of Celtic's goals in a 9-0 win. Alec Thomson (who was pretty handy too) got the other one. The *Evening Times* led with the headline 'Rat-Tat-Tat Scoring'; the *Glasgow Herald* went with the more characteristically phlegmatic 'Celtic Centre's Record'.

McGrory's multi-goal haul on that day is still a British top-flight record. And, remarkably, apparently not one of his goals in that game was a header.

Because, despite only being 5ft 6in tall, McGrory scored almost a third of his goals with his head. He was so renowned for his diving headers that he was nicknamed 'the Mermaid', and journalist Hughie Taylor said he could head the ball as fiercely as most players could kick it. Queen's Park goalie Jack Harkness was reported to have once broken three fingers trying to save one of McGrory's headers.

McGrory's haul against Dunfermline serves as evidence of his relentless goalscoring excellence, rather than a freak one-off achievement. He finished that season on 47 league goals, but even that wasn't his best. In one season he got 49; in another he grabbed 50. In both of those seasons he was Europe's top scorer.

McGrory's first ever Celtic goal was a bittersweet one, coming on the same day as his father's funeral. The Mermaid had already scored 13 goals on loan at Clydebank, including a winner against Celtic. He would end up on 398 league goals and 74 Scottish Cup goals for Celtic, as well as 53 in other cups.

He only got seven Scotland caps – although, to be fair, at least part of the reason for that was the fact that he was in direct competition with the almost equally great Hughie Gallacher for the centre-forward spot. In those seven international games he scored six times, including a winner against England. His six goals for the Scottish League XI brought his total in top-level football to 550, a British record.

The Mermaid's playing career was consistently excellent, but his exploits against the Pars on that one winter's day stand out among all others as the ultimate example of joyous goal-hungry gluttony.

36

Tuesday, 23 March 2021

Brora Return from Lockdown to Knock Hearts Out of the Cup

The result itself makes it one of the biggest Scottish Cup upset of all time: a Highland League side knocking one of the country's biggest clubs out.

But Brora's defeat of Hearts is all the more impressive for the fact that it was the part-timers' first game for two months, with the Highland League suspended because of the Covid-19 pandemic.

The Jam Tarts may have been, temporarily, surprisingly consigned to the Championship after the previous season finished early because of lockdown, but they were 16 points clear at the top of the table, had been finalists in the previous two seasons' cups, and could still call upon experienced top-flight players including Christophe Berra, Craig Halkett, Peter Haring, Gary Mackay-Steven, Liam Boyce and Jamie Walker.

But after just 12 minutes under the Dudgeon Park floodlights – in one of 12 cup ties taking place on this Tuesday evening – the Cattachs took the lead as Andy MacRae fed Jordan MacRae on the edge of the box, and the young goal machine blasted a great diagonal shot past Hearts goalie Ross Stewart and into the top corner. The strike later won the award for the best goal of the second round.

The visitors, playing in light blue, created some decent chances but their finishing wasn't good enough, while Brora created more chances of their own. Another Jordan MacRae shot was deflected wide, and home defender Tom Kelly had a penalty claim waved away when Stewart came out to challenge him for a through ball, and Kelly went down.

Hearts defender Halkett came close to equalising, but veteran keeper Joe Malin made a great reflex save from his strong header. In the 70th minute Berra did scramble home the equaliser, but the favourites were only level for five minutes because midfielder Martin MacLean thrashed a shot into the top of the net from a tight angle, following a corner.

Hearts' best chance in the remaining 15 minutes came from a Boyce cut-back across the face of goal, but there were no light blue shirts there, and Brora held out to claim their historic victory.

Hearts boss Robbie Neilson called the result an embarrassment for his club, while Brora manager Steven Mackay said, 'We had no right whatsoever to win this game. I'm just so privileged to be manager of such an incredible team.'

Unfortunately, there were no Brora fans in Dudgeon Park to celebrate the club's best ever result, with Covid dictating that the game was played behind closed doors, but after the final whistle the players ran to applaud supporters who were gathered on the other side of the wall behind one goal, and the team celebrated with gusto in the dressing room afterwards.

Club director Ben Mackay said, 'About two minutes before the end of the game, my mind turned around to "we've got no alcohol to celebrate". So we were running to the local shop before it closed, trying to get some alcohol into the dressing room and we managed to do that!'

37

Saturday, 16 January 1982

Scotland Star in a Calamitous World Cup Draw

The draw for the 1982 World Cup was shown live on STV straight after *Game for a Laugh*. Viewers could have been forgiven for thinking that the bloopers show had continued straight through. And Scotland had an unwitting starring role in the farce.

FIFA clearly wanted the draw to be a big spectacle. They hosted it in Madrid's impressive Palacio de los Congresos, accompanied by elaborate opening speeches, with three huge rotating silver cages for the (mini Tango) balls with the team names in them. They roped in six boys from a local orphanage – dressed in suits and purple sashes – to carry the balls around, and created a huge screen where the teams would be allocated to their groups.

This being FIFA, it was also hugely over-complicated, and accompanied by two days of political horse-trading and controversy, from well before a gilded cage had been spun. England wanted to be one of the six top seeds – despite being not very good – because they'd previously won the World Cup, and so had been good, albeit 16 years earlier. Belgium and France weren't keen on that idea. FIFA were understood to be offering the Belgians a compromise, of being drawn in a group in the milder north of Spain.

Although that didn't happen in the end.

Initially, Belgium were drawn into Italy's group, in temperate Vigo and La Coruña. But hang on – according to what journalists had been told, as the first European third seed out of the cages, Belgium should have been placed in either Argentina or Brazil's group, to help keep South American third seeds Chile and Peru away from their fellow South Americans.

And then Scotland were drawn into Argentina's group, even though, according to what FIFA had told journalists, they should have ended up with Brazil.

Up on stage, FIFA executive Hermann Neuberger and a young Sepp Blatter debated what to do. One of the orphans was told to stick a ball back into a cage, while some whistles started to come from the crowd of football administrators. Graeme Souness and Alan Hansen, watching on, shook their heads incredulously. And then Belgium got moved to Group 3 with Argentina, and Scotland to Group 6 with Brazil, based in Málaga and Seville, as FIFA had originally said they would.

Then a ball split open inside one of the cages and a cage stopped spinning. While officials prodded balls with their fingers and sticks, the orphans tried not to laugh.

Afterwards, Scotland boss Jock Stein said that his team's group – which, as well as 9/4 tournament favourites Brazil, included the Soviet Union – couldn't be any harder, and he called the draw 'very confusing and very disappointing'.

To make matters worse, when SFA officials arrived in Málaga the next day to book their accommodation for their matches against the Soviet Union and New Zealand, they discovered that the Soviets had booked their rooms there before the draw had even been made.

The *Daily Mirror* asked, 'What leak did the Russians get that enabled them to steal a march on the Scots?' and added, 'The Scots are secretly simmering over the whole business of a draw that looked as rigged as a Kremlin election. One official said, "What a cock-up to make a wrong draw and put the Scots with Argentina, and then to have to change it. I thought the Scots' president, Willie Harkness, was going to faint. And no wonder.'"

So Scotland faced the best team in the world in the hottest city in Europe. And they could be forgiven for thinking that the draw that put them there was about as random as the Earth's orbit around the blazing sun.

Dave Narey wasn't caring about any of that though, as he blasted Scotland into the lead with a fierce 20-yard drive, which seemed to take him by surprise as much as anyone else. But then, in the blazing heat, Zico, Sócrates and co. turned on the style and scored four without reply. Scotland had already beaten New Zealand 5-2 but when they drew with the Soviet Union in their last group match, they went out on goal difference.

Scotland met Brazil so often in the World Cup that it often seemed predestined to happen. In 1982 more so than ever.

38

Wednesday, 22 March 1933

Caledonian, (Brief) Floodlight Pioneers

Until the 1950s, floodlights in football were only really seen in experiments – including at Celtic Park as early as 1893 – initially without much success due to the limitations of early systems. Indeed, neither the SFA nor the English FA sanctioned floodlights in competitive football until the '50s.

But 20 years before that, floodlight pioneers Caledonian FC were – briefly – playing under lights at their Telford Street ground in Inverness.

The benefits were clear, so far north, in the winter. The lights, which resembled modern floodlights, mounted on three tall pylons down either side of the pitch, worked well, but were only used for two matches.

A crowd of 2,500 turned up for the first game under lights, a 2-1 defeat of Clachnacuddin. Previously, midweek matches had had to take place in the afternoon, when most supporters were at work.

A white ball was used, and was replaced whenever it became too dirty. A few weeks later, Caledonian beat Aberdeen University 4-3 under the lights.

So why were they then removed, if they'd been a success? They were wanted elsewhere. And it's a story that sounds like a cliche based on lazy outside perceptions of Highland life, but it's actually true.

Nessie-hunting mania peaked just as Caledonian were successfully showing the rest of Britain how to enable midweek evening football. A supposed sighting of the beast was reported in the *Inverness Courier*, then a hefty reward was offered for the monster's capture. And Caledonian's floodlights were taken to the Loch to help with the search.

It would be more than 25 years before Caledonian played under lights again. And that's another story.

39

Wednesday, 11 March 1959

Rangers and Celtic Unite

A quarter of a century after Nessie inadvertently curtailed
Caledonian FC's initial floodlight experience, they started
playing under lights again, and their opposition in a special
match to inaugurate the new system was a rarity in Scottish
football history: a combined Celtic and Rangers select.

With the obvious exception of Scotland internationals, it was
one of just a handful of times when Celtic and Rangers players
have joined forces. But the most remarkable thing about the game
is that the Celtic players – goalie Dick Beattie, Jim Conway,
Paddy Crerand, Jim Kennedy and Charlie Tully – had to sign for
Rangers because of SFA regulations. And Celtic just had to trust
Rangers to give them their players back after the game.

Celtic missed those five; on the day before the match in
Inverness, the Bhoys lost 2-1 against Airdrie in the league.

Although the Rangers and Celtic players typically got
on well, the clubs weren't on great terms with each other and
Glasgow was particularly divided at the time, which made
Caledonian's achievement in securing the combined side's
opposition all the more remarkable.

And the Celtic players who would be turning out for a side
managed by Gers boss Scot Symon probably weren't cock-a-
hoop about the strip they would be playing in: Rangers' away
kit. The only good news for the Celts was that there was quite
a lot of white on the shirt. But it was an unmistakably Rangers

kit, with the black socks with red turnovers of disputed significance, blue shorts and red and blue on the shirt.

Rangers' Sammy Baird grabbed a hat-trick and Conway scored the other in a 4-2 victory for the Glaswegians, with Rod Clyne and Jimmy Ingram getting Caley's goals. The match was a big success for the home team, drawing a capacity crowd, while Conway later said that it helped to improve relationships between the Celtic and Rangers players.

The two clubs' players had played together in combined selects a couple of times before: in Welsh superstar Billy Meredith's testimonial at Maine Road in 1925 – a 2-2 draw with a Lancashire select; and in a charity match in aid of the Granton Trawler Disaster Fund in 1933, when they beat a combined Hibs and Hearts XI 3-2. The Glasgow team simply wore Celtic strips while the Edinburgh side played in Hearts' kit.

And after their shared Inverness floodlight experience, Celtic and Rangers joined forces again in 1971, in a fundraising match for the Ibrox Stadium Disaster Fund. In a captivating match in front of 80,000 fans at Hampden, the Rangers and Celtic select – a team that played in all-white and that also featured Chelsea keeper Peter Bonetti, and Bobby Charlton and George Best – lost 2-1 to a Scotland select, which also included Celtic and Rangers players. The logic of players from each side of Glasgow's divide lining up together was much more obvious then than it had been in Inverness.

And finally, Rangers and Celtic players from each team joined forces again at Hampden in 1977, for the Queen's Silver Jubilee, in a Glasgow select team that also included Partick and Queen's Park players and that played in an eye-catching, specially designed strip incorporating all the clubs' colours. The Glaswegians beat an English football league select 2-1, with goals from Celtic's Kenny Dalglish and Rangers' Sandy Jardine.

Although you have to think that Celtic might not have agreed to that one if they'd had to play by the 1959 rules and let Rangers have King Kenny's registration.

40

Saturday, 28 April 1962

Gordon Smith Wins the League with Three Different Clubs

Some players – including Kenny Miller, Mo Johnston, Tommy McLean and Richard Gough – have won the Scottish league with two different clubs. Bobby Wishart achieved that same distinction without ever playing for Celtic or Rangers. But only Gordon Smith has won the league with THREE different clubs, and he also did it without ever playing in hoops or light blue.

Smith's remarkable achievement is made even more amazing because he did it despite spending the first 18 years of his career as a one-club man, during which he won three titles with Hibs. He was in his late 30s when he won the league with Hearts and Dundee, thanks to his exemplary fitness and absolute professionalism.

Two of the five titles in particular stand out – the first and the last – although the second was the most impressive.

For almost ten years after World War II, Scotland's top two teams were undoubtedly Rangers and Hibs. Inspirational manager Willie McCartney and visionary chairman Harry Swan had elevated the Leith side to the very top, and the first piece in their formidable front line was Smith.

In 1946/47 they missed out on the league title by just two points. The next season initially looked like it might go the same way. Rangers won 17 of their first 19 games, during which their famous 'Iron Curtain' defence conceded just 13 goals.

But Hibs – and Smith in particular – were attacking with the same quality as Rangers were defending. In August Smith scored five goals in three days, against Aberdeen and Clyde.

In November he scored possibly the best goal of his career, beating several Motherwell players before placing the ball between the full-backs and past the keeper. On the train back to Edinburgh, an excited McCartney promised the players £100 each if they won the championship. According to Smith, Swan 'quickly disassociated himself from such reckless enthusiasm'.

A week later, Smith scored five in one game, an 8-0 win over Third Lanark, then, after the match, criticised his own performance. Centre-forward Alec Linwood got a hat-trick in that match; he only spent one year at Hibs before young Lawrie Reilly broke into the side, but in that one season Linwood was a key part of the league-winning team.

At the end of January Rangers were still in the driving seat, three points ahead of Hibs with two games in hand. And then Hibs' season was struck by a terrible tragedy.

Willie McCartney collapsed during a cup match at Albion Rovers. He was taken to his home and said he was feeling better, but he died hours later. Some of the players learned about his death from newspaper vendors as they left dance halls that night. He was just 59.

The *Glasgow Herald* said, 'When he laughed the whole world laughed with him. When he had occasion – as he often had – to make a serious pronouncement on the game that he loved, everyone listened with respect. Mr McCartney never minced his words. In his 11 years at Easter Road, Mr McCartney played a great part in raising Hibernian from a comparatively lowly club to one of great powers and ability.'

His funeral was so well attended that 200 mourners had to wait outside.

Hibs' next match was the key game of the season, against Rangers, in front of 57,750 fans at Easter Road. Trainer Hugh Shaw took over as manager. Hibs won it 1-0 with a last-minute goal from John Cuthbertson. The *Herald* said that Hibs' 'superb courage in mastering adversity was born of a desire to play tribute, by defeating their great rivals, to one who has gone – and no less his successor'.

Hibs won their next seven league matches, while Rangers started to drop points, and Hibs' league victory was virtually guaranteed when Rangers drew a must-win match with Motherwell – just five days after Hibs had thrashed the Steelmen 5-0.

Hibs lost their last match of the season, against a strong Dundee side, while Rangers won the first two of their three games in hand, leaving the Ibrox side needing to beat Hearts 20-0 away in their last game to win the league. Swan said that, if they did, his club would never set foot in Tynecastle again. Hearts won 2-1, and Hibs were champions for the first time in 45 years; a title masterminded by McCartney and Shaw but dedicated completely to the memory of McCartney.

The next season, Bobby Johnstone broke into the team, to complete the Famous Five forward line alongside Smith, Reilly, Willie Ormond and Eddie Turnbull – almost certainly the best front five ever fielded in Scotland. But it was the only season out of seven consecutive years when they didn't really compete for the title.

The next year they lost out to Rangers by one point.

The 1950/51 championship was Hibs' most impressive victory. With the Famous Five at the top of their game, they won the title by ten points, despite losing two of their first three games. They clinched it with four matches to spare, by beating Clyde 4-0 away – despite Smith and Ormond being out injured, while Johnstone and Reilly were away in London on international duty. In the last two games of the season they beat Rangers 4-1 and Celtic 3-1. And Harry Swan dished out some pretty generous bonuses for the league winners.

Sunday Post writer Jack Harkness – that Queen's Park goalie who'd broken his fingers trying to save a Jimmy McGrory header – summed it all up: 'Hibs – best I have ever seen. What an attack. A shot in every locker and a bright idea in every head.'

Hibs' – and Smith's – next league title came just a year after, when they scored 96 goals in just 30 games. Legend has it that, as Smith drove up past Abbeyhill after the last game of the season (a Wednesday night win against Motherwell), boys ran alongside his car to congratulate him, men left their pints in the pub to come and see him pass, and even the police horses smiled.

They almost won the next year too – when, remarkably, they scored seven goals in five different league matches – but a Rangers equaliser against Queen of the South on the last day of the season sent the title to Govan on goal average. If the league had been decided on goal difference in those days, it would have been three in a row for Hibs.

Harry Swan had guarded Smith – the jewel in his forward line's crown – like a lioness guards her cub. When Arsenal made an inquiry for him, Swan named his price: Highbury.

But even the fittest players can't avoid injury for ever, and in his 30s Smith was no exception. By 1959 Swan was convinced that his right-winger could never properly recover from recent injuries and should leave Easter Road. Swan was in a minority on that one.

Smith was devastated, but he wasn't short of offers – including from Bill Shankly at Huddersfield and Bob Shankly at Third Lanark, and from Kilmarnock, Dundee, Newcastle, Fiorentina and Cannes. And he paid for his own ankle operation, before crossing Edinburgh's divide to sign for Hearts – not a decision that he took lightly, but he needn't have worried about that. Hibs fans lost none of their love for him and Hearts supporters were glad to have his services.

And it helped Gordon that his new boss was his childhood hero, Tommy Walker, who he'd lined up against 18 years earlier in his Hibs debut.

Hearts went unbeaten in the first 26 league and league cup matches of Smith's first season at Tynecastle, during which they won the League Cup and scored 91 goals, with Smith getting his fair share. The Jam Tarts only lost four games in all competitions all season, as they finished the league four points above Kilmarnock, and a whopping 12 ahead of third- and fourth-placed Rangers and Dundee.

Not bad for Smith, who'd supposedly been past it. But he still wasn't finished – not by a long way.

Almost exactly 20 years after he'd signed for Hibs, and once again in the North British Hotel – where he'd put pen to paper with Hibs – Smith was snapped up for his third and final top-flight Scottish club, Dundee, by Bob Shankly.

Two years after he'd tried to sign Smith for Third Lanark, Shankly was assembling a top side at Dens Park, from defenders Bobby Cox and Ian Ure to teenage midfielder Andy Penman, young winger Hugh Robertson and excellent young strikers Alan Gilzean and Alan Cousin, who was combining part-time football with studies at St Andrews. Smith's experience would greatly benefit this talented young side.

Writer Bob Crampsey said, 30 years later, that this Dundee side 'could fairly claim to be the best pure footballing team produced in Scotland since the war'. Smith said they were on a par with Hibs at their best. And the veteran winger was happy about working alongside former Hibs trainer Sammy Kean again at Dens Park; one of the factors that took the edge off his commute to Dundee from North Berwick, before the Forth Road Bridge existed. Owning and driving a Porsche probably made it more palatable too.

On the pitch, with Cousin and Gilzean both playing as centre-forwards and feeding off Smith and Robertson's crosses, Gilzean got 24 league goals that season, with Cousin scoring 15 and Penman grabbing 17.

In November Dundee travelled to Ibrox to play Rangers, who were unbeaten in 21 games. There were no goals in the first half, but six in the second – five of them for the visitors. Gilzean got four.

The game was played in such dense fog that Dundee keeper Pat Liney couldn't see the goals: 'I kept hearing the roars and thinking, "Well, it hasn't gone past me, so it must be at the other end."'

After the match, the Rangers players went to the away dressing room to congratulate their rivals for their performance.

The next week, Dundee came back from 4-2 down against Raith Rovers to win a dramatic, entertaining match 5-4.

The Ibrox match was one of Dundee's best ever performances; the Raith game was all about securing the result even when everything wasn't going your way. These were the sorts of results of which champions are made.

The Dark Blues went 19 matches unbeaten but then lost four in a row and Rangers overtook them and went three points ahead. Next up was the key game: Rangers again. It was a draw, and Rangers maintained their lead.

Dundee had seven games left. They won them all. And when Dundee United and Aberdeen both beat Rangers 1-0 and Dundee goalie Pat Liney pulled off a great save in a key game against St Mirren, it was all set up for the final day, when Dundee easily beat St Johnstone 3-0 away, in front of about 20,000 travelling fans, to seal their first ever league title.

Sir Alex Ferguson, who was in the St Johnstone team that day, later recalled that his team-mate Lawrie Thomson was constantly trying to foul Smith, but couldn't get close enough to the 38-year-old.

Thousands of Dundee fans invaded the pitch at full time and carried their heroes shoulder-high. The team coach returned to Dundee at walking pace, with Smith in his Porsche behind, and fans marching triumphantly alongside them.

It was a great achievement by an excellent team and a fitting finale to Gordon Smith's incredible career.

41

Wednesday, 1 May 1963

Dundee, European Cup Semi-Finalists

In 1962, Dundee stepped into European competition for the first time, and did incredibly well against top teams in the flagship tournament, in spite of incredible adversity in one game in particular.

Their adventure started with a home tie against the tournament's second-favourites, Cologne, who had ten internationals in their team. The first leg result, at Dens Park, was beyond Dundee's wildest dreams.

To be fair to the Germans, there was one mitigating factor: their goalie Fritz Ewert was injured early on, in a collision with Dundee forward Alan Cousin, and couldn't play on. Nevertheless, Dundee's triumph was still astonishing: they beat the West German champions 8-1, with a hat-trick from Alan Gilzean.

The *Evening Telegraph* said, 'The massacre at Dens Park was like fiction gone wild ... Dundee made up their minds that attack was the only way to set about the task,' and that the German defenders 'were completely baffled'. It's still Cologne's worst ever defeat.

The German press published a photo from an angle that made it look like Cousin had punched Ewert, although he hadn't, and the Dundee players endured a torrid time in Germany. They were given nowhere to train before the away leg; an underhand tactic that would look very innocent compared to what followed. Cologne manager Zlatko Čajkovski had said that if something happened to Dundee keeper Bert Slater in the return leg, there might be a reversal of fortunes in the scoreline.

And ominously, an ambulance was parked behind Slater's goal, with stretcher bearers standing by. Then, after 27 minutes, Slater made a diving save, and Christian Müller followed through on his challenge, kicking Slater in the head and cutting him badly. The stretcher-bearers tried to get Slater into the ambulance, as he, bleeding badly and heavily concussed, tried to get off the stretcher. They kept putting him back on, he kept getting off and eventually he managed to get to the dressing room, while young midfielder Andy Penman went in goal.

Cologne went in 3-0 up at half-time and suddenly it was looking like that incredible first-leg lead might not be irreversible.

But Slater came out, heavily bandaged, for the second half, initially on the wing, before switching places with a relieved Penman and going back in goal, where – despite his concussion – he made several good saves. Cologne only scored one more goal.

But the kick to Slater's head was far from an isolated incident. The Dundee players were being kicked up and down the park. Ian Ure later said that a German forward aimed a kick at his head that would have killed him if it had connected, then he described his response: 'I stuck the boot right into his ribs and he went down in a heap. But there was so much going on nobody noticed.' Thirty-nine-year-old Gordon Smith in particular ended up covered in bruises.

And even worse was to come from the crowd. Towards the end they poured towards the touchline – it became almost impossible to take throw-ins – and at full time there was a huge pitch invasion. Dundee players had to be rushed off the pitch to safety by hundreds of off-duty British soldiers who were fortunately in the crowd, as fans punched them and hit them with folding chairs. Smith was so badly bruised by this point that two of his team-mates had to help him from the pitch. Fists flew between players in the tunnel, where Cologne players threw water on the Dundee team.

Unsurprisingly, the Dundee players and officials didn't go to the post-match banquet. They'd been through the wringer, but they'd learned from it. Beating Cologne 'did our morale a power of good' said Gilzean in the *Sporting Post*. 'We felt we could hold our own now with any club. That was far from how we felt before Cologne came to Dens Park.'

Their experience in Lisbon in their next match was much more pleasant. Although there was controversy – Sporting scored the only goal of the game with a last-minute shot that looked like it didn't cross the line – the encounter was fair and clean, the training facilities were excellent and the fans were friendly. This time the players did go to the post-match banquet, where they were treated to brandy, wine, caldo verde (a Portuguese soup), bacalhau (dried and salted cod) and more.

And then, on Halloween, Dundee got another great result, beating Sporting 4-1 in the home leg. Gilzean got his second hat-trick of the tournament, but the *Aberdeen Evening Express* said that Smith was 'the real architect of victory' as he set up three of the four goals.

Sporting captain Hilário, the man who had to try and mark Smith, agreed, saying, 'He gave me a much harder game than Garrincha.'

Dundee's quarter-final opponents were Anderlecht, who had knocked out Real Madrid and had nine internationals in their team. Dundee's build-up was hampered by Scotland's terrible winter; they'd only played two games in the seven weeks leading up to the game in Brussels (see also iconic moment 71).

Nevertheless, the men from Dens turned in possibly an even better performance in Brussels than they did in either of their home matches against Cologne or Sporting.

In the first minute Smith and Cousin combined to set up Gilzean to open the scoring. Seventeen minutes later Gilzean made it 2-0. A couple of minutes after that he picked up a foot injury that bled heavily and later needed six stitches but he played on anyway. The *Evening Telegraph* later reported, 'The Belgians were amazed when they heard the extent of the injury, for he had never flinched at any time.'

Anderlecht pulled one back from the penalty spot, but in the second half Gilzean set up Cousin and then Smith to make it 4-1. At full time overjoyed Dundee fans carried Slater – who'd been brilliant between the sticks yet again – shoulder-high off the pitch, while the home fans and players gave the Scots a standing ovation. The *Press and Journal* said that Dundee 'wiped the floor with Anderlecht'.

Dundee boss Bob Shankly said, 'I had full confidence in my players, but I did not expect such a success.' Smith later said that it was the best football that that great Dundee team ever played.

At the after-match dinner this time, the Dundee players were given inscribed silver cigarette lighters and cigar boxes.

Dundee won the home leg 2-1 with late goals from Cousin and Smith, while the Belgian markers were doubling up on Gilzean. Anderlecht coach Pierre Sinibaldi said that Dundee were better than Real Madrid.

At the first time of asking, Dundee had reached the European Cup semi-final, where their opponents were a Milan side that included Cesare Maldini, Giovanni Trapattoni, Gianni Rivera and José Altafini.

The final was scheduled for Wembley, but unfortunately it was a bridge too far even for this brilliant Dundee team, as it all fell apart in the San Siro second half. A Cousin header from a perfect Penman cross had made it 1-1 at half-time, but Milan scored four after the break.

It was a physical game but referee Vicente Caballero seemed to turn a blind eye to fouls by Milan players. He had accepted extravagant gifts from Milan before the game, and events later in his career illustrated his unsuitability for his role, as he was later banned from refereeing for accepting bribes.

The ball seemed to go out of play before the first of Milan's second-half goals, and their next was initially given as offside before that decision was changed.

At the post-match banquet this time, the disappointed Dundee players were given watches – with the Milan badge on them.

In the home leg, the *Press and Journal* reported, 'Dundee started the game in death-or-glory style but they found the Milan defence cool.' With their characteristic calm and confident defending, Milan never looked in any danger, although Dundee were arguably unlucky not to get a penalty or two, and Gilzean got the only goal of the game just before half-time, with a towering header from a Smith cross. It was the ninth goal he'd scored in Dundee's eight European Cup games. The Dundee fans went wild with joy.

Unfortunately it was another dirty game, and Gilzean ended up getting his first ever red card, for his reaction to a foul on Smith. 'For me, it was a particularly sad end to our European Cup bid,' he later said.

But the semi-final exit shouldn't detract from Dundee's incredible achievements. Gordon Smith alone now had the incredible distinction of playing in European Cup semi-finals for Hibs and Dundee. The whole team had been superb throughout the eight matches. And a couple of decades later, Dundee would become one of a select number of cities to have two clubs who played in European Cup semi-finals. They're by far the smallest of those cities and it's inconceivable that anywhere could ever take that distinction away from them.

42

Saturday, 11 September 1965

The Dens Park Massacre

Dundee United were struggling in the league in 1964 when manager Jerry Kerr went on a scouting mission to East End Park to watch Dunfermline play Swedish side Örgryte in the Fairs Cup. Kerr was impressed by the visitors' winger Örjan Persson, and he soon bought him, and, for good measure, three more Scandinavian players – Lennart Wing, Mogens Berg and a name that still strikes fear into Dundee fans who are old enough to remember: Finn Døssing.

Kerr's Scandinavian signings helped United move up to an eventual mid-table finish, three places and 12 points behind their hitherto dominant neighbours, Dundee. It was the beginning of a steep upward curve for the Tannadice men, a trajectory made abundantly clear when they crossed the road for the first league derby of the 1965/66 season.

Persson, Wing and Døssing were all influential that day, as was 17-year-old full-back Frannie Munro. Munro should have scored in the seventh minute, when Døssing set him up, but instead of shooting quickly, the young Scot took the ball round Jim Easton and left himself with a too-difficult angle.

Seven minutes after that, though, United were ahead thanks to the three Scandinavians. Døssing was brought down; Wing fired the free kick into the box; Persson flicked it on; and 'deadly Dane' Døssing headed it home.

For all of United's dominance, it was only 1-0 at half-time, as Ally Donaldson saved well twice, from Dennis Gillespie and Benny Rooney. But the one-way traffic continued in the second half.

Just ten minutes after the break, it was 2-0. That man Døssing controlled the ball with his back to goal, spun and smashed it past Donaldson. Nine minutes later Bobby Cox cleared a Persson shot off the line but Munro squared the ball to Gillespie, who cracked it home.

Just a few minutes from the end, it was still a just-about-not-humiliating 3-0. But then Døssing got his hat-trick. His second had been spectacular; this one was an average shot that Donaldson should have saved.

And in the last minute, Cox pulled Persson down in the box and Wing converted the penalty, to score his first United goal and make the final score a 5-0 thrashing, which the United fans commemorated in song.

Dundee had fielded a new forward that day, who they'd bought from Clyde earlier in the week. The *Sunday Mail* said he 'looked wasted on the left wing'. It never worked out for him as a player at Dundee, but he would go on to become an extremely successful manager in the City of Discovery. That man was Jim McLean.

And he wasn't the only player in that vanquished dark blue side to end up successfully plying his trade at United.

Doug Houston and Kenny Cameron were young Dundee players in the match. Houston played at Dens for 11 years and became captain, before McLean brought him to Tannadice in 1974, when he was 30. He still had plenty left in the tank, and made over 100 appearances for United.

And striker Cameron signed for United in 1968, where he made 170 appearances and scored 83 goals, before becoming a coach and one of McLean's key scouts.

Of course, McLean, with help from many great players and coaches like Houston and Cameron, took the Tangerines to previously undreamed-of highs. But he was forever grateful for the excellent foundations that he inherited from Jerry Kerr, whose managerial skill was rarely more evident than it was on the day when his Scottish and Scandinavian stars humbled their neighbours at a packed Dens Park.

43

Wednesday, 18 March 1987

Dundee United Beat Barcelona
– Yet Again

Under Jim McLean, Dundee United were brilliant in Europe. Highlights from their 14 consecutive seasons in continental competition included reaching a European Cup semi-final, which they lost controversially against Roma, getting to two UEFA Cup quarter-finals and beating Monaco 6-4 on aggregate, with Grace Kelly and her husband Prince Rainier of Monaco in the stands in both legs, and dispatching Borussia Mönchengladbach 5-2 on aggregate.

But their greatest European night was probably their third UEFA Cup quarter-final, in the Camp Nou in 1987.

It's true that Barcelona weren't quite at their imperious best at the time. Mark Hughes in particular was struggling to live up to the fans' high standards, but they had played in the previous season's (admittedly dire) European Cup Final, and boasted players like Gary Lineker, Andoni Zubizarreta – the world's most expensive goalie – and Víctor.

Meanwhile, United had laboured to a draw against Forfar in the Scottish Cup just days earlier.

But the Terrors' record against the Catalan giants was outstanding. They'd become the first – and by 1987 still the only – British side to win a European match in Spain when they'd beaten Barça home and away in the Fairs Cup in 1966, and they won the first leg of their 1987 quarter-final, with Kevin Gallacher getting the only goal of the game.

The away leg was widely anticipated to be a different kettle of *peix*. In their famous ground – six times the size of Tannadice, with their bowling green-flat, wide-open pitch, the home leg would surely favour Terry Venables' men. They even watered the pitch beforehand, presumably to suit their slick passing game. But most of the best passing, especially in the second half, came from the men in tangerine.

And the atmosphere in that vast theatre seemed to hinder rather than help the home team. 'Only' 42,000 fans turned up – among them 1,000 Scots up in the gods, and Manchester United boss Alex Ferguson, to run the rule over potential signing Hughes – and the *cules* weren't reluctant to harangue any poor efforts or suspect decision-making from their players.

The first half wasn't a classic. United defended well and played on the break. Billy Thomson made a good save early on from Lineker, and Zubizarreta also had to get down low once, to save a Gallacher effort. Barça were too often resorting to high balls into the box, and Thomson collected them all with ease.

But then, on 40 minutes, from a corner, the ball ricocheted to Ramón Calderé on the edge of the box and he smacked it into the net to level the tie on aggregate.

United now needed to score, and they were much more attacking in the second half, which tore the game open, raised the tempo and led to more action and chances at both ends.

Paul Sturrock was constantly heavily involved on the left wing. Lineker started dropping back into midfield to try and make things happen for Barça.

With 15 minutes left, the Barça fans were clearly getting impatient with their team's inability to find the winner, and United fans' voices became clear, singing 'You'll Never Walk Alone'.

In the 85th minute the tension was blown away. Maurice Malpas picked up a loose ball in the middle of the park, made a brilliant run forward, laid the ball off to the left, where it ended up with Sturrock on the wing. The elfin magician from Ellon cut inside characteristically and was brought down on the edge of the box. Ian Redford fired in the free kick, and an onrushing John Clark rose to power a header past Zubizarreta. The away goals rule meant Barça had to score twice in five minutes. They couldn't score one. But United could.

In the last minute, Sturrock – naturally – got himself into loads of space on the wing, raced into the box and clipped the ball back to Iain Ferguson, who headed home United's second.

It was the best of United's four consecutive victories against Barcelona; an incredible performance and achievement for one half of Scotland's fourth city, once again deservedly beating the biggest club in the world. And now they were in the pot for the UEFA Cup semi-final.

McLean said his players 'were all simply magnificent. This is without a doubt our greatest ever night in Europe.'

Venables said, 'United could go on and win the UEFA Cup now.' They nearly did. More on that later.

44

Saturday, 24 April 1965

Captivating Title Race
Last-Day Showdown

The 1964/65 Scottish Division One title race was one of the most dramatic ever: a captivating tussle between four clubs, with a thrilling last-day winner-takes-all showdown and underdog champions.

Those four clubs were: Rangers? No. Celtic then? No. They were Kilmarnock, Hearts, Dunfermline and Hibs.

The great '60s Dunfermline and Hibs sides both had Jock Stein's fingerprints all over them. In 1964/65, he was managing the Easter Road side – for most of the season – and the Pars were going well under his talented successor there, Willie Cunningham. Hibs also boasted the extreme talents of striker Willie Hamilton.

Over at Hearts, manager Tommy Walker had recently secured two league titles and a haul of cups.

Kilmarnock manager Willie Waddell had developed a team who defended strongly and played well on the break but had acquired an always-the-bridesmaid tag. As well as being runners-up in the 1960 International Soccer League (see iconic moment 33), they'd finished second in a whopping four seasons in the first half of the decade and lost two League Cup Finals – including one against Hearts. There was no reason to suspect that the 1964/65 league would be any different, until the last day of the campaign. Inspired by captain Frank Beattie – who made 600 club appearances, as well as working as a miner – and, in his debut season, sparkling 17-year-old winger Tommy McLean, Killie won their first six league matches and sensationally beat Eintracht Frankfurt 5-1 at home in their first ever European tie.

But in October, Waddell surprised everyone by announcing that he would be leaving Killie at the end of the season to move into football journalism. Regardless, the next day they beat Celtic 5-2. At the end of the month they were top of the league, with nine victories and a draw from their first ten games.

In the winter their form stuttered, with one notable exception: a convincing 3-1 defeat of leaders Hearts in December, the Gorgie men's first defeat in the league. According to the *Glasgow Herald*, 'It was the small men of Kilmarnock's attack who did the damage. [David] Sneddon, [Tommy] McLean and [Brian] McIlroy wriggled like eels and distracted Hearts' defence with the neatness and speed of their incisive running and passing.'

But after that, Killie's first win of 1965 didn't arrive until 17 February and they dropped back to fourth place. But that first victory of the year, against Hibs, rekindled their dwindling title hopes. Killie scored three goals in a remarkable second-half eight-minute spell as they won that key match 4-3 and went level on points with Hibs, two behind Hearts.

The *Herald* reported, 'The transformation in Kilmarnock's fortunes after the interval was astonishing and exhilarating,' and said their 'spirit and opportunism were justly rewarded. Their morale for the important matches to come must have been greatly restored.' So it proved.

In March, Stein left Hibs for Celtic. He was replaced by Bob Shankly but the men from Leith lost three of their last four games, scuppering their title challenge. Stein later admitted that leaving Easter Road during the title race was a huge regret and embarrassment for him.

Meanwhile, Killie switched keepers, bringing in 20-year-old Bobby Ferguson. It was an important change.

Dunfermline kept up the pace for longer than Hibs and had a great goal average, but drew their penultimate game of the season, against St Johnstone, with their young star striker Alex Ferguson missing a good chance, while Killie were beating Morton 3-0.

Which all meant that the title would be settled by a last-day top-of-the-table clash at Tynecastle in front of 37,500 fans. Killie needed to win 2-0 to take the title on goal average; or, if Hearts scored, Killie had to win by three clear goals.

Hearts hit the post early on, but 20 minutes later the visitors grabbed the lead, as Sneddon headed home a McLean cross, and just three minutes after that McIlroy got the all-important second goal, with a great turn and low strike from just inside the penalty box.

Hearts, of course, fought back, and their best opportunity to get the one goal that would have given them the title came in the last minute, when Alan Gordon's point-blank shot was heading just inside the post until young shot-stopper Ferguson sprang across his goal to somehow pull off a vital miracle save.

Since coming into the side, Ferguson had played eight games, during which he'd only conceded five goals. He would eventually play for Scotland seven times and in 1967 was the world's most expensive goalie when he moved to West Ham, for whom he would make over 200 appearances.

But at Tynecastle his wonder save ensured that Killie won their first league title, thanks to a goal average that was just 0.04 better than Hearts'. Waddell celebrated on the pitch with the players, like a man who really didn't look like he was so keen to leave his job.

The celebrations continued in the away dressing room, where the players drank champagne from mugs.

If the title had been decided on goal difference, rather than goal average, Hearts, instead of Killie, would have won it. Three years later that rule change was made at a Scottish Football League meeting. It was Hearts who proposed it.

Killie's remarkable triumph marked the end of an era; the finale of a 20-year period in which seven different clubs won the league. It was the last season before Stein's Celtic embarked on their nine-in-a-row title march.

Even by that captivating era's standards, this rare four-way title race stands out as uniquely enthralling, with its captivating neck-and-neck winner-takes-all finale, and – following their frustrating period as heroic nearly men – a great Killie side's overdue crowning glory.

45

Wednesday, 20 October 1999

Nuts Match 1: Motherwell 5 Aberdeen 6

Andy Goram and Jim Leighton are both surely near the top of any Scotland fan's list of best ever Scottish goalies. But both of those renowned veteran custodians had a night to forget when they played against each other in one of the SPL's most memorable, remarkable matches.

Aberdeen took to the Fir Park pitch in black; Motherwell in white. The Steelmen had won only one of their first seven league matches; the Dons had taken just one point from their first nine, scoring just three goals and conceding 29 in the process. It wasn't surprising that Leighton picked the ball out of his net five times on that Wednesday night in Lanarkshire; what no one was expecting was for Goram to have to do it more.

Goram wasn't the only notable veteran in the Steelmen's ranks; under their ambitious new chairman John Boyle, they'd been investing in quality players including Pat Nevin and John Spencer, who both played against Aberdeen that night. Spencer got a hat-trick. To no avail.

Aberdeen's Robbie Winters scored three too. His first, after just eight minutes, was the Dons' second of the night. Andy Dow had opened the scoring with a shot that took a wicked deflection off a defender's heel, wrong-footing Goram. It wasn't the only time that night that Goram resembled a statue. Then Dow turned provider for Winters, who raced in unmarked in the middle to simply slot the ball past the exposed ex-Rangers keeper.

Former Scotland striker Spencer pulled one back with a characteristic bustling turn and low shot from the edge of the area. But then Winters turned in a rebound after a shot cracked off the post, and another skilled veteran, Eoin Jess, blasted home Aberdeen's fourth from outside the box, to give the visitors an unlikely three-goal lead. Goram was looking angry.

Just before half-time, Don Goodman pulled one back for the Well, when Aberdeen couldn't clear the ball; 4-2 at the break, and still plenty more goals to come.

The sides traded four more goals in a 12-minute spell in the second half. Winters sprung the offside trap to restore Aberdeen's three-goal lead. Goram raged at either the linesman or one of his defenders. Spencer latched on to a long punt, held off defenders and slotted the ball past Leighton. Paul Bernard raced through to slide Aberdeen's sixth past Goram; 6-3 with 20 minutes to go and surely there was no way back for the Steelmen now?

But just three minutes after that, Spencer got his hat-trick, stooping to head, unmarked, past Leighton from about four yards out.

And then, with ten minutes left, the home side earned a freak penalty. Aberdeen tried to clear a free kick but the ball, on its way back out, hit a defender – who was still facing upfield, in the wall – on the arm.

Shaun Teale sent Leighton the wrong way from the spot. There were ten minutes to go and just one goal in it. But the home side couldn't find an equaliser.

Aberdeen had somehow trebled their goals-for column and quadrupled their points column in their tenth league match of the season. To be fair to Goram and Leighton, they'd both been repeatedly left horribly exposed by their defenders, and, from Nevin to Jess and Winters and Spencer, there was a lot of experienced Scottish striking talent on the pitch that night.

But despite their headline-grabbing defeat, Motherwell then won six and drew one of their next seven games. They finished fourth in the league that season and Goram earned a brief move to Manchester United soon after.

Leighton retired at the end of the season, after breaking his jaw in the cup final. Aberdeen finished bottom of the league.

46

Saturday, 12 September 1885

Arbroath 36 Bon Accord 0 – The Record that Almost Never Was

One of the most famous results in world football very nearly became a footnote in history; a coda to someone else's glory and merely the second most remarkable of two astonishing Scottish Cup first round results on the same day, in the same wee corner of Scotland.

Arbroath 36 Bon Accord 0 is a scoreline that's familiar to football fans around the world. More than 135 years later it's still a record win for a ratified competitive game in senior football.

The *Arbroath Guide* called it the most amusing football match ever seen in Arbroath and said that the goals accumulated at an alarming rate, with five early goals before a brief respite. But after that short pause, according to the publication, 'The Arbroath forwards seemed to get thoroughly into the fun of the game, and before the call of half-time had scored another ten goals ... The second half was simply a repetition of the first, with five goals in the first 15 minutes and 16 during the other 30 minutes.'

Apparently Bon Accord only got anywhere near Arbroath's defence once in each half. The *Arbroath Guide* concluded, 'The Aberdeen men cannot play football, but this lesson will show them how it's done.'

Teenage winger – and shoemaker – John 'Jocky' Petrie scored 13 of the goals, which is still a British record.

Incredibly, the score could have been even more ridiculous. The *Scottish Athletic Journal* reported that the home side had five goals disallowed for offside. Referee Dave Stormont later said that it was seven, and he admitted that he doubted whether he'd got all those calls right, so hard was it to be sure when the Arbroath forwards were moving so quickly.

There's an apocryphal tale that Bon Accord were actually a cricket club who'd received another club's invitation to play in the cup in error, but that's not true; they were a football club, just not a very good one. They'd been formed a year earlier, and would last just until 1892, playing occasional cup matches without much success.

On that incredible day in 1885 they never really stood much chance against a strong Arbroath team, since they'd reportedly turned up at Gayfield without appropriate footwear and with just nine players, so had to get two volunteers from the crowd. Their goalie, Andrew Lornie, was usually a midfielder and had never played in goal before. Apparently he retired soon after. At the other end of the pitch, the Red Lichties' keeper, Jim Milne, spent most of the match sheltering under a spectator's umbrella.

Coincidentally, on the same day, just down the road and the 15 miles to Dundee, Dundee Harp recorded an almost identical massive scoreline, beating Aberdeen Rovers 35-0.

The *Dundee Courier and Argus* reported that Murphy scored the first goal 'in less time than it takes to write it … It is needless to give the play in detail, as it was from start to finish all on one side … Suffice it to say that the Harp scored ten goals in as many minutes.' They concluded, presumably with understatement, that Rovers' play 'was of the mediocre type' and, less diplomatically, that 'their custodian especially gave a particularly weak-kneed exhibition of goalkeeping. The Harp had the game all their own way, as from start to finish it was only a case of walking up to their opponents' goal and putting through the leather.'

Like Bon Accord, Rovers had travelled down from Aberdeen short of players, but didn't recruit anyone from the crowd and played with just ten men.

And Rovers were as inexperienced as Bon Accord too. Their shocking defeat by Harp was just their second ever match (their previous opponents were Bon Accord). Rovers played one more Scottish Cup tie in 1888, again in Dundee, against Wanderers. They lost that one 10-0.

But there's one more extremely intriguing point from that goal-laden day: contemporary reports state that the referee in Dundee initially recorded the Harp score as 37-0, but the Harp secretary told him that he had it as 35-0, and that was recorded as the official result. Presumably if the Dundee club had known that someone else would win 36-0 that day, they might not have been so honest.

And if they had let the referee's goal count stand, Arbroath 36 Bon Accord 0 would now be a little-known result, and Harp 37 Rovers 0 would instead be the globally famous world record today.

47

Wednesday, 16 November 2016

East Kilbride's 30th Consecutive Win

In early November 2016, a representative from Ajax turned up at East Kilbride's Lowland League match against BSC Glasgow to present them with a crate of Jupiler beer and show them a congratulatory video from former Ajax goalie Edwin van der Sar.

Because, by beating BSC Glasgow 3-1, the Kilby had broken the great 1970s Ajax side's world record winning run, which had stood at 26 matches.

East Kilbride's winning streak started shortly after an impressive Scottish Cup run, in which they knocked out clubs including League One side Stenhousemuir on their way to the fifth round and a respectable 2-0 defeat by Celtic.

As well as umpteen league matches, the run was trophy-laden, including cup ties and finals, as the club won the East of Scotland Cup, the Lowland League Cup and the East of Scotland Qualifying Cup.

And towards its record-breaking end, the run included more Scottish Cup success – a 9-1 win over Vale of Leithen and a 1-0 victory over League Two Cowdenbeath in the second round.

A couple of weeks after Ajax's congratulations, the Kilby made it 30 wins in a row with a 4-0 defeat of Civil Service Strollers, but three days later Spartans brought their long run to an end, with a 1-0 victory.

Despite the efforts of Spartans, who finished third, and East Stirling, who also had a great season, East Kilbride comfortably won the league, then, in the League Two play-offs, beat Buckie Thistle before losing on penalties to Cowdenbeath in the final.

Unfortunately, our *Guinness Book of Records* overlords decreed that the Lowland League was too low a level of competition for East Kilbride's amazing winning run to count as an official world record, but that should do nothing to deflect from the fledgling club's remarkable achievement. Not even a draw in sight, for nine months.

48

Saturday, 9 July 1921

Canada Play Their First Ever
International – Against Third Lanark

For more than two months in the summer of 1921, Third
Lanark undertook an epic groundbreaking tour across the
Atlantic and around North America, as they taught Canadians
and Americans the joys of football, playing 25 games, winning
24, drawing one, scoring 112 goals, conceding just 19, and
enjoying a succession of receptions, banquets, dinners, dances
and sightseeing interspersed among their relentless travels.

Although they went under the banner of the Cathkin Park
club, they were more of a Scottish representative side, with just
four Third Lanark players, as well as four from Dunfermline,
two each from Partick and Motherwell and the rest from Ayr,
Dumbarton, Aberdeen and Albion Rovers.

That Albion Rovers player, Alec Bennett, became
Third Lanark's manager after the tour. He certainly would
have known the four travelling Thirds players very well by
then. Five of the players in the squad of 16 were Scottish
internationals.

Third Lanark shouldn't really have taken one of those
internationals, Andy Wilson, with them, as he was in
the middle of being transferred from Dunfermline to
Middlesbrough, and the Glasgow club didn't have Boro's
permission to take him. But they were glad that they risked

the Teessiders' wrath, as he scored a whopping 60 goals on the tour.

But the tour didn't get off to a great start. The Scots arrived two days late into Halifax, on the *Cameronia*, which had been delayed by ice, so some matches had to be rearranged, including a high-profile fixture in the capital, Ottawa, 'to the huge disappointment of lieutenant-governors, city mayors, members of Parliament, bagpipe players and football enthusiasts in general' according to the *Evening Times'* correspondent in Montreal.

Instead of facing Ottawa, the Scots played Halifax first, and beat them 7-0, with four goals from Wilson.

More than 10,000 fans – including large numbers of expat Scots – turned up for the next game, at Montreal: a record for football in North America (which was itself broken a few days later). Locals hung lion rampant flags from their windows as spectators arrived three hours early for the game.

The *Evening Times'* man reported, 'The famous scarlet and gold Scottish bunting flitted all over the place and a great Scottish standard hung gracefully over the stand. Many [fans] wore little Scottish flags in their buttonholes or carried them in their hands.'

In ideal weather, a pipe band and Montreal's mayor led the Scottish team out on to the pitch. Apparently there'd been so much hospitality the night before the game that the Scots barely got any sleep, but that didn't stop Willie Rankin from opening the scoring in the first minute.

In what the *Evening Times'* man said was 'the finest exhibition of football ever seen on this side of the Atlantic', the Scots won 6-2.

Next up were three games in Ontario and a visit to Niagara Falls. First, the Scots beat Hamilton 6-0, in front of 8,000 fans. Rankin played well again and Wilson scored four. Then they squeezed in a trip to the races, where a 'lady admirer' (the words of the *Evening Times'* correspondent) gave

Jimmy McMenemy a tip – Irish Jig – which he shared with his team and which did indeed come first. The touring party, evidently, could do nothing wrong.

And then that record attendance was smashed, on a hot day in Toronto. Fifteen thousand fans squeezed into ferries for the short crossing to the match, on a small island in Lake Ontario. Toronto's mayor, Tommy Church, kicked off the game, and the locals opened the scoring. But the Scots won 4-1.

Next up was that rearranged match in Ottawa. On a cool evening on a waterlogged pitch following an afternoon thunderstorm, it wasn't a mere mayor kicking off the match this time, it was one of the most aristocratic of aristocrats: the ninth Duke of Devonshire, in his capacity of governor general of Canada.

Multiple members of parliament were in the crowd that saw the Scots win 7-0. The rearranged Ottawa match had a knock-on effect on another game, against Fort William, which was supposed to be played the day before but had been moved to more than a month later.

First though, the Scots set off on a two-day journey to Winnipeg, the first stop on a visit to each far-flung corner of the great Canadian prairie, where they apparently had eight banquets to look forward to, and would be welcomed in each city by enthusiastic Scottish expats and pipers.

The prairie-criss-crossing Scots beat Winnipeg, Regina, Saskatoon, Calgary and Edmonton, before crossing the Rockies to the Pacific coast, where they won 3-0 against a Vancouver 'all-stars' team, which locals didn't think was as strong as it might have been. So, five days later, the Scots played against a different Vancouver select, and won 3-0 again.

Between those two games, the tourists crossed to Vancouver Island where they beat Nainamo 4-0 and Victoria 4-1.

Their travelling was epic, but the next leg made their previous journeys seem like popping to the shops. They boarded a boat up the Pacific coast to Prince Rupert – 500 miles away – and then went overland to Prince Albert, another 1,200 miles to the east.

Despite – or perhaps because of – the long trip (it was five days since their match in Vancouver), the Scots, according to the *Evening Times'* correspondent, 'were in their happiest mood and gave a sparkling exhibition of trick football, which many of the fans in the other large centres would have gone many a long mile to see. The locals put up a good fight but were obviously not in the same street with the visitors, and the score – three goals to nothing in favour of the Scots – might easily have been larger.'

Three days later they were in Winnipeg again, where they won 6-1. Three more sleeps after that they won their rearranged match in Fort William, 7-1. Then – in baking heat – they were back in Toronto, for a 3-1 win, before the highlight of the whole epic business, in Montreal.

In our final instalment from the *Evening Times'* correspondent, he said that First Nations people from Kahnawake, near Montreal, were planning to make Scots captain Jimmy Gordon an honorary chief ahead of the Scots' last game in Canada.

And that game was highly significant. It was Canada's first ever international match, as the tourists faced a team composed of the very best 11 players that the Dominion Football Association had to choose from. Nevertheless, the Scots maintained their perfect record, with a 1-0 win.

But that wasn't the end of the adventure. The tourists crossed the border and, one day after beating Canada, beat New Jersey Celtics 4-2, in the first of six games in the States.

They beat Bethlehem Steel 8-1 and Philadelphia 3-1 – and were taken on a sightseeing trip by the Football Association of Eastern Pennsylvania – before beating New York 2-1 and Massachusetts 6-3. That Massachusetts game was their third match in three days. Which perhaps explains what went wrong in the very last game of the whole huge tour.

The Scots had played 24 games and won 24, but drew their final match, 2-2 with Fall River, losing their perfect record. They were probably very tired by that point though.

Gordon Smith, one of
Scotland's greatest ever
players, who won the league
with Hibs, Hearts and
Dundee.

World Cup-winning Argentine hero Claudio Caniggia, playing for Dundee.

Jock Stein, Billy Bingham and Ron Greenwood share a laugh after the farcical 1982 World Cup draw.

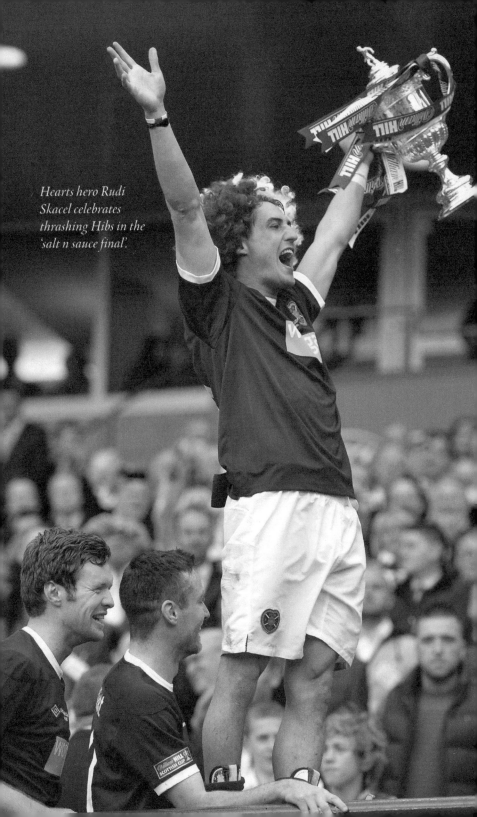

*Hearts hero Rudi
Skacel celebrates
thrashing Hibs in the
'salt n sauce final'.*

Teenager Tony Watt celebrates his blistering winning goal against Messi and co, on Celtic's 125th birthday.

Scott McTominay and Kieran Tierney celebrate McTominay's second goal against Spain in 2023.

Willie Johnston stretches Rangers' lead in the 1972 Cup Winners' Cup Final.

World Cup winner Rose Reilly, in her Milan strip.

Scotland celebrate becoming the only team to ever beat the CIS.

Partick Thistle celebrate humbling Celtic 4-1 in the League Cup Final.

Motherwell goalie Ally Maxwell — complete with ruptured spleen and broken ribs — after the best ever Scottish Cup Final.

Denis Law and Jimmy Johnstone: two top talents in Scotland's excellent 1974 World Cup squad.

49

Wednesday, 15 April 1970

Celtic Outclass Leeds

When Celtic drew Leeds in the semi-final of the European Cup in 1970, plenty of English commentators didn't give Jock Stein's men much of a chance against Don Revie's star-studded First Division champions.

Journalist Alan Smith wrote that Celtic's five successive titles 'merely established them as the biggest fish in surely the smallest pond ever dug'.

But the Scots utterly dominated their English rivals over both legs, and the 'home' meeting – in Glasgow but not at Parkhead – was one of the greatest nights in Celtic's history.

Revie – a good friend of Stein and Celtic assistant boss Sean Fallon – tried some cheeky mind games in the first leg, at Elland Road. The clubs were told that they couldn't both wear their usual white socks. Fallon later said that Revie had told him that Leeds would wear a different colour, although he added, 'But when we got there, he insisted that he had made no such agreement. We had to wear socks from one of Leeds' change strips and there were two options: blue or orange. I think he possibly thought it would cause a bit of consternation in our dressing room and unsettle everyone. But we just laughed it off.'

George Connelly, in his orange socks, scored in the first minute, as Celtic won 1-0 in Yorkshire, in front of a full house. Celtic officially had 6,000 fans there; the true figure was considerably higher. British Rail had planned to run one special train but had to put on three.

One fan in particular, from Methil, was enjoying himself so much that he was fined £5 for repeatedly trying to climb on to a police horse, in spite of his defence that he was so drunk that he surely wouldn't have been able to get up on to it.

More importantly, on the Elland Road pitch, Jimmy Johnstone turned in one of his top-class performances, full of his characteristic swerving runs. Billy McNeill was a rock at the back, and Bobby Murdoch, Bobby Lennox and Bertie Auld were all outstanding in midfield.

The *Press and Journal* praised Celtic's 'brilliant attacking' and said that, after their early goal, they 'scorned defence to protect their lead and thoroughly outplayed the English champions'.

But all that paled into insignificance compared to the glory of the second leg.

Demand for tickets was so high that the match was shifted to Hampden. Leeds were allocated 10,000 tickets but returned half of them. Celtic fans snapped them up too. There were 136,505 at the game. It was and still is the record attendance in any UEFA competition.

Bobby Lennox called it 'the biggest sea of faces I've ever seen'. Sean Fallon said, 'You could have reached out and touched the atmosphere.'

Jimmy Johnstone played the game of his life. Leeds full-back Terry Cooper later admitted, 'I couldn't get near him. I still have nightmares … I could do nothing to take the ball off Johnstone.'

But Billy Bremner opened the scoring, against the run of play, to level the tie on aggregate.

After that, though, as the *Press and Journal* reported, 'Celtic surged back into the game with a skill and fury that completely destroyed the challenge of the English champions. This was Celtic at their brilliant best. From first to last they carried the fight to Leeds and the final outcome was never seriously in doubt.

'Leeds must have been shocked and dismayed by the speed and build-up of Celtic's scoring moves. It was a magnificent John Hughes header from a Bertie Auld cross that brought the first goal and a brilliant right-foot shot by Bobby Murdoch in 52 minutes that made the aggregate 3-1. Celtic's direct and busy style never gave Leeds a chance to settle ... this was Celtic at their most adventurous and how the crowd loved it.'

After the match, Revie said Johnstone was better than George Best and continued, 'Celtic were great at Elland Road, but they were out of this world before their own fans.'

'Jock and myself were so proud,' Fallon later remembered. 'He had to leave the dressing room because he was worried he was going to cry in front of the players. I don't think I've ever seen him happier.'

Quite something, considering how many other achievements the big man had to celebrate in his illustrious career.

50

Wednesday, 4 November 1992

Rangers Outclass Leeds

When Leeds were drawn against Rangers in the second round of the 1992/93 Champions League, it was an opportunity for English club football to assert its dominance over the Scottish game, in just the second season since English teams had returned to UEFA's premier competition following their European ban.

And there was more than bragging rights at stake. The winners of the tie would qualify for the group stage, in its second year, which would earn them a flat £4m plus £217,000 per point. A lot of money in those days.

This 'Battle of Britain' wasn't simply England v Scotland. Rangers lined up with Englishmen Trevor Steven and Mark Hateley in their ranks, while Leeds' midfield consisted of just one Englishman, David Batty, plus young Welsh maestro Gary Speed and two prominent Scots, Gordon Strachan and Gary McAllister. And up front Leeds had a certain French genius named Eric Cantona, shortly before Alex Ferguson signed him for Manchester United.

Both matches were frenetic and action-packed.

In the first leg, Leeds struck first, after just two minutes, through Rangers fan McAllister's brilliant long-range volley. With no away fans allowed at either leg, Ibrox fell silent. But that was as good as it got for the men in white. Twenty minutes later the Gers equalised when goalie John Lukic turned an Ian

Durrant cross into his own net, and 15 minutes after that Ally McCoist turned home a rebound.

The *Mirror* singled out Durrant – who'd recently returned from long-term injury – for particular praise, calling him a miracle man. The match finished 2-1, leaving the tie finely balanced.

Rangers fans were determined to break the fan ban for the return at Elland Road, paying well over the odds to ticket touts. The *Daily Record* reported that about 3,000 travelled, and said, 'Most travelled by road and many avoided motorways in case they were turned back at police checkpoints. Some wore suits and ties in a bid to avoid suspicion. And hundreds used Leeds United scarves to complete the disguise. One load of Rangers fans had a "Stirling Leeds Supporters Club" banner on their bus.'

For all their trouble, some fans only saw a couple of minutes of the match. In those action-packed first two minutes Andy Goram saved well from Cantona, before Hateley blasted home from just outside the box and celebrated deliriously, as he left Leeds needing to score three to go through. Some Rangers fans who weren't meant to be there couldn't contain their glee and were soon led away by police.

There was loads more action but just two more goals, as Goram played a blinder between the sticks. In the second half McCoist extended Rangers' lead with, incredibly, his 29th goal of the young season, hurling himself at Hateley's lovely cross. Coisty's flying header left Lukic 'perplexed and bewildered', according to the *Record*, as Elland Road fell silent.

Cantona got a consolation goal five minutes from the end, but it was all over long before that. At full time the Leeds fans gave Rangers a sporting round of applause as the Scots marched on to the group stage.

Midfielder Ian Ferguson summed up exactly how much the two-leg victory meant: 'I wouldn't go as far as saying it's better than beating Celtic. But it's close.' High praise from a Rangers-supporting Rangers player.

The men from Ibrox carried their good form into the group stage, where they finished unbeaten but missed out narrowly on a place in the final, with Marseille ending up one point above them.

The French team beat Milan in the final but their victory has long since been indelibly tainted by a subsequent European ban for domestic match-fixing in the same season. There's never been any proof that they fixed any matches in the Champions League, but Rangers fans have for ever been left wondering what could have been, having missed out so narrowly to the dubious eventual winners of that season's Champions League.

51

Friday, 16 November 1979

George Best Signs for Hibs

In 1979 George Best signed for Hibs. Thousands of extra fans turned up to games – to start with, at least – to see the most famous footballer to ever play in the Scottish league.

Three days before Christmas, he charmed fans of every persuasion when he picked up a beer can that a Rangers fan had thrown at him and took a swig from it. When Derek Johnstone repeatedly fouled him in the same match, he jokingly handed the Rangers man the ball, as if to say 'if you want it that badly ...'

Three weeks after that, he repaid the fans' trust in him when he scored the goal of the season, against Celtic – a blistering shot from the corner of the penalty box.

It was all classic Georgie boy, but that was as good as it got.

His manager, Eddie Turnbull, hadn't even wanted Best there. It was nothing personal – Turnbull, like the Hibs players, found the Irish star to be a lovely, and quite shy, guy. And it was no reflection on Best's quality – the Hibs boss rated the Belfast boy, at his best, right up there with Pelé, Maradona and Cruyff.

But Best was 33, was struggling with alcohol, and hadn't achieved anything of note anywhere in the five years since he'd left Manchester United. Meanwhile, Hibs were bottom of the league, and Turnbull thought the money should have been spent elsewhere to strengthen the team for the relegation battle.

Hibs chairman Tom Hart – who'd been tipped off about Best's availability by *Edinburgh Evening News* reporter Stewart Brown – signed him from Fulham against Turnbull's wishes.

The mercurial Irishman scored on his debut, a 2-1 defeat to St Mirren. It was one of just three goals that he would score for Hibs.

He was splitting his time between his London home and Edinburgh, where Hibs were putting him up in the North British Hotel – an establishment with 50 pubs within a square mile.

It wasn't surprising when Best was photographed by journalists the worse for wear in the Jinglin' Geordie pub. As any Edinburgh local could have told him, it was the worst place to try to have an anonymous drinking session, as it was about ten feet away from the back door of the *Scotsman* and *Evening News* offices.

Best was providing just occasional flashes of inspiration on the pitch, and was missing training too often. Turnbull was frustrated, but Hart was happy about all the extra money coming through the turnstiles as fans initially flocked to see the troubled star.

But in February 1980 – after Best had played just six games for Hibs – even Hart's patience was shattered.

Best called in sick to a game against Morton, was suspended by Hart, then apologised, rushed back to Edinburgh for an extra Monday training session that was just for him, and was reinstated.

But just one week later, on the night before a Scottish Cup tie against Ayr, he befriended French rugby players who were drowning their sorrows after losing a Five Nations match at Murrayfield. You can guess what happened next.

Best was far too hungover to face Ayr, and Hart announced, 'The marriage between Hibs and Best is over.

The divorce took place this morning. Eddie Turnbull and I have agreed that George Best is available for transfer.'

But – no doubt with a mind on those bumper gate receipts – Hart relented just days later, and Best came back, starting with back-to-back games against Dundee. In the second of them, at home, he scored one and set up the other in a 2-0 victory, in what some papers described as his best Hibs performance. But the attendance was back down to 5,000.

In April Hart clearly decided that enough was enough, and Best was transferred to San Jose Earthquakes, although he returned to Easter Road to play four more games the next season – in the second tier – and two in the League Cup.

Before flying out to California, he thanked the Hibs fans for everything, over the Tannoy at Easter Road, at a league game against Killie. But only 2,650 fans were there to hear his thanks. And Hibs lost 2-1.

Signing George Best didn't save Hibs from relegation. But the fans who flocked to see him will always remember his occasional flashes of genius.

52

Saturday, 17 April 1999

The Dundee Clubs Almost Merge

In early 1999 Dundee were struggling, on the pitch and off it. The SPL were threatening them with automatic relegation if they didn't renovate dilapidated Dens Park, and the club certainly didn't have the money to fund those works. The only good news for the dark blue half of the city was that their tangerine rivals weren't exactly charging up the league table either.

So the men in charge at Dens reached for one of the worst possible solutions to their temporary problems, and, in the February, opened 'informal' merger talks with United.

Dundee chairman Peter Marr said, 'We are all Dundonians but we are battling against each other to achieve the same thing and to me that is quite silly.' But Jim McLean – the former manager was by this time chairman at Tannadice – said the only possible way of joining forces would be a takeover of Dundee by United, who had the better ground and healthier finances.

So Dundee briefly turned to another terrible way out of their money woes: investment from Anglo-Italian businessman Giovanni Di Stefano. Unfortunately, the man who the *Daily Record* likened to describe as a 'Belgrade wheeler-dealer' had been a friend of Željko Ražnatović – better known as Serbian war criminal Arkan. He'd also met Saddam Hussein and was an admirer of Benito Mussolini (and of Alex Salmond). By now, he'd also been convicted of fraud multiple times.

Thankfully, the Dundee board saw sense and discarded Di Stefano as an investor, and just about managed to find investment from other sources to bring Dens Park up to SPL standards.

But on Friday, 16 April, the *Record* reported, '[Marr] has made moves to reopen merger talks with arch rivals Dundee United. The view, however, of commerce and industry is that Dundee's position is now financially so weak that any joint venture would be a United takeover rather than a merger of equal partners.'

And, indeed, on the Saturday, they followed that up with a quote from a United spokesman: 'At the moment the only basis on which we could consider joint working with Dundee FC will be a takeover by us.'

And by the Monday it was all off. 'Dundee have shelved plans for a merger with Dundee United' was the latest update from the *Record*, adding, 'Dundee are determined to complete their £2.9m project to build two new stands, although financing still appears to be fraught with difficulties.'

Apparently the possibly actually pretty cool name of Sporting Club of Dundee had been mooted for a merged club.

Some years later, Roger Mitchell, who was the chairman of the SPL at the time, claimed that 'the deal was done'. Surprisingly, Mitchell claimed that McLean – who always saw it as United taking over Dundee – was a driving force and that Marr pulled the plug at the last minute.

Mitchell said they'd come up with the new name – apparently Dundee United City – and decided on their strip. He added that the deal was agreed on the Friday night, but cancelled on the Monday, following 'some incident in a nightclub'. Marr said Mitchell's claims were 'total nonsense'. Most fans weren't sure who to disbelieve more.

This wasn't the first time that the merger talk had reared its head. In 1991, then Dundee chairman Angus Cook went as far as registering the name Dundee City for an amalgamated club, which he hoped to have operating within a year. Dundee United Supporters Association spokesman Finlay McKay said, 'When we first heard about it we treated it as a bit of a laugh. But I know a lot of fans will be worried.'

But Sporting Club of Dundee, Dundee United City and Dundee City all remain hypothetical beasts. Both sets of fans still have their own clubs to support and hopefully always will.

53

Saturday, 9 May 2015

The Pyramid Is Finally Introduced

Until 2015, the only way for non-league clubs to be elected into the SPFL (Scottish Professional Football League) was to wait for a vacancy to arise – which didn't happen very often – and then go up against other ambitious clubs for election from the SPFL's existing members.

A Highland or Lowland League club could hypothetically go on a record-breaking years-long winning streak with no realistic prospect of promotion. Meanwhile, the bottom end of SPFL League Two was moribund, with no threat of relegation, which left some clubs sleepwalking into embarrassing worst-club-in-the-country territory.

But SPFL clubs resisted opportunities to change the situation, voting in short-term self-interest against reconstruction proposals – until 2015, when the first ever play-offs for league membership finally, belatedly, happened.

Highland League champions Brora Rangers – despite having logistical concerns about playing in a nationwide league – faced Montrose in the play-off final. Brora won the home leg 1-0, and the return match in Montrose was delayed by 15 minutes to let in a crowd that was four times the League Two average. The Highlanders were still in the driving seat until 16 minutes from the end, when former Trinidad and Tobago international Marvin Andrews equalised for the

Gable Endies, before Garry Wood got the winner for the men from Angus a minute later.

It had been a close-run thing, and 12 months later, Lowland League winners Edinburgh City – who'd lost to Brora in the 2015 semi – became the first club to be promoted to the SPFL based purely on results on the pitch. Edinburgh City had applied for league vacancies in 2002 and 2008 but lost out to Gretna and then Annan. But this time they beat Cove Rangers 4-1 on aggregate in the play-off semi-final and then beat East Stirling in the final, thanks to a penalty five minutes from the end of the second leg.

The Citizens started a trend. Cove – who'd won the Highland League seven times since 2000 – Kelty Hearts, Bonnyrigg Rose and The Spartans have all followed them into the SPFL, with Berwick Rangers, Brechin City, Cowdenbeath and Albion Rovers going the other way, and discovering that life carries on in the fifth tier.

And the promoted clubs have done well in the SPFL. Edinburgh City, Kelty and Cove were all fairly quickly promoted into League One – Kelty in just one season – with Cove briefly reaching the Championship.

Not everyone is keen on this tweaking of the guard; the word 'ambitious' is often used as a loaded term, particularly against Cove and Kelty, with envious glances cast towards some of the players they've managed to attract.

But, like the clubs who've been in the SPFL for longer, the newcomers have history, heritage, community and the right to compete on a level playing field, and they've freshened up Leagues One and Two. Better late than never.

54

Friday, 13 June 1986

The Fastest Red Card in World Cup History

In 1986, Scotland became one half of a piece of World Cup history: the quickest ever sending-off in the tournament.

The foul that led to the card wasn't quite the horror show that would have been apposite for the match's date, but the way that the remaining 89 minutes of the game unfolded was pretty disquieting for the men in dark blue (and iconic hooped shorts).

It was Scotland's crucial final match in the group that the Uruguay manager Omar Borrás had labelled the 'group of death': Scotland, Uruguay, West Germany and Denmark. After playing well in their first two games but narrowly losing both, Scotland needed a win to reach a last-16 match against Argentina, while Uruguay only needed a point.

After just 49 seconds of play at the Estadio Neza 86 on the edge of Mexico City, José Batista launched himself into the back of Gordon Strachan's calves. It was the first foul of the game, but referee Joël Quiniou – in the first minute of his first ever World Cup match – whipped out his red card. Although it was a fairly bad foul, it was a harsh decision; even a yellow card would have been a bold choice.

In the commentary box, a surprised Billy McNeill confessed that he thought Quiniou had accidentally pulled out the wrong card. But if he had, he wasn't about to admit it. As the shocked Uruguay players harangued the French whistler, he reiterated his decision by flourishing the card in Batista's general direction two, three – actually, six – times and pointing to the sideline for good measure.

The Uruguay players had good reason to be worried about how this surprise development could affect the game. In their previous match, against swashbuckling Denmark, their captain Miguel Bossio had been sent off after 20 minutes, they lost 6-1, and Borrás's home was given police protection after fans threatened to kill him.

But the Copa América holders – through means both fair and foul – dealt much better with the changed circumstances than the Scots did. They went ultra-defensive, even whenever they got corners or free kicks, and remained very well organised, and the great Enzo Francescoli was excellent throughout, playing on the break.

There was some more tasty tackling – although not as much as has been typically reported, and Richard Gough, Dave Narey and Steve Nicol dished it out a bit too – and a masterclass in time-wasting, which was very frustrating for Scotland but probably more or less what most teams would have done in Uruguay's situation, especially when they'd just seen a European referee give a big, strange decision in favour of their European opponents.

The Uruguay players really crossed the line in two respects though. Throughout the match, they harangued Quiniou, who'd clearly tried to impose his authority early on but who then never booked anyone for dissent, although he did eventually flash two yellow cards for time-wasting. He received especially terrible treatment at half-time, not just from players and fans but from the bench too, as FIFA officials struggled to help him down the tunnel safely.

And, as Scotland full-back Arthur Albiston later said, Uruguay players stood on fouled players' ankles, nipped

Scottish players, pulled their hair – a photo captured goalie Fernando Álvez grabbing Graeme Sharp's mullet – and threw their elbows around.

All of which didn't leave much room for much football of note. Scotland only really carved out one good chance, a low Paul Sturrock cross finding Nicol in the box, but the Liverpool man's shot was very weak and Álvez scrambled across to claw it away. After that, Uruguay created the best chances, with Jim Leighton saving well from Francescoli and then Wilmar Cabrera.

A late Narey blast from outside the box flew narrowly over the bar. It was Scotland's last chance. Uruguay went through to face Maradona and co., without winning a match and with a goal difference of minus five.

The bad blood continued in the post-match press conference. Borrás described Batista's sending off as 'murder by the referee', to which Alex Ferguson responded by saying, 'They seem to have no respect for anyone. That was a debacle out there. I know we are out of the World Cup, but honestly I'm glad to be going home because this is no way to play football. I have to sit here and listen to Borrás lying and cheating. My players are very upset and I will not criticise any one of them. I cannot say "good luck" to Uruguay, because they don't deserve it.'

SFA secretary Ernie Walker was even more forthright, describing the Uruguayans as cheats, cowards and 'the scum of world football'.

Two days later, FIFA fined Uruguay, threatened to kick them out of the tournament if they did it again, and banned Borrás from the touchline for the Argentina game. What may have galled Uruguay even more was the fact that FIFA later appointed Quiniou for seven more World Cup matches, across 1990 and '94.

Meanwhile, Scotland went home, finished off by the group of death and their own inability to score in a match where they played against ten men for 89 minutes.

55

Saturday, 30 December 1995

Gazza Books the Ref

Rangers v Hibs at Ibrox, just before half-time: the home side are 2-0 up. Paul Gascoigne gets on the end of a Gordon Durie pass in the box but Jim Leighton forces him wide and the chance is gone.

Which is when it gets interesting. Gazza spots referee Dougie Smith's yellow card lying on the turf by the goal line, where it must have fallen from the whistler's pocket slightly earlier.

The twinkle-toed Geordie picks up the card and trots 25 yards to give it back to the man in black, but before handing it to him, he flourishes it above his head, as if he's booking him.

Unfortunately for the wayward genius, Mr Smith is probably the only person inside Ibrox who doesn't see the funny side, and he swiftly returns the gesture in a much more officious manner, while the cheeky Englishman jogs away, still smiling.

Gazza could afford to see the funny side. This match was 1990s Rangers at the top of their game. Already well on their way to their eighth consecutive title, they were playing with verve and style and dominating the only team who'd beaten them so far that season.

And Gascoigne was to have the last laugh in this match. Although it was Durie who scored four in an eventual seven-goal destruction of the Edinburgh men, Gazza grabbed the pick of the bunch – a brilliant solo run from midfield, dancing past defenders into the box and slotting the ball past Leighton. He ran to celebrate joyfully with the Rangers bench, but they urged him not to leave the pitch in case he got a second yellow card.

It's tempting to think that Gascoigne was past his prime when he moved to Rangers – so much had already happened in his career and he'd had a tumultuous time at his previous club, Lazio. But he was only 28 when he signed at Ibrox. He scored 19 goals in that double-winning season and won both the players' and writers' player of the year awards.

But it's perhaps appropriate, for a player whose genius was matched by his rebellious unpredictability, that the image that sticks in the mind is him pretending to caution Dougie Smith.

56

Wednesday, 27 April 1938

East Fife Win the Scottish Cup

East Fife were playing in Division Two when they won the Scottish Cup in 1938: a remarkable achievement that was well-earned via an epic cup campaign: they played in five replays and two periods of extra time, scored 23 goals and performed in front of a grand total of 375,000 fans in the process.

But their whole cup campaign initially looked like it would be over as soon as it began when they were 1-0 down away to Airdrie in the first round with 15 minutes to go, before a Robert McCartney double took the men from Methil through to the second round, where they beat Dundee United 5-0.

It was an impressive result against Division Two opponents who'd surprisingly knocked out Hearts in the first round. But even so, no one gave the Fifers much hope in the next round, against Aberdeen.

Again East Fife came from behind, to set up a replay four days later at Pittodrie, where they came from behind yet again, and beat their illustrious opponents 2-1. They received a heroes' welcome when they got off the train back in Methil.

Quarter-final fever was augmented by the identity of their opponents: local rivals Raith Rovers, who were also competing with their neighbours for promotion. The match, at home, was made all-ticket and, although the club increased ticket prices for it, all 17,000 tickets sold out in one hour. So space was somehow found for 2,000 more fans inside Bayview and 2,000 more tickets were sold.

This time it was East Fife's turn to surrender a lead, going 2-0 up but eventually drawing when Jock Whitelaw scored a late penalty for the men from Kirkcaldy. At Stark's Park, in front of another bumper crowd, the replay was 2-2 in the dying minutes when a Raith man blocked a shot with his hand. The East Fife players thought it had crossed the line first, but the referee gave a penalty. Andy Herd fired it home and East Fife were in the semi-final.

Their opponents at neutral Tynecastle were another Division Two team, St Bernard's. They drew 1-1. The replay finished 1-1 too, after extra time, so they had to play each other for a third time in Gorgie.

That replay was also 1-1, with six minutes to go (future Dundee United manager Jerry Kerr scored the Edinburgh side's goal), when Danny McKerrell scored the winner with a header, on his East Fife debut, days after joining on loan from Falkirk. When the final whistle went, joyful Fifers spilled on to the pitch to celebrate with their heroes.

Six special trains took East Fife fans to Hampden for the final, against Division One Kilmarnock. Eddie McLeod gave the underdogs the lead but Killie equalised soon after and it finished 1-1.

The cup final replay took place four days later. Writing in the *Courier*, Don John celebrated a 'never to be forgotten' replay that was 'nerve racking in its countless incidents'. McKerrell gave East Fife the lead after 15 minutes 'with a goal that was of gilt-edged cup stock' but Killie came back and then took a 2-1 lead.

But McLeod equalised for the Fifers in the second half with 'one of the cutest goals scored in a cup final – a wonder hook' and yet again East Fife were playing extra time. And McKerrell and Larry Miller secured black-and-gold glory with two goals in the last 11 minutes.

As Don John said, it was a 'wonder finish to a wonder game ... No thrill-satisfied enthusiast in a remarkable midweek crowd of 91,710 could dispute the merit of East Fife's memorable triumph.' Time for another – massive – black-and-gold pitch invasion, as Killie president James Henderson praised East Fife's 'wonderful football'.

With so many fans at Hampden, you could be forgiven for thinking that Methil would have been left empty, but cheering crowds were back home too, when the team got back at midnight. But they had to squeeze their celebrations in around a packed schedule of rearranged league matches that had been delayed by all those cup ties. They played five games in just seven days.

On the Monday between the cup final and the Wednesday replay, they'd faced East Stirling away in the league, and now, on the day after the victorious replay – and after that late-night return home – they beat Forfar. And just one day after that – on the same day as they celebrated their cup triumph at a dinner and ball with local dignitaries – they fired seven past Dundee United.

Unfortunately, with the distraction of the cup, East Fife missed out on promotion, despite scoring 104 league goals that season.

And despite the excellent excuse of such extreme fixture congestion, the league fined the Methil men for playing an under-strength team in their match against East Stirling. Not that they'd have been too worried about that. They made a hefty £12,000 from their epic, victorious cup run.

57

2014/15

The Most Unlikely League Season Ever

The Scottish Championship in 2014/15 had quite possibly the most unlikely assortment of teams for any second-tier division in the world ever; an unusual combination that led to an incredibly eventful season.

Remarkably, three of the five biggest clubs in the land met up there, for one year only. Rangers had earned back-to-back promotions after starting again in League Two following their liquidation in 2012. Hearts had just been relegated after their own financial troubles, which resulted in a 15-point deduction and a transfer ban in 2013/14. Hibs fans' joy at their rivals' travails turned sour in the spring of 2014 when their own terrible form on the pitch – one win in their last 18 league games, then a lost play-off against Hamilton – led to their relegation too.

At the other end of the scale, three part-time teams were also in that same league of ten: Dumbarton, Alloa and Cowdenbeath were all going strong.

As if to reinforce the fact that this was to be a season like no other, on the opening day, new Hibs player Mark Oxley scored on his league debut, against Livingston. Debut goals may not be particularly remarkable, but this one was, because Oxley was Hibs' goalie.

The next day, there was late drama when the other two big clubs met up, at Ibrox. Hearts led until Rangers got an injury-time equaliser, but just one minute later the Jam Tarts' striker Osman Sow blasted home the winner.

That late winner in that big game was a clear and accurate signal of Hearts' intent. In 36 matches they scored 96 goals and earned 91 points, and they had a 20-game unbeaten run. If Rangers had thought they could breeze through all of the lower leagues, the men from Gorgie shattered that misconception, ultimately winning the league with seven games to go. This was very much Hearts' season.

Ten of Hearts' 96 goals came in one match in February – including a three-minute hat-trick for Género Zeefuik – when they thrashed Cowdenbeath.

Rangers travelled to Cowdenbeath a week later – and one day after an Ibrox boardroom revolution that new non-executive chairman Dave King described as a turning point in the future of the club. In conditions so windy that ground staff had to hold down the empty dugouts at half-time to stop them from blowing over, the Glasgow giants could only manage a goalless draw against the team who Hearts had so recently hammered.

Big clubs experiencing the challenges of the weather at Cowdenbeath's ramshackle but iconic Central Park characterised the idiosyncrasy of this season beautifully. Ahead of another match against Hearts, the Fifers had to drive a van on to the pitch to use its engine heat to defrost their goalmouths.

Rangers' struggles to keep up with Hearts weren't for want of trying. They changed managers twice. After they put Ally McCoist on gardening leave in December, Kenny McDowall and then Stuart McCall were only in the job for three months each. They signed a bumper-pack of five players on loan from Newcastle in January. One of them – Haris Vučkić – was a brief success but the other four played just a handful of matches between them.

So it wasn't really a surprise that Hearts pulled so far clear from Rangers, but what about Hibs? Following their disastrous run under Terry Butcher at the end of the previous season, they brought in new boss Alan Stubbs. Young striker Jason Cummings came of age, finishing as the division's top scorer, while Stubbs signed midfielder Scott Allan, who was one of the best players in the Championship that season, and was particularly instrumental in a 4-0 victory over Rangers in December. Hibs won two of their other three league matches against the Gers and finished second to Hearts.

Meanwhile, what of the part-time clubs?

Dumbarton finished seven points above the relegation play-off spot, under manager Ian Murray.

Alloa made a shock signing in March, former England youth international Michael Chopra, who played well in their relegation battle. The Wasps' fight to stay up was helped by drawing with Rangers three times in the league. And during the same season, in a remarkable Challenge Cup tie, the Clackmannanshire minnows came back from 2-0 down to beat the Glasgow giants 3-2.

The title race may have been done and dusted before 2015's lambs were being born, but the last day of the season boasted a three-way relegation battle between Cowdenbeath, Alloa and Livingston, who had been deducted five points and given a transfer ban for tax-related transgressions.

With Livi beating Queen of the South 1-0, Alloa needed to beat Cowdenbeath to avoid automatic relegation, and they did it, 3-0, with Chopra getting the first goal. The Blue Brazil went down, and then Alloa won their play-off matches to stay up.

After all their turmoil off and on the pitch for most of the season, under McCall's leadership Rangers came good at the right time, beating Queen of the South and then Hibs in the play-offs to set up a final with Motherwell. But that's when the Gers' brief renaissance conclusively petered out.

The Steelmen won 3-1 at Ibrox, and then 3-0 at Fir Park, in a game that finished in a full-scale boxing match between Rangers' Bilel Mohsni and Motherwell's Lee Erwin. It was an appositely dramatic conclusion to a unique season.

58

Saturday, 27 October 2007

Julie Fleeting Scores Her 100th Goal for Scotland

Ally McCoist scored 19 goals for Scotland, Lawrie Reilly 22. Hughie Gallagher got 24 in just 20 games. With 30 each, Denis Law and Kenny Dalglish sit atop the scoring charts; the men's scoring charts, that is.

Jane Ross has scored more than 60 goals for Scotland, but head and shoulders above any other Scottish footballer is Julie Fleeting, who's in the world's top ten goalscorers in women's football, even though she's played far fewer games than almost every other player in that – mostly American – list.

All this despite playing at a time when women's football in Scotland was still desperately lacking support and funding. She was the only female player in her primary school's whole league, and she helped her school to win the Scottish school championships. But when she turned 12 she wasn't allowed to play in boys' teams any more.

Like Rose Reilly, she considered other sporting options, thinking of mainly playing basketball or hockey instead, but stuck with football. And – again, like Reilly before her – she didn't let any of the challenges facing female footballers at that time hold her back.

She made her international debut aged just 15, when she came on at half-time against Wales. She later said that the game left her in a bad mood because Scotland lost and she didn't score. Then she crossed the Atlantic on tour in a young Scotland side that played against Brazil three times, while her mates back home were sitting exam prelims at school. Her first Scotland goals – four of them in one match – came in a World Cup qualifier against Estonia when she was 16.

She moved briefly to San Diego to play professionally. She was the first Scot and just the second British player in American women's football. The goals kept coming, as her team-mates nicknamed her 'Air Scotland' and she won her team's player of the year and golden boot awards.

Most of Fleeting's club success came later, at Arsenal, where she spent nine years and won 17 major trophies. All while working as a PE teacher in Scotland and flying down to London and back for games.

But it was in dark blue that Fleeting had her most remarkable and inspirational success, maintaining an average of a goal a game until she reached that incredible triple-figures landmark in a 3-0 victory away against Slovakia in a Euros qualifier in 2007, her 99th game for Scotland. Her boot sponsor gave her a pair of golden boots to commemorate the achievement, and later that year she won Scotland's Sports Personality of the Year award, which was swiftly followed up with an MBE.

She was only 26 when she scored her 100th Scotland goal, and said that she hoped she still had 'a few more goals' in her. She did, although her appearances became sporadic, interrupted by her first two pregnancies.

She eventually scored her 116th – and last – official goal for Scotland in 2011, in her 121st official cap. Why do I keep emphasising 'official' so much? Because she also scored 16 goals in one unofficial international, against the Isle of Man. But even without counting that, she's one of the greatest goalscorers the world has ever seen.

59

Monday, 10 July 1989

The Most Shocking Transfer of All Time

It was more than a shock. It was a bombshell. It was the unlikeliest possible marriage between player and club. It was also a breathtaking, audacious coup, as that club snatched the player out of the grasp of their greatest rivals.

On top of all that, it was also the signing that finally, belatedly, dragged that club's recruitment policy out of the Dark Ages.

It was a football transfer that dominated the front and back pages, and several in between, of not just the tabloids but broadsheets too. The *Daily Record* called it the 'transfer of the century' and dedicated ten pages to it.

Mo Johnston was a Celtic fan. He had played for Celtic, scoring 52 goals in 99 games. After a couple of pretty successful years at Nantes, he wanted to return to Scotland.

He took to the Parkhead pitch, a week before the Scottish Cup Final, wearing a Celtic strip, and he shared an unambiguous message, as he said that returning to the club that he supported was a dream come true.

It was meant to be a signal that Celtic's penny-pinching days were behind them; it was going to be Scotland's record transfer. Which was all crucial, exactly when Rangers' spending was starting to open a gulf between the two clubs. Johnston, Celtic boss Billy McNeill and the player's girlfriend Karen Bell were all smiles for the cameras.

Johnston continued with his clear messaging, as he said, 'I had six or seven offers from Italy, France, Germany and England, but there was only one place I wanted to go. I always wanted to play for Celtic and I still do,' while a clearly thrilled McNeill praised his new signing's maturity.

The day before the final, Celtic captain Roy Aitken said, 'His arrival has given everyone a massive lift,' and said the signing indicated that 'things are starting to swing in our favour'. Paperwork was completed. Everyone thought it was a done deal. Celtic beat Rangers in the cup final and Celtic-minded people were starting to feel pretty positive.

But soon it was reported that a wrangle with Nantes over tax payments was causing problems, and fans' fears that the transfer would fall through started to look more and more likely.

And then, suddenly, it got far worse for the green-and-white half of Glasgow, in ways that they would never have dared imagine. Just two months after he'd been all smiles with McNeill, Johnston was back in Glasgow, but cosying up instead with Rangers boss Graeme Souness, who was making the shocking announcement that Mo was signing instead at Ibrox.

Just a year earlier, the striker had said in his book *Mo: The Maurice Johnston Story* that he would only ever consider signing for Rangers if they offered him £1m and Stirling Castle. Another pretty clear statement. But in the event, it seemed that they met him in the middle – no castle, but significantly more cash than Celtic could offer.

Although he wasn't moving into Stirling Castle, Johnston did notably admit that he wouldn't be living in Glasgow. And not just because Celtic fans would be livid to be snubbed and humiliated by a man who they'd thought was one of their own. A large section of the Rangers support were equally angry. Johnston wasn't simply a high-profile former Celtic player, who also supported Celtic and who had also once annoyed

Rangers fans by blessing himself when he left the pitch in front of them. He was also a Catholic.

Rangers had never knowingly signed an openly Catholic footballer. Thankfully, Souness didn't have any time for any of that sort of so-called tradition. But some Rangers fans were still belligerently proud of their discriminatory signing policy, and were consequently disgusted that the club had signed a high-profile Catholic.

A wreath saying '116 years of tradition ended' was quickly placed outside Ibrox. Some supporters burned scarves. Some demanded a refund on their season tickets. David Miller, the general secretary of the Rangers Supporters Association, said, 'I don't want to see a Roman Catholic at Ibrox.'

Rangers were painfully aware of the outrage they would face from some of their own fans but had reached a point where they could no longer pander to such irrational beliefs. When they very nearly recruited Jim McLean as their potential new manager a few years earlier, they had agreed to his demands that he could sign Catholic players. Meanwhile, there was speculation that European clubs may refuse ambitious Rangers the opportunity to compete in anticipated money-spinning European competitions if they didn't mend their ways.

In the end, it was Souness and Johnston who took that big step. And although they were motivated by straightforward football and financial reasons, it was also a brave move to be the public faces of Rangers' long-overdue step towards equality.

FIFA weren't about to congratulate Rangers for that belated improvement though. They fined Johnston £3,000 for pulling out of the initial transfer to Celtic: a tiny dent on his new-found fortune, and small recompense to Celtic fans, especially as their former hero went on to score 31 goals for their fierce rivals.

60

Wednesday, 7 November 2012

Great Goals 2: Tony Watt Beats Barcelona

Tony Watt was 18 years old and ten minutes into his Champions League debut when he scored probably Celtic's most memorable goal of the 21st century so far.

It was the day after Celtic's 125th anniversary and what a birthday present young Tony's first ever goal at Parkhead was. The opposition? Barcelona. And this was not just any Barcelona team. This was possibly the greatest Barcelona team of all time: Messi, Xavi, Iniesta, Dani Alves; one of the greatest football teams ever assembled.

The *Blaugrana* hadn't lost a Champions League group match for three years. But that record couldn't last for ever, in the cold November rain.

Two weeks earlier, Celtic had succumbed to glorious defeat at the Camp Nou, taking the lead but eventually losing to an injury-time Jordi Alba strike. And for the home game the Bhoys were missing four key players in Scott Brown, James Forrest, Gary Hooper and Emilio Izaguirre.

In Glasgow, Barcelona's passing was metronomic, almost hypnotic. Their possession, passing and shots stats were mind-boggling. Celtic defended deep, and defended narrowly, and defended brilliantly, deliberately and effectively restricting their aristocratic guests mostly to crosses and long shots. Barça's dominance had no impact on the buzzing atmosphere, which went up a few more notches in the 20th minute.

Victor Wanyama – who was imperious throughout the match – rose brilliantly to head a Charlie Mulgrew corner past Victor Valdés; 1-0. Celtic Park went wild. But still Barcelona pushed forward, again and again.

The Catalan giants created umpteen chances and half-chances, but very few heart-in-mouth moments, until Messi forced Fraser Forster into a brilliant save in the 70th minute. The Argentine genius later described the big Northumbrian stopper's performance that night as the greatest goalkeeping performance he'd ever seen. And he'd come up against a lot of top keepers.

But the truth was that the whole back four: Mikael Lustig, Efe Ambrose, Kelvin Wilson and Adam Matthews – who was playing out of position filling in for Izaguirre but doing a brilliant job on the great Dani Alves – were relentlessly excellent too. They had to be.

But then another injury for Celtic, as Lustig limped off. Surprisingly, Neil Lennon replaced his right-back with a third striker, Tony Watt, who he'd recently bought from Airdrie for £50,000 – about four days' wages for any of the Barcelona players.

Ten minutes after young Tony came on, Forster easily gathered a Messi free kick and launched a long ball down the middle. The bounce deceived Xavi, while Watt reacted instantly and precisely, bursting forward and blasting the ball past Valdés; 2-0. The atmosphere was cranked up to 11. The delighted crowd sang their hearts out to 'I Just Can't Get Enough', and did a massive Poznań celebration.

It was a direct, route-one goal but Tony did everything exactly right and it was absolutely electric.

Incredibly, five minutes later, he almost did it again, but Javier Mascherano grabbed the teenager's left arm and he went down, but the referee waved play on.

There was still time for a nervy four minutes of injury time, after, in the last minute, Messi finally got the goal that his performance and tenacity deserved when he turned home the rebound after Forster had saved from Pedro.

But Celtic held out for more joyous scenes at full time. On their way out, home fans grinned and waved at their Catalan counterparts, and threw scarves to them. The Barcelona supporters waved back. They were still top of the group, after all.

Rod Stewart wept tears of joy.

The result meant Celtic finished above Benfica and went through to the knockout stages. But the match is more memorable for itself than for the valuable points that it delivered.

Spanish paper *Marca* christened Forster 'the Great Wall'. Other outlets were universal in their praise of the Celtic crowd, and expressed semi-concerned awe at the fact that Celtic Park physically swayed with the fans' movement. Xavi, Gerard Piqué and manager Tito Vilanova all waxed lyrical about the fans and atmosphere. Vilanova said, 'I have been lucky in my career to have been to many grounds, but I have never seen anything like it.'

Reaction to Celtic's performance was almost universally positive, in spite of Barcelona's stats, although the Barcelona website did brand Celtic lucky and point out how good Barça's passing was and the fact that they hit the woodwork a few times. Celtic probably were lucky that Barcelona only scored once, but the main reason for that was their excellent performance and tactics, and they certainly weren't lucky with the number of injuries that they had to overcome. And Barcelona were lucky that the ref missed Mascherano's last-man foul on Watt, and that Alex Song didn't get a second yellow card for a very clumsy foul on Miku. Barcelona were pass masters, but Celtic defended better and were more clinical up front.

It was a great team performance, but the main glory belonged to one raw teenager. After the match, Lennon said Watt was 'still learning, but he's written himself into the history books of the club tonight'.

61

Sunday, 30 May 1982

Scotland Win the Under-18 Euros

No one – not even the Scottish players – thought that Scotland were among the favourites at the 1982 European Youth Championship, especially since Bryan Gunn, Neale Cooper, Eric Black, Dave McPherson, Kenny Black and Billy Davies weren't available because Aberdeen and Rangers were playing in the Scottish Cup Final at the same time.

Goalie Gunn and both the Blacks had played against England in both legs of the qualifier and McPherson had played in the home match, and Cooper away, but management team Andy Roxburgh and Walter Smith would have to do without those key players in Finland.

But they still had plenty of talented kids to pick from, not least Pat Nevin, Ally Dick, Gary Mackay, Jim McInally, the Daves – Bowman and Beaumont – and Celtic duo Paul McStay and Jim Dobbin, who were responsible for creating and scoring all three goals against England.

Nevin decided to travel even though he had exams at Glasgow Tech the day after the final. He didn't think there was much chance of Scotland reaching the final. But the nation would be glad that the part-time Clyde player decided to risk the potentially tight schedule.

He was outstanding from the word go, and throughout the tournament. He had a hand in all of Scotland's goals in the opening game against Albania, with Brian Rice, Sammy

McGivern and Mackay scoring in the 3-0 victory. Two days later, Mackay scored again, against Türkiye, but it was Nevin again who was the man of the match, scoring the other goal in a 2-0 victory and getting a standing ovation from the crowd of 5,000, in the small town of Hamina, near the Russian border.

The win left the young Scots just needing a draw in their final group game – against the Netherlands, including Marco van Basten – to reach the semis. The Dutch had already booked their hotel for the semi-finals.

That final group game didn't start well. Captain McStay was missing with a foot injury. Van Basten opened the scoring after just four minutes. Another heroic near miss for Scotland? No. Dundee United defender Gary McGinnis – making his debut in the dark blue – volleyed home from a late Dick back-heel to put Scotland through. It was the toughest match Scotland would face in the tournament.

There were still two games to go, but Dutch coach Ger Blok visited the Scottish dressing room after the draw, to offer his congratulations to 'the champions of Europe for 1982'. Hopefully he put some money on his prediction.

McStay was back for the semi, against Poland, but now Dobbin was out injured.

Scotland had no recognised centre-forward, so Mackay played in the middle, slightly behind the wingers, who were outstanding yet again. Dick scored both of the game's goals, but Nevin – as was starting to seem inevitable – was the man of the match.

McInally was booked for time-wasting in the semi, so was added to the list of players missing for the final against Czechoslovakia in Helsinki's iconic Olympic Stadium – which was mostly empty for the big match – but again Scotland were comfortable, with Mackay reprising his striking role behind Dick and Nevin.

The *Glasgow Herald* reported that around 100 Scottish oil workers cheered every attack, and Stirling Albion defender

John Philliben opened the scoring just before half-time, set up by Dick from a Nevin corner.

Not long after the break came the decisive moment of the final, and the goal of the tournament, from the player of the tournament, Nevin. The wee teenager who split his time between playing for Clyde and studying at Glasgow Tech dribbled past three defenders before chipping the ball over the keeper and into the net.

The team had one hand on the trophy, but their opponents pulled one back two minutes later. It was only the second goal that Scotland had conceded in the whole tournament, although Mackay restored the two-goal margin with 25 minutes left, beating the keeper from the edge of the box.

The young Scots were champions of Europe – the only collection of Scottish players ever to be able to make such a bold claim. Over ten days they had played five matches, winning four, drawing one, and scoring 11 goals. And yes, Nevin did make it back to Glasgow in time for his exams.

By virtue of reaching the semi, the team had also qualified for the 1983 World Youth Championship in Mexico, where they reached the quarter-finals in a tournament featuring the likes of Dunga and Bebeto, as well as Van Basten again.

Unfortunately, Ally Dick's immense promise was badly hampered by injury, although he did, coincidentally, briefly team up with Van Basten at Ajax. Most of the rest of the team had long, successful football careers, with several household names among them, five of whom played for Scotland – as did three of those aforementioned absentees, Bryan Gunn, Eric Black and Dave McPherson.

And the Aberdeen teenagers' disappointment about missing out on the glory in Finland was tempered by their 4-1 win in the Scottish Cup Final, in which Cooper played from the start and scored, and Black came on as a sub. That regular exposure to first-team football is probably what gave Scotland's young class of '82 their edge.

62

Saturday, 13 February 1993

The Worst Refereeing Decision Ever

At Firhill in 1993, Les Mottram made one of the world's worst refereeing decisions ever. Or, more precisely, he somehow completely missed two incredibly glaring and important events.

Dundee United completely dominated Partick Thistle for the first half but were only leading 1-0. Two minutes before half-time, from a United corner, Paddy Connolly prodded the ball into the net, then wheeled away in celebration, congratulated by his happy team-mates, while Thistle players started to amble sadly upfield to take their positions for kick-off.

Everyone in the stadium – all the players, all the fans, both managers – knew that United had doubled their lead. Everyone except one man. One particularly important man. Mottram didn't blow his whistle. He wasn't pointing to the centre spot. He waved his left arm in the air. He surely couldn't have been waving play on, could he? Err, aye, he was.

Despite being well positioned in the box, the hapless whistler hadn't realised that the ball was in the back of the net, where it hit the stanchion before bouncing back out again.

Perhaps the most incredible aspect of the whole incident is that Mottram also missed Thistle defender Martin Clark catching the ball and handing it to his keeper. But the man in black didn't award a penalty for handball either.

So unbelievable was Mottram's double howler that it was a good few seconds before everyone realised what he had/ hadn't decided. The players from both teams surrounded him, gradually becoming more doubtful and confused, like dogs who aren't quite sure if their master's going to throw a ball for them or not. The Terrors players weren't protesting because the ref's blunder was too monumental to have sunk in yet.

But then they realised. They pointed, they remonstrated, and, as the match stopped for half-time, Jim McLean angrily chased Mottram up the tunnel.

Fortunately for United, Mottram's cock-up had no bearing on the result as they scored three more goals in the second half, with Connolly grabbing two of them. Thankfully, Mr Mottram let them stand.

FIFA's response to the incident? They selected Mottram to referee at the 1994 World Cup.

63

Saturday, 30 November 1872

Queen's Park Teach the World to Pass

When football was first codified, in England in 1863, it was very different to what it soon became. With its roots in private schools and their emphasis on pluck, bravery, strength and courage, passing wasn't initially a part of the game.

Victorian football was initially more about charging forward in a group, tackling and 'backing up' – trying to win back possession if your team-mate had lost it.

Passing was viewed with suspicion in the cloisters of Charterhouse and Westminster, as not within the spirit of their vision for the game, as unwelcome and ungentlemanly a prospect as the grubbiness of impending professionalism.

But the private schools were powerless to thwart progress, and one club, up in enlightened Glasgow, did more than any other to force the skilled short-passing game, which would become football's *lingua franca*, to the fore: Queen's Park.

Key to this difference was the fact that early versions of the offside rule were implemented differently in different places, which dictated teams' scope for forward passing. Initially, in the south of England, all forward passing was outlawed. Queen's Park, on the other hand, played in their first few years under rules where no one could be offside if they were more than 15 yards from the goal; rules that encouraged passing.

And in their early days the Glasgow side had trouble finding regular opposition, so they often played among themselves, with that isolation conducive to developing their own particular style.

It was at the first ever official international match, on St Andrew's Day in 1872, in Partick, that Queen's Park's revolutionary short passing game caught English attention.

England lined up with seven forwards; Scotland just six. Scotland were simply Queen's Park under a different name, and they were, man for man, a stone lighter than their opponents, which was an additional reason for them to favour skill over a physical contest. The Scots could dribble as well as pass, and gave birth to what became known as the combination game.

The match was a 0-0 draw, but the press praised the Scots' passing, and that was the point when they became known and respected for their innovation. Queen's Park's passing game spread, especially in Scotland, including via exhibition matches that they played in Dunbartonshire, Edinburgh and Dundee. And Scotland won ten of the next 15 matches between the two nations – including 7-2, 6-1 and 5-1 victories – and lost just twice.

By the last of those matches, the old purely dribbling game was obsolete everywhere but short passing was still more synonymous with Scottish football.

And northern English clubs capitalised on Scottish players' greater proficiency in the passing game. Throughout the final years of the 19th century and the first of the 20th, hugely successful Preston, Sunderland, Aston Villa and Newcastle sides all included multiple 'Scotch professors', so called because of Scotland's more scientific approach to football.

Preston's 'invincibles' double-winning side won their first ever FA Cup Final with six Scots in their side. Sunderland sometimes played with an entirely Scottish team, and their Scottish striker John Campbell was top scorer in the league in three seasons when the Wearsiders won the title.

This headhunting did not go down well in Scotland, to the extent that Sunderland co-funder Samuel Tyzack had to disguise himself as a priest on his scouting trips north of the border, to avoid detection and ire.

Scottish football had become a victim of its own success, which is all testament to the fact that the style of football that the whole world plays today was invented in Glasgow.

64

Saturday, 23 October 1971

Partick Thrash Celtic in the League Cup Final

No one gave Partick a hope in hell of beating Celtic in the 1971 League Cup Final.

That was only partly down to ignorance about quite how good this young Jags team – who'd been promoted from Division Two mere months earlier – were. Most neutrals liked them, albeit in that slightly patronising, condescending way, and they'd scored 30 goals in 11 games to get to Hampden, but it still seemed unnatural to think of them as serious contenders.

It was also because the Jags – who hadn't won a major trophy for 50 years – were facing one of the greatest Celtic teams of all time. A mixture of Lisbon Lions and Quality Street Kids. The Scottish Cup holders. Six-in-a-row league champions on their way to nine in a row, who would win the same season's Scottish Cup Final 6-1 against Hibs a few weeks after playing in a European Cup semi-final. Gemmell, Murdoch, Johnstone, Hay, Dalglish and Macari were among the stars who faced Partick's young team – average age of 21 – that day.

Meanwhile, half of Partick's youngsters juggled trades with part-time football, but these kids were full of potential; six of them – Alan Rough, John Hansen, Alex Forsyth, Ronnie

Glavin, Jimmy Bone and Denis McQuade – would later go on to play for Scotland. And this fast, attacking Partick team – with two strikers, two wingers and attacking full-backs – were as unpredictable as any other Partick vintage. Which is really saying something.

Teenage goalie Rough travelled to the game by bus, surrounded by confident Celtic fans. Twenty-one-year-old defender Hansen had to catch two buses and a train to get from his Tullibody home, just to meet up with the team coach.

Before kick-off, *Football Focus* presenter Sam Leitch said, bluntly, that Partick 'have no chance'. The bookies agreed; they would have given you 8/1 that morning on any Thistle win.

As Partick took to the Hampden pitch in their all-yellow shirts, with red shorts, red socks and – nice early '70s touch – red numbers, they had one piece of good fortune: Billy McNeill was out. Although Celtic missed him, Partick played well enough to surely win even if he'd been there. It's also true that Jimmy Johnstone went off injured after 20 minutes. But Thistle were already two up by then.

Just ten minutes in, Alex Rae fired a lovely 20-yard lob into the top corner. Not what was in the script, but surely no need for their illustrious opponents to panic.

Just five minutes after that, Bobby Lawrie cut inside Davie Hay, dashed into the corner of the 18-yard box and fired the ball across Evan Williams into the bottom corner. Now this was getting interesting.

It really started to look like a major upset could be on the cards on the half-hour mark. With the ball ricocheting around in the box after a Thistle corner, McQuade was quick to react and turned it into the net.

And shockingly, just six minutes after that, Lawrie chipped a free kick in from the right, and Bone ran through the middle of Celtic's static back line and blasted it home.

Rough later said that he could have been sitting on a deckchair reading the *Daily Record* for the first half. He was only exaggerating slightly.

It was 4-0 to the underdogs at half-time, but Partick's players were probably as conscious as anyone else of their infamous unpredictability. Hansen later said, 'The general consensus in the dressing room was that we would probably lose 5-4.'

Meanwhile, back at the BBC, Frank Bough was no less surprised. When he announced the half-time score, he added, 'We'll get that checked.'

Celtic stepped it up in the second half but could only pull one goal back, from Kenny Dalglish, as Rough made some great saves. The Jags didn't lose 5-4 – they won the final 4-1, and thousands of Celtic fans stayed behind to applaud them.

John Hansen's wee brother Alan was in the Hampden crowd that day. Legend has it that the match inspired him to become a footballer rather than a professional golfer. He went on to play more than 400 games for Liverpool and win the European Cup three times.

But this story isn't about him. So back to Glasgow in 1971, where Thistle had some unanticipated celebrations to get on with. Unfortunately, nobody had prepared for such an eventuality, so they couldn't get hold of an open-top bus, and had to make do with a single-decker. Some of the players managed to get on the roof with the trophy but their victory parade was sparsely attended, as most of the Thistle fans were still celebrating gleefully in pubs near Hampden. It was a fittingly eccentric finale to Partick's day of unexpected joy and glory.

65

Sunday, 3 June 1979

Europe Learns that Diego is the Real Deal

The wee 18-year-old seized possession in the middle of the park. In a split second, in one fluid motion, he controlled the ball under his left foot, flicked it with his right and spun in the opposite direction, leaving his opponent chasing clear air.

In the congested midfield, another player snapped towards him, but the diminutive trickster knocked it sideways and was immediately away again, leaving his would-be tackler in a heap on the ground.

With his original opponent close behind him, and two others closing in ahead, he caressed the ball with the outside of his left foot, just enough to beat the next man, and then – with yet another opponent racing towards him, he flicked an instant perfect pass to a team-mate.

The whole intricate, precise, apparently effortless series of subtle flicks and tricks took less than five seconds but the 60,000 Scots packed into Hampden knew their football and they knew world-class quality when they saw it.

For his next trick, Diego went on another run down the middle, beat Paul Hegarty and Alan Hansen and neatly flicked the ball to Leopoldo Luque, who slotted it home past Alan Rough, who was – appropriately, given the quality of his opponents – wearing the number 13 shirt.

The wonder boy also smacked a shot into the post and had another cleared off the line by George Burley.

After Luque had doubled the South Americans' lead, Diego claimed his first international goal, which was characteristically impudent. He received a pass from José Valencia wide inside the box, then stopped, as Scotland's second-half goalie George Wood came out to meet him. Then the teenage sensation simply slotted the ball through the tiny gap between Wood and the woodwork. He ran and celebrated with all the elation of a player playing for the sheer joy and beauty of the game.

Diego Maradona's skill and potential were no secret, but this Hampden friendly was arguably the match where he – probably the world's best ever footballer – announced himself on the global stage.

While the Scots fans stayed behind to cheer their opponents, Jock Stein labelled the Argentinian side as 'perhaps even better than the one that won the World Cup' – and that was without Mario Kempes or Ossie Ardiles, but with a certain young man from Villa Fiorito.

Meanwhile, Argentina boss César Luis Menotti sang the praises of the Scotland fans, saying that the most important thing in sport is 'to return with friends'.

And Scotland's journalists were also happy to participate in the mutual love-in. Ian Paul described Argentina's display as the best at Hampden since Real Madrid in 1960. Jim Reynolds said that 'torturer in chief' Maradona's 'speed and skill left the Scots gasping'. And Allan Herron called Diego 'the complete inspiration of the Argentinians, living up to every expectation. This little, bouncing ball of a kid paralysed us with his control, pace on the ball and laying it off. With Maradona around, the world champions just don't need Kempes or Ardiles.'

Herron was right to evoke the expectations placed on Diego; although he was just 18 and hadn't previously scored for Argentina, he'd been well known back home since he was at primary school, when, as an Argentinos Juniors youth player, he would showcase his skills on the pitch at half-time in league matches, with the fans apparently chanting for this ridiculously talented wee boy to play in the second half. He was furious when he was left out of the 1978 World Cup squad, even though he was just 17 at the time (and they did not do bad without him).

But the game at Hampden was one of his very first outside of South America, on a short tour of Europe. In the previous game, against Ireland, he came on as a substitute and was Argentina's best player.

It's tempting to speculate about the significance that his experiences in Glasgow had for the footballing genius.

There's a beautifully evocative photo of young Diego on the day of the match, leaning out of his window at the Central Hotel and taking in the view of Hope Street. He'd moved uptown in Buenos Aires by then, so wasn't wide-eyed or naive, but was still so young, and only just starting to explore the world whose greatest sport he would soon dominate.

And the story of Maradona's relationship with Glasgow has an intriguing epilogue. When he returned to Scotland almost 30 years later, for his first match as Argentina's manager, he landed their federation with an unexpected £10,000 bill when he suddenly changed the team's hotel. They were booked into a five-star countryside hotel but he decided that they should stay in the city centre instead, so they flitted to new digs in town.

Perhaps memories of his first international goal and the spellbinding performance that went with it gave Glasgow a permanent special place in El Diego's *corazón*.

66

Saturday, 19 May 1951

77,650 Fans Turn Up for the Junior Cup Final

As if Scotland's senior football clubs, leagues and cups didn't already have enough character, history, intrigue and heritage, there's also – just for good measure – long been a whole other level of club football: the Juniors. A separate league and cup setup from the senior game.

It's drastically slimmed down now – more on that later – but it's historically been big enough to attract attendances comparable to the senior leagues, to watch passionately supported part-time local teams, with famous names like Auchinleck Talbot, Pollock, Linlithgow Rose and Cambuslang Rangers.

And the jewel in the Juniors crown has always been – since it was established in 1886 – the Junior Cup. In 1922, an incredible 412 clubs entered the cup, but the biggest moment in the iconic tournament's history was undoubtedly the final in 1951 between Petershill and Irvine Meadow, when – in good weather on the king's birthday holiday weekend – 77,650 fans turned up at Hampden.

The *Evening Times* reported that 'the whole of Ayrshire seemed to be on the road to shout on the Meadow in their great bid to win the cup for the first time in 53 years of junior football'.

As a mark of the importance of the match, Meadow flew their right-back Frank Muir, who was stationed in Germany for his National Service, home for it.

And there was a lot of interest in the men on the field. Chelsea, Portsmouth, Notts County, Everton, Sheffield United and Manchester City all had scouts there. Ipswich and Third Lanark sent their managers. Two Petershill teenagers who played that day – goalie George Stewart and left-winger Ronnie Clark – had already signed for Raith and Killie.

And the bumper crowd weren't disappointed by the match itself, which the Glasgow side won 1-0, with Jimmy White getting the only goal 12 minutes from the end, and captain Jimmy Shaw imperious at centre-half.

According to the *Evening Times*, it was 'a game of fast exchanges and good, honest endeavour with plenty of incidents to keep the crowd roaring. Petershill were the better and smarter team and were due their victory. The man chiefly responsible for preventing Petershill from taking the cup until well on in the second half was Jock Murdoch the Meadow goalkeeper. His saving was magnificent, but he had no chance with White's shot.'

It was the fourth time that Petershill had won the cup. Meadow could take solace from the fact that, in that same season, they won the West of Scotland Cup, the Western Junior League, the Ayrshire League Cup and the Ayrshire District Cup. The team were given a civic reception to mark their season and were made Freemen of the Royal Burgh of Irvine.

And eight years later, Meadow finally won the big cup for the first time, in front of a relatively modest crowd – 65,000.

67

Saturday, 15 April 1967

Jim Baxter Plays Keepie-Uppie Against England

When Scotland comprehensively outplayed and beat the world champions on their own turf just nine and a half months after the Three Lions had lifted the Jules Rimet Trophy, and ended the Englishmen's 20-match unbeaten run, the enduring, iconic image wasn't of any of Scotland's three goals, but of Jim Baxter casually playing keepie-uppie as he slowly advanced down the left wing.

Baxter's nonchalant bravado perfectly encapsulated exactly how dominant Scotland were that day and also Slim Jim's own gallus personality. But the match – one of Scotland's greatest performances, in spite of the modest 3-2 scoreline – was about so much more than that moment of impudent skill; it was about a total team performance from a collection of top players.

In fact, as manager Bobby Brown later said, 'I was doing my head at Baxter, because we were so much on top at that time. Denis Law had two great efforts wonderfully saved by Gordon Banks and I felt I wanted to rub it in, because there was only one team on the field.'

Remarkably, for a match with such a complete performance, this was Brown's first game in charge of Scotland, as the first ever Scotland manager to pick the team himself. Previously, it had been chosen by selection committee. The improvement was immediate.

Brown had great players to pick from – Celtic, Rangers and Kilmarnock were all confidently motoring through the European competitions after all – and he assembled a finely tuned side, from Ronnie Simpson in goal, making his debut at 36 years old, through top defenders like Tommy Gemmell and John Greig (although, of course, it feels unfair to label Gemmell simply as a defender, and he played a key attacking role that day, as he so regularly did), to Baxter and Billy Bremner in midfield, and Law, Bobby Lennox and Willie Wallace up front. Possibly the pick of the bunch, though, was another debutant, 20-year-old Jim McCalliog, bustling between midfield and attack. Brown described him as the lynchpin of the team that day.

It's not as if England played badly. The world champions – with just one change, which was probably an improvement, from the World Cup Final team: Jimmy Greaves replaced Roger Hunt – were simply outclassed. As Sir Alf Ramsey said after the match, 'I warned it would take a great team to beat England. And it did.'

The *Sunday Mirror*'s Sam Leitch praised the Scots' skill, ideas, pace, penetration and urgency, and said, 'No England forward could compare with the frisky, impertinent genius of Denis Law. There were no England men in midfield so clever at holding the ball and adjusting the pace and tempo of play as Beatle-cropped Jim Baxter and that skilled toiler from Leeds, Billy Bremner. Neither England full-back could compare with the long-legged Celtic thoroughbred Tommy Gemmell. England did have equality in goal although Gordon Banks let in three.'

Scotland's first two goals were both the result of straightforward, brave and penetrating attacking play. Law turned home the first midway through the first half. Fifteen minutes later, Law was brought down in the box by his

Manchester United team-mate Nobby Stiles, but the German ref inexplicably waved play on.

Surprisingly, it wasn't until the 78th minute that Lennox made it two. After that, *Press and Journal* man Norman MacDonald lamented, 'The Scots became over-casual. They were so much in command that they slowed the tempo, and Baxter, in particular, was inclined to start "kidding" the opposition ... it turned out to be a dangerous brand of impertinence. It cost a couple of goals in the final six minutes.'

In those frantic minutes, England scored twice, either side of McCalliog claiming the best goal of the game. After the match, the young debutant said that he then ran towards where he knew his dad was in the stand.

'When the final whistle signalled Scotland's triumph,' added Leitch in the *Mirror*, 'the Wembley pitch was invaded – danced on, prayed on, kissed, cuddled and finally cut up – by the joy-crazed, tartan-drenched fans. It was one of the most fantastic sights I have seen in football.'

Thirty thousand Scots were in London for the game. When they got back to Euston station, they found entrepreneurial compatriots selling chunks of the Wembley turf for ten shillings per divot, or twice as much for a piece of the centre circle.

And the match was even more than a British Home Championship clash against Scotland's greatest rivals. It put Scotland in the driving seat for qualification for Euro '68, with the combined results from two consecutive Home Championships forming one qualifying group. Scotland won the first, England won the second and unfortunately Scotland missed out on qualification by just one point. England came third in the finals. A Scotland side playing how they did on that day at Wembley would have been an excellent addition to the tournament.

68

Sunday, 13 May 2018

Nuts Match 2: A Game of Three Halves –
Hibs 5 Rangers 5

Some matches swing from extreme glory to painful despair. Not many then also move on to redemption. But that's what Hibs experienced in this rare match – where defending seemed to be an afterthought for both sides – while, of course, their opponents, Rangers, had the exact opposite experience: despair first, then glory, and ultimately disappointment.

Both sides had recently returned to the top flight from the Championship. Rangers had got through three managers in one campaign but, going into the last game of the season, they were aiming for second place, if they could win at Easter Road and if Celtic – who had already won the league and had nothing to play for – did them a favour against Aberdeen. Meanwhile, Hibs had their own faint hopes of leapfrogging the Gers into third place – if they could beat them 6-0.

Hibs boss Neil Lennon sent his team out with a simple instruction: go for it.

Halfway through the first half in the Leith spring sunshine, with the Hibees going all-out attack, their unlikely ambition was beginning to look surprisingly attainable. Florian Kamberi fired a penalty past Jak Alnwick after David Bates grappled Jamie MacLaren to the ground on the edge of the box; Scott Allan found space six yards out to knock home after Vykintas Slivka set him up with a neat header. That second goal had come from a Lewis Stevenson cross, and three minutes later Stevenson provided a carbon copy, which MacLaren headed past Alnwick; 3-0.

The capacity crowd were jubilant. For about three minutes. Then it all started to go badly wrong for them, as Rangers started to find the gaps in their defence, and scored, scored and scored again.

First James Tavernier knocked home a Jason Holt cut-back, then, two minutes later, Jordan Rossiter collected a Jamie Murphy pass on the edge of the box and turned it past Ofir Marciano. Meanwhile, Gers boss Jimmy Nicholl took off Sean Goss and brought on Bruno Alves, to try to sort out his own leaky defence. And just before half-time, it was substitute Alves who blasted a curling free kick into the net; 3-3 at the end of an action-packed first half of two halves.

And the goals kept coming after the break. A Holt effort deflected off Efe Ambrose and wrong-footed Marciano, and then another Holt blast, from distance, clipped his own team-mate, Josh Windass, on its way into the net. Nicholl was looking pretty chuffed; 5-3 to the visitors, after being 3-0 down. A historic comeback. Some home fans started to leave. But there were still 20 minutes left.

Rangers' two-goal margin lasted just two of those minutes, as MacLaren got his second, cracking home an effort from near the penalty spot to cap a slick passing move.

And with just five minutes left, Holt got a second yellow card for almost managing to pull John McGinn's shirt clean off his back.

In the third minute of stoppage time, speedy substitute Brandon Barker left Tavernier trailing far behind him, sprinted into the box, and cut the ball to MacLaren, who completed his hat-trick from six yards.

As the home crowd roared, Lennon ran on to the pitch and celebrated like an aeroplane, and ref Andrew Dallas promptly sent him to the stands, to cap off a unique, action-packed, unforgettable match.

69

Wednesday, 15 May 1974

A Wee Fishing Trip

Jimmy 'Jinky' Johnstone was probably Scotland's most skilful player ever. He also had a wickedly cheeky sense of humour and loved to enjoy himself. Which is one of the main reasons why he never fulfilled his potential in a dark blue shirt.

And never was his carefree attitude more evident than it was in the Firth of Clyde at six o'clock on a May morning, a month before he was due to star at the 1974 World Cup.

After a good win over Wales and a few days before the annual fixture against England, the Scotland team were staying in Largs, and most of them went out drinking – and stayed out until six in the morning. It was on their way back to their hotel that Johnstone spotted a boat and had a fun idea.

He got in, left the shore, lost an oar and started drifting out to sea. It was windy, the currents were dangerous and he couldn't swim, but he was singing merrily, merrily, merrily.

But, despite the mammoth session, Davie Hay and Eric Schaedler were sober enough to realise the danger and got into another boat to rescue him. 'I don't know what I was thinking about! We were using blocks of wood to try to steer it,' Hay later said. 'Wee Jimmy was heading to America.'

They belatedly realised that it would be better to call in the experts so returned to shore and Schaedler ran off to raise the alarm, while Jinky got caught in a worse current and quickly drifted further out.

He was half a mile from shore when a local boatman reached him and brought him safely back. Jinky told national team boss Willie Ormond that he'd just intended to go on a wee fishing trip. Ormond didn't seem too bothered about the escapade, but the SFA and the press were.

'The selection committee will want to know what happened in this matter,' Ernie Walker ominously proclaimed.

'I've spoken to the players and as far as I'm concerned the matter is closed. I've got more to worry about than newspaper stories,' said Ormond.

Like Ormond, a police spokesman introduced a level of calmness that was at odds with the concerns of the SFA and the press: 'This sort of thing often happens here because of the tide and the wind. We are quite used to it. I think it has been all exaggerated.'

Either way, Jinky made the team for the England game and – naturally – turned in possibly his best ever performance for the national team, in an impressive 2-0 win. Hay reckoned the experience (albeit ill-advised) and criticism (albeit justified) had helped the players bond.

Journalist Ian Archer singled out particular praise for Johnstone, saying, 'He checked, turned, cavorted and struck balls the like of which brought back shades of little wingers long dead but not forgotten.' The *Press and Journal* said 'Johnstone reaffirmed his return to top form'.

But before they'd had a chance to print their praise in the latest twist in their relationship with the mercurial, controversial winger, he'd demonstrated his contempt for their criticism.

At full time at Hampden, Ormond ran straight to Johnstone, embraced him, then pointed to the press box. Jinky's unmistakable hand gesture made his feelings clear.

Sadly, that was as good as Jinky's international career got. In Oslo for a pre-World Cup warm-up game against Norway, he and captain Billy Bremner were involved in another drunken incident, and the SFA's patience was wearing thin.

Jinky's off-pitch indiscipline was probably linked to him surprisingly not featuring in West Germany. He was only 29, but he would only play twice more for the national side.

70

Wednesday, 14 September 1955

Hibs, European Trailblazers

When Gabriel Hanot, the editor of French sports magazine *L'Équipe*, launched the first ever European Cup, in 1955, he invited the champions of 15 countries – and Hibs – to contest it.

Hibs weren't champions of Scotland; Aberdeen were, and the men from Leith had finished fifth in the league, 15 points behind the Dons. But Hanot had a lot of respect for Hibs' forward-thinking, outward-looking attitude at the time, characterised by the many international tours that they'd been on, and by chairman Harry Swan's long-held belief that exactly such a competition would eventually happen. It also probably helped that Swan was SFA president at the time, and that Hibs had floodlights.

It's not clear whether Aberdeen would have taken part anyway, but they had every right to feel aggrieved by the snub. It was far from clear at the time that this new cross-border competition would have much of a future. Prevailing British attitudes towards the new tournament were characterised by the fact that the FA forbade English champions Chelsea to have anything to do with it.

Hibs were well past their triple-league-winning heyday though. Bobby Johnstone had been sold to Manchester City, Eddie Turnbull, Gordon Smith and Bobby Combe were in their 30s, and recent recruitment had been patchy. But they were well up for this new competition.

Hibs' first-round tie was a tough one, against West German champions Rot-Weiss Essen. Boss Hugh Shaw urged his team to play cautiously in the away leg, but, in heavy rain and with 1,000 Scottish squaddies in the crowd, Hibs' experienced forward line – Smith, Combe, Lawrie Reilly, Turnbull and Willie Ormond – soon realised their own superiority, took the game by the scruff of the neck, and were 2-0 up at half-time, as Turnbull became the first British player to score in Europe, with a characteristic fierce shot, and Reilly the second, which he later said was one of his best ever: a long run from the halfway line before beating the keeper.

Turnbull scored again after the break, Ormond made it four, and Smith had the ball in the net right at the end, but the Dutch referee chalked it off because he said he'd blown the full-time whistle while the goal-bound ball was flying through the air. Still, a 4-0 away win against the champions of the country that had just won the World Cup wasn't bad, and the German papers were full of praise for the Scots, even if most of the British press was relatively disinterested.

After that, the home leg was less impressive. Smith, Reilly and goalie George Younger missed out because they'd been playing for the Scottish League XI away in Denmark two days earlier, and all flights were grounded because of heavy fog so they couldn't get home in time. They eventually landed in London about five hours before kick-off in Leith, but mist in Britain affected domestic flights too.

Young striker Jock Buchanan deputised for Smith, and opened the scoring after just five minutes – made all the more impressive by the fact that, because he'd thought he wouldn't be playing, he'd eaten a huge portion of mince and tatties just before the game. In Younger's absence, teenage keeper Willie Adams made his only appearance for Hibs in the match, which finished 1-1.

Hibs were comfortably through to the second round, and again were away first – at Firhill. Because of the Swedish winter, their opponents, Djurgården, chose to play at 'home' in Glasgow, and it initially seemed a good choice as they scored in the first minute and then also hit the bar, before Hibs again seized control, with Combe and Jimmy Mulkerrin giving them the lead before a late own goal made it 3-1 to the Scots.

Just five days later – presumably so that the Swedes didn't have to make two trips to Scotland – Hibs won the second leg 1-0 at home, with a Turnbull penalty. The men from Leith were into the semi-final two weeks before any of the other quarter-final first legs had even been played.

The four clubs in the first European Cup semi-finals were Hibs, Milan, Real Madrid and Stade de Reims. Harry Swan wanted to play the Spanish aristocrats but his team were drawn against Reims; less famous but packed with quality players (including future France manager Michel Hidalgo) and led by Raymond Kopa, one of the world's greatest at the time.

Reims had moved their quarter-final home leg 100 miles to the west, to the Parc des Princes in Paris, and they did the same for the semi. Hibs played well and created chances but couldn't take them, and Kopa was influential as his fellow French internationals Michel Leblond and René Bliard scored the only goals of the game, with Bliard's goal – set up by Kopa – coming in a last-minute counterattack, as Hibs were chasing an equaliser.

It was a disappointing result but not an insurmountable defeat. A crowd of 45,000 turned up at Easter Road for the home leg. Hibs created multiple chances but couldn't make any of them count, and Léon Glovacki – another French international – got the only goal of the game, again set up by Kopa.

So it was Reims, and not Hibs, who faced Real Madrid in the first ever European Cup Final. It was a disappointing end to a ground-breaking adventure, but Hibs can always say that they were the first British club to play in Europe, Eddie Turnbull was the first British player to score in Europe and

Jock Buchanan was the first player to score in a European match in Britain – with his stomach full of mince and tatties. And they can always say that they were the first club to qualify for a European Cup semi-final.

71

Monday, 11 March 1963

Big Freeze Cup Havoc Finally Ends

The 'Big Freeze' of 1963 sent Scottish football into extended cold storage and – despite the inventive efforts of ground staff around the country – caused huge fixture congestion, especially for the Scottish Cup, and for Airdrie and Stranraer in particular.

Saturday, 12 January was meant to be Scottish Cup first round day but as icy weather swept the land – cold enough to freeze the diesel in lorries' tanks in Lanarkshire – only a handful of ties went ahead, in Fife, Angus and Inverness.

Two days later, the *Evening Times* reported that pipes cracked and ceilings crashed in with the weight of water when the Big Burst followed the Big Freeze as temperatures rose slightly in Glasgow. Despite that brief thaw, the cup outlook was still grim.

The icy conditions weren't a problem for all sports; the big curling match between North and South Scotland went ahead on Lake of Menteith. The convenor of the ice committee said the conditions were excellent. Hockey clubs in Aberdeen got round the freeze by playing their matches on the beach at low tide.

Many cup ties were postponed on almost a daily basis, with constant rearrangement eventually sending the number of postponements well into double figures for many clubs, and for some well over two dozen. With so many postponements across Scotland and in England too, the Pools Panel was invented that winter.

Dundee United used tar-burning flamethrowers to thaw out the Tannadice pitch. The ice melted but repeatedly re-froze, so it had to be melted again and again, which destroyed the grass. Forty men worked on the pitch all day to ensure that their tie against Albion Rovers went ahead, but it was played on so much sand that – according to legend – the club's fans earned their 'Arabs' nickname, because their heroes performed well on sand.

St Johnstone boss Bobby Brown, his ground staff and 50 fans spiked and broke up the Muirton Park pitch and removed ice, to no avail.

Partick Thistle used acetylene burners on their pitch, while Arbroath spread tonnes of agricultural salt on theirs.

Most attempts to get pitches playable were unsuccessful but eventually, by early February, most of the first-round ties were played – after the third-round draw had gone ahead as planned in late January. But two remained: St Johnstone v Stenhousemuir and Airdrie v Stranraer. The Broomfield pitch was under solid ice for the whole time.

And then, on Tuesday, 5 February, a blizzard came to Scotland. Nine children and their teacher were trapped in their school near Portpatrick for four days before they were rescued by an RAF helicopter.

Now four inches of snow lay on top of the ice at Broomfield. Despite an all-day session with shovels, barrows and lorries, Airdrie's league match against Rangers was called off. And then, on the Friday night, frost turned Scotland's roads into icy death traps.

And every football match on the Saturday was cancelled. Partick v Falkirk was called off just ten minutes before kick-off, with 4,000 fans inside the ground. Parts of the pitch were under three inches of water, which had emerged from the previously frozen undersoil when the sun came out.

Nine cup ties rescheduled for the Monday were all called off. The same thing happened on the Tuesday, Wednesday and Thursday – when most of the following Saturday's fixtures were also cancelled early.

The big problem now was the sort of flooding that Partick had experienced. The groundsman at Queen of the South tried repeatedly hammering a crowbar deep into the frozen ground, so that the water could drain away, but it took 15 minutes to make just one hole through the thick underground ice. Partick used pneumatic drills in an attempt to do the same thing.

Then, on Friday, 15 February, there was lots more snow. The white stuff blocked 33 Scottish main roads and almost caused a milk crisis when lorries couldn't get to farms in Ayrshire.

For the second Monday in a row, nine ties were postponed, and so was the draw for the fourth round, since it was so unclear who would still be in it by then.

As the snow kept Scottish football in hibernation, Celtic and Morton flew to Dublin to play each other in a friendly, for much-needed match practice.

Inevitably, the freeze led to a lot of discussion about a potential move to summer football – starting with the very next season. Hearts, Kilmarnock, Dunfermline and Motherwell led the campaign for change; the Glasgow clubs – especially Rangers – were opposed. A vote was held on Monday, 25 February. If 25 of the 37 league clubs had voted 'yes', it would have happened. Instead, 25 voted against change.

On the same day as that vote, all 11 cup fixtures were either postponed or abandoned. Thick ice was still a huge problem everywhere. It kept thawing, flooding and then re-freezing.

The only cup match that kicked off that day – Third Lanark v East Fife – had to be abandoned, after 90 minutes! The thawed water had re-frozen during the match, so extra time couldn't be played after it had finished 1-1. Several players left the pitch with bruises caused by falling on the hard ground.

But by the first Saturday in March the conditions – almost everywhere – had finally settled down and football was suddenly almost back to normal. The cup and league fixture backlog could start to be cleared. No cup matches had been played to completion for almost four weeks.

But the Muirton Park and Broomfield pitches were still in bad shape and those two first-round ties still hadn't been played, almost two months after they were originally scheduled.

On Thursday, 7 March, St Johnstone finally got their cup match played. They beat Stenhousemuir 1-0. But throughout that week Airdrie v Stranraer was still being repeatedly postponed, as the latest thaw caused yet more flooding.

Until, on the Saturday, Airdrie finally played their first home game since 15 December. But it wasn't their long-postponed cup tie. They had a league fixture with Dundee, which they won 1-0.

And just two days later – long after several second-round games had taken place, and on the same day as Queen's Park and Dundee United met in the third round – Airdrie and Stranraer's first-round cup tie finally went ahead. The wait had been so long that Airdrie had a new manager in the dugout.

The match wasn't a classic. With Rangers boss Scot Symon scouting his second-round opponents from the crowd, Airdrie won 3-0. Two of their goals were penalties.

Airdrie's reward for winning the cup tie? A home tie against the Gers, just two days later. They lost 6-0.

72

Thursday, 4 May 1967

Kenny Dalglish Signs for His Heroes' Bitter Rivals

Kenny Dalglish is probably Scotland's best ever player. In the first half of his club career, he scored 167 goals for Celtic and helped them win four league titles and four Scottish Cups, before moving to Liverpool for a British record transfer fee.

But it could easily have been very, very different. Dalglish was a Rangers fan and would much rather have played in the light blue. How differently would Scottish league football have been in the '70s if Celtic hadn't signed him, and Rangers had him instead?

He ended up plying his trade in the East End because of one man: Sean Fallon.

Jock Stein was undoubtedly Celtic's best manager of the 20th century, but Fallon, his assistant, was a huge part of Celtic's incredible success in the 1960s and '70s, and he was more responsible than anyone, including Stein, for Celtic's recruitment of top-quality young players, like Lou Macari, Davie Hay, Danny McGrain, Tommy Burns – and Dalglish.

The big, genial Irishman was tireless in his pursuit of prospects and had a huge network of informants. A bookie told him about Macari, he heard about McGrain from a publican, a priest tipped him off about Hay, and a car dealer was the source of Fallon's knowledge about Burns.

But Dalglish was hoping for – and expecting – a call from Rangers. He was playing for Scotland Schoolboys and he later said that he had heard that Rangers' chief scout, Jimmy Smith, was telling people watching him play in those schoolboy matches that he thought he would end up playing for the Govan side. If they had ever asked him to, he would have done.

Liverpool and West Ham invited him for trials, but nothing came of them, partly because Dalglish didn't really want to leave Glasgow.

So the 16-year-old kept playing for Glasgow United, where one of his team-mates was fellow future Celt Vic Davidson. They were invited to play in a match at Celtic's training ground, where apparently Stein liked the look of him.

And Celtic's interest was cemented when Fallon saw him play again on a red ash pitch in Cambuslang, when Vic Davidson's mum wrote to him, asking him to scout young Kenny. Although mothers' recommendations should often be taken with a pinch of salt, Fallon put in the effort and was rewarded with two excellent prospects: Davidson and Dalglish.

So Fallon headed to Dalglish's flat – overlooking Ibrox – to sign him. It was Fallon's wedding anniversary, and he'd promised to take his wife Myra and three daughters to the coast, at Seamill. He told them he had something to do on the way though, but it wouldn't take long. So they waited outside in the car while he visited the Dalglishes.

But the visit took longer than Fallon had expected. He sensed that Kenny's dad was worried about what would happen if it didn't work out for Kenny as a player, so it took a couple of hours to reassure them, and then, once everything was finally arranged, his mum offered to show Fallon round the family home, so the player desperately dashed into his bedroom first, to rip down the Rangers posters that he thought could put off Fallon.

About those posters, Fallon later said, 'I hadn't even noticed but, even if I had, I wouldn't have cared one bit … If anything, it was quite nice to know that we had brought in this great player right from under Rangers' noses.'

Fallon reckoned that Rangers had thought that young Dalglish was too slow, and apparently Stein had similar concerns, but Fallon was sure, and was proved very right, as Dalglish – after a bit of a slow start – became a great player for Celtic; albeit one who, initially at least, continued to go and watch and support Rangers, after training at Celtic.

So 4 May 1967 was a good day for Sean Fallon – from a work perspective. Domestically, not so good. 'I'd completely forgotten about Myra and the kids down in the car,' he later confessed. 'And I'll tell you, I wasn't popular. Myra told me to forget about Seamill – that the day was ruined – and to just drive home. I don't think she spoke to me for the rest of the week.' Myra's recollection was similar: 'I could have killed him. I remember saying to him "whoever this boy is, he'd better be worth it". Just as well for Sean he was.'

Dalglish's recollection is less conflicted: 'Sean was a huge influence on my career. Really, it was him who started it all off.'

73

Wednesday, 12 September 2007

Great Goals 3: James McFadden's French Thunderbolt

Scotland have had some very tough groups in the finals of the Euros and the World Cup. Outside of the actual finals, probably the toughest group ever in qualifying was the one we were pitched into for Euro 2008, alongside both of the 2006 World Cup finalists, Italy and France, and also another 2006 World Cup quarter-finalist, Ukraine.

But Alex McLeish's men won their first three games in the group, including a 1-0 victory against France at Hampden, when Gary Caldwell grabbed the only goal of the game, from short range, to send Vieira, Henry *et al.* home with *nul points*.

By the time of the return leg at the Parc des Princes, Scotland had won three more games but lost away to Italy and Ukraine, and France had gone top of the group.

But Scotland won again, with one of the simplest goals you'll ever see and one of the best, and it was all about probably the most talented Scottish player of his generation, James McFadden, who, about 35 yards out, effortlessly controlled Craig Gordon's long clearance, turned, took one more touch to set himself up and blasted the sort of shot that's often labelled 'speculative'.

But McFadden's aim was immaculate, his shot blistering, and goalie Mickaël Landreau could only get half a glove to it

231

as the ball burst into the top corner and the huge travelling support went wild.

It was a gallus strike from a gallus player, possibly his best ever goal (and he scored quite a few good ones, of many different types) and one of Scotland's greatest results of a generation. It was a where-were-you-when moment for Scotland fans.

Scotland leapfrogged France at the top of the group and maintained the momentum in their next match, a 3-1 win over Ukraine at home, which meant that four points from their last two games would guarantee them a place in the finals.

But they snatched disappointment from the jaws of success by meekly losing 2-0 away against Georgia, which meant that they needed a win at home against world champions Italy in their last game to have any chance of edging into the qualifying spots.

Despite an improved performance, it was a bridge too far for Scotland, and McFadden's Paris piledriver was destined to be remembered as the ultimate example of Scottish glory in defeat: an excellent goal that secured a brilliant result but that ultimately led to missing out by just two points on miraculously qualifying from possibly the toughest qualification group the world has ever seen.

74

Tuesday, 22 December 1964

Denis Law Wins the Ballon d'Or

Denis Law was in the middle of a 28-day suspension and staying back home in Aberdeen when he got an unexpected phone call just before Christmas. A call from a journalist telling him that he'd been voted European Footballer of the Year and won the greatest individual award in football: the Ballon d'Or. The young Scot initially thought it was a joke.

During his suspension, communication between Law and his club, Manchester United, was forbidden, and it was only when he returned to Manchester after the suspension that his victory was officially confirmed.

A few months later, the editor of *France Football* magazine popped in to Old Trafford to present Law with his award. He hadn't been expected to win it. Inter's Spanish midfielder Luis Suárez – who'd already won it in 1960 – was the favourite, but Law beat him by 61 points to 43, with six of the multinational panel of 21 voters putting the Scot top and six more having him as their second choice.

It shouldn't have been a surprise. Law scored 50 goals in 51 matches in 1964. In October 1963 he'd scored for the Rest of the World against England at Wembley, in a match to commemorate the 100th anniversary of the FA. Simply getting picked for the team confirmed Law's status as a global superstar: he lined up alongside the likes of Lev Yashin, Josef Masopust, Raymond Kopa, Alfredo Di Stéfano, Eusébio and

Francisco Gento. Ferenc Puskás and Uwe Seeler came on as subs, as did another great Scot, Jim Baxter.

Law's Ballon d'Or victory came in spite of frequent high-profile run-ins with authority. As *France Football* announced his victory, they celebrated the voting panel's decision to reward his raw talent and genius rather than dwell on questions around his temperament.

They ascribed an increase of 5,000 to United's home attendances to Law's arrival at Old Trafford in 1962, credited him with 'the energy of a giant in his adolescent body' (Law was just 24 when he won the award), and praised his 'colossal left foot', his ability to shoot from apparently impossible angles, his superb timing and his 'astonishing' headers.

'Denis Law is definitely not English,' *France Football* concluded. 'He is a Scot with all their characteristics and defects. But, for the British crowds, he is a hero, even if he makes mistakes which are precisely the price of his unique character.'

Scottish and Irish football heavyweights were more straightforward – and, unsurprisingly, less inclined to national stereotypes – in their praise.

United boss Matt Busby said, 'I've never in my life seen goals to equal those scored by Law for bravery or sheer unexpectancy.'

Leeds midfielder Johnny Giles, who frequently had to try and contain Law's genius, said he was 'the most dynamic player I have ever seen'.

But it was – again, unsurprisingly – probably Bill Shankly who summed up Law's talents with most eloquence, when he said the Aberdonian genius 'could dance on eggshells'.

75

Saturday, 29 March 1884

The Scottish English Cup Finalists

When Queen's Park entered the English FA Cup in 1883/84, they scored 44 goals, struggled to balance competing priorities, participated in a highly controversial semi-final and almost won the whole thing.

The first ever FA Cup tie to be played in Scotland, in December 1883, was a huge mismatch. Six thousand fans saw Queen's Park beat Manchester (Manchester's first recognised football side, who were affiliated to the city's rugby club) 15-0. The *Sheffield Independent* reported, 'The Manchester players were the weakest lot of English football players that ever visited Scotland,' and added, 'The Glasgow goalkeeper never handled the ball during the whole of the contest.'

Queen's Park had entered the FA Cup before, but their efforts had been hampered by travelling expenses. This time, before hammering Manchester, they beat Crewe Alexandra 10-0 away in the first round.

In the third round the Scots scored seven more goals, away at Oswestry Town, to set up a mouth-watering last-16 tie against Aston Villa.

Three special trains brought 1,200 fans from Birmingham to the match, played in front of a crowd of about 10,000 at the Titwood cricket ground, while the second Hampden Park was being built. The *Dundee Courier* reported, 'Play during the first period was very fast and exciting, the Queen's securing a couple of goals,' and although the Scots scored four more after the break and Villa got a consolation goal, the *Courier* bizarrely labelled the second half 'uninteresting'.

Because of the cross-border competition, Queen's Park's Scottish Cup semi-final against Hibs had to be postponed by two weeks. And the *Blackburn Standard* reported on surprising priorities for the Spiders, stating that a letter sent from a Queen's Park player to a member of Aston Villa said, 'If one of the two ties has to be abandoned, it will be that for the Scotch Cup, the feeling being that the Queen's Park must at all hazards go on with the English cup competition.'

But they managed to balance both competitions. One week after beating Hibs 5-1 in Edinburgh, they dumped Old Westminsters 1-0 in London, to set up an FA Cup semi-final against Blackburn Olympic – who'd won a match against Dumbarton the week before – at the Trent Bridge cricket ground in Nottingham.

The semi-final crowd of 16,000 did not behave themselves. There was a large break in play in the first half as supporters moved on to the pitch and had to be moved back, but the Scots managed to take the lead after half an hour.

In the second half there were four more large-scale fan incursions on to the field of play, sometimes with the crowd spilling ten yards on to the pitch, and it often took five or more minutes to get them back. More importantly though, Queen's Park scored three more times, without reply. Well after five o'clock, the match finished 4-0 to the Scots. But Olympic weren't happy, and appealed to the FA about the crowd trouble. The FA committee turned down their protests, and the Scots were in the final, against the other half of Blackburn: Rovers.

If the semi had been controversial, the final – in the eyes of the *Referee* newspaper at least – was a celebration of all things great about football and a lovely day out. And 15 of the 22 players were Scottish.

'In beautiful weather, the ground being in first rate condition, this,' *Referee* reported, 'the final tie of the 13th competition for the much-coveted Association Cup, was decided at Kennington Oval, in the presence of about 10,000 spectators, which ultimately resulted in favour of the English team, after as fine a contest as could possibly be witnessed, by two goals to one. The Scots were dressed in jerseys with black stripes across the chest, while the Rovers were clad in light blue and white, which made each side pleasantly distinguishable.

'At length, after some brilliant play in the centre, the passing being admirable on both sides, [James] Brown, having received the ball from the right wing, rushed down the left side and kicked a goal for the honour of Blackburn, and very shortly afterwards, [Jimmy] Forrest, who played grandly throughout the match, gained a second for his [Blackburn] comrades amidst terrific applause from all parts of the ground. The Scots, no doubt feeling somewhat nettled by their two losses, advanced to the attack with renewed energy, and their exertions were presently rewarded with success, through the instrumentality of [Bob] Christie, who kicked a goal for the representatives of Fair Scotland, the applause being equally as vehement as when their opponents gained theirs.'

It was 2-1 to Blackburn as 'this splendid match came to a conclusion amidst tumultuous applause'.

It was so near but so far for Queen's Park, but they did win their seventh Scottish Cup that season, as their opponents in the final, Vale of Leven, pulled out because of a dispute with the SFA.

And Queen's Park also reached the following season's FA Cup Final, losing to Blackburn Rovers again, after knocking out both Notts County and Nottingham Forest.

Queen's Park were by far the most successful Scottish club in the FA Cup but far from the only ones to enter it. The next season, Partick joined the fun, but their first-round opponents were none other than their local rivals Queen's Park, who beat them 5-1. Hearts, Rangers and Third Lanark also briefly took part that year.

And in the final year of cross-border competition, in 1886/87, the same five Scottish clubs were augmented by Cowlairs and Renton, with far more success, as Rangers made it to the semi-finals.

But then, because of professionalism in English football, which had started in 1885, the SFA brought an end to the fun, ordering Scottish league clubs not to compete in the FA Cup any more (although, over a century later, one more Scottish club, English Northern League members Gretna, would lose narrowly against Rochdale and Bolton in it in 1990 and 1993).

Queen's Park and Rangers had come close to winning the FA Cup, but no Scottish club ever got their hands on it.

76

Thursday, 17 December 1987

Dundee United Fans Win the First Ever FIFA Fair Play Award

After beating Barcelona (see iconic moment 43), Dundee United were drawn against Borussia Mönchengladbach in the UEFA Cup semi-final.

They drew 0-0 in the first leg, at Tannadice, and then turned in one of their greatest European performances, winning 2-0 away with goals from Iain Ferguson and Ian Redford, to set up a final against a strong, talented IFK Gothenburg side.

The second leg of the final was United's 67th game of the season (or 70th, if you include the Forfarshire Cup), and took place just four days after they'd played 120 minutes in the Scottish Cup Final. It was a step too far for the Terrors, as they lost 2-1 on aggregate.

It was a so-near-but-so-far season for United, but they did, a few months later, win one piece of silverware. Or at least the fans did.

Despite their UEFA Cup Final disappointment, most of the 21,000 United fans in Tannadice stayed in the stands, waving their flags, for an hour after full time – to applaud their own players and manager but also to applaud their Swedish opponents. The Gothenburg players ran around the pitch, applauding the home fans in response. United supporters threw their scarves to Gothenburg players, who picked them up and waved in salute.

About 70 million TV viewers saw the United fans' generous act of respect. Perhaps one of them was FIFA president João Havelange, because the world governing body were clearly impressed. They created the Fair Play Award, and, in December, gave the very first one to those United fans, accompanied by £20,000 for the club.

Manager Jim McLean said, 'It's a great tribute to our fans, in fact to the Scottish fans as a whole ... this is the first time this season our fans have got what they deserve.'

FIFA complimented the fans' 'rousing ovation'.

Sixteen years later the award went to Scottish fans again, when it was presented to the many tens of thousands of Celtic supporters who went to Seville, again for a UEFA Cup Final. Scotland remains the only nation whose football fans have won the award more than once.

77

Saturday, 3 May 1986

Albert Kidd Day

No one was expecting Hearts to be title challengers in 1985/86; they'd only returned to the Premier Division three years earlier, and had finished the previous season in seventh place, 28 points behind champions Aberdeen.

Celtic weren't exactly favourites either; Alex Ferguson's Dons were firmly in pole position again, and Jim McLean's Dundee United were also considered at least as strong as Davie Hay's Hoops.

But, by the end of the season, Hearts and Celtic were the teams going for the title on a dramatic last day – and if their identities were a surprise, no one could have predicted the player who would settle their race: a journeyman Dundee striker who hadn't scored all season.

Hearts started the season like the also-rans that most people thought they were. For the first three months, Aberdeen, Celtic and Rangers gingerly passed the top spot to each other.

And then Jock Wallace's Gers imploded spectacularly, going on to win only six games between November and the end of the season, and heralding Wallace's imminent replacement, in the Graeme Souness Ibrox revolution.

Aberdeen topped the table until Christmas, when the season's surprise package from Gorgie, fired by the goals of fans' favourite John Roberston – he got 20 in 1985/86 – and with highly talented defensive partnership of veteran Sandy Jardine and youngster Craig Levein at the back, overtook the men from Pittodrie with a momentum that in the new year seemed as unstoppable as it was unexpected.

The Jam Tarts went an incredible 27 league games unbeaten, but Celtic and Dundee United were still clinging on to their coat tails, until, on the last day of the season, Hearts just needed a draw – at home, against sixth-placed Dundee – to claim their first league title since 1960.

Celtic needed to beat St Mirren, hope that Hearts lost – for the first time in 32 games in all competitions – and overturn a four-goal goal-difference deficit.

They found the first task straightforward, winning 5-0 in Paisley, which sorted out the goal difference too, but it would all count for nothing if Hearts didn't lose.

With ten minutes to go at Tynecastle, it was still goalless. Dundee – who were still in with a chance of claiming a spot in the next season's UEFA Cup, if they won and Rangers didn't – had brought on substitute Albert Kidd.

Many Hearts fans probably had no idea who Kidd was. He'd scored less than one goal for every ten Dundee appearances he'd made, and none at all in the season so far. He was only in the matchday squad because he'd pleaded with boss Archie Knox to include him, and he'd only come on because of an injury to young full-back Tosh McKinlay.

With the title within touching distance, the Gorgie fans were nervous but surely Kidd's introduction was no extra reason for them to worry?

Football can have the unlikeliest heroes.

Kidd prodded home the ball from a corner. Now Hearts needed to score. But instead Dundee – and Kidd – scored again.

At Love Street, Celtic supporters with transistor radios spread the news among the delirious away section, and the Hoops, who'd only been top for two weeks in the autumn, and then for these last ten minutes of the season, were suddenly champions.

The next week, Hearts lost the Scottish Cup Final to Aberdeen, and the 'I'm for ever blowing doubles' jokes rang out around Scotland's playgrounds.

Kidd – a Celtic fan – became an instant hero to other Hoops supporters, and to Hibs fans too, given his part in their great rivals' dismay.

Dundee apparently had no more use for him though, and sold him to Falkirk – where he scored precisely two goals fewer than he had in those ten minutes at Tynecastle.

After Brockville, the next stop for Kidd was West Adelaide Soccer Club, and he settled in Australia, where in the mid-90s he was involved in a surprise celebrity encounter – in which it wasn't clear who was hero-worshipping whom the most.

'I met Billy Connolly on the steps of a hotel,' Kidd later said. 'When I told him I'd scored a couple of goals that helped Celtic win the league, he said straight away, "You're Albert Kidd!" He invited me to his show that night and backstage afterwards.'

Celtic and Hibs fans still celebrate Albert Kidd Day to this day.

78

Saturday, 23 February 1901

Scotland 11 (Eleven) Ireland 0

Nowadays any win over Ireland is a good result, but Scotland utterly dominated their early matches against their neighbours, going unbeaten in the first 17 fixtures. In spite of that dominance, the result of the 18th – their opening game of the 1901 British Home Championship – was still incredible.

At Celtic Park, Celtic fans' favourite Sandy 'the Duke' McMahon and Scotland captain and Rangers hero Robert Hamilton grabbed four goals each, while Hamilton's fellow Rangers forward John Campbell scored twice, and Celtic half-back Davie Russell got one.

As well as the four scorers, five more of Scotland's players came from the ranks of the Glasgow giants, while – in pre-partition days – eight of their opponents played for Belfast clubs and three for teams from Dublin.

Remarkably, the visitors started brightly. The *Glasgow Herald* said, 'With a little more dash they should have scored early in the game.'

But then McMahon scored two quick goals, after which, the *Belfast Newsletter* reported, 'The Irish defence now fell away greatly, and made a poor show against the strong half-back and back divisions of the Scots, with the result that the forwards of the latter were always on the aggressive. Russell went through several men, finally scoring a pretty goal.' That made it 3-0.

By half-time it was 5-0, with Campbell getting his first, and McMahon completing a first-half hat-trick. The *Belfast Newsletter* declared that Ireland goalie Sam McAlpine was 'decidedly weak'. This was the unfortunate custodian's international debut. He never played for Ireland again.

The *Glasgow Herald* said that the second half 'was even more one-sided than the first, and with the exception of half a dozen times, the Irishmen were never beyond midfield, and goals were put on by the home side at regular intervals in a somewhat easy manner'. Hamilton scored all four of his in the second half, while Campbell and McMahon got one more each.

According to the *Belfast Newsletter*, Scotland were also awarded – and missed – a second-half penalty. They commended Hamilton's 'very pretty forward play', as the Irish forwards and half-backs seemed to 'completely lose their heads'.

You would think that the Scotland selectors would have kept faith with the multi-goal heroes from the national team's record victory, but Campbell never played for Scotland again, and McMahon got just one more cap after this game, bringing his total number of international appearances, for a man who scored over 170 goals for his club, to just six.

Thankfully the selectors stuck by Hamilton for a bit longer, and he ended up with a remarkable 15 goals from 11 international appearances.

Unfortunately, despite this incredible result, Scotland finished second to England in the Home Championship, after drawing with the Englishmen and also with a tough Wales team.

79

Friday, 13 July 1990

Hands Off Hibs

In the summer of 1990, Hibs very nearly ceased to exist. One of Scotland's biggest clubs was almost lost, and with them one of the oldest derbies in the world.

The protagonists in the drama read like characters from Shakespeare: Hibs chairman David Duff as the ambitious, naive and questionable young prince facing a crisis of conscience. Assorted heroes including fans, former players and musicians. Property developer David Rowland, the shadowy behind-the-scenes puppet master. Car care millionaire Tom Farmer as the knight in shining armour. Supporters of fierce local rivals lending their support, like Montagues-turned-Capulets. Above all – and in the eyes of Hibs fans clearly the villain – Hearts chairman Wallace Mercer. And to top it all off nicely, Rowland's ex-wife Sheila Rowland, who falls for Hibs and joins the good guys. Oh, and, in a supporting role, Rangers chairman David Murray.

Hibs were in a right financial mess in 1990. They'd raised millions in 1988 when they were the first Scottish club to be floated on the stock exchange, but had then bought a nightclub, a country club and 15 pubs in the south west of England from Rowland – who had lent moustachioed 30-something Duff the money to buy Hibs in 1987. And the businesses, which were supposed to raise money for Hibs, made big losses and plunged the club into £6m of debt.

It was against this backdrop that Rowland summoned Duff and Hibs chief executive Jim Gray (Duff's brother-in-law) to a meeting with a prospective buyer, in a suite at the London Hilton on Park Lane on Sunday, 3 June. But that investor was the last man Duff and Gray would have expected. They were shocked when Mercer walked into the room and told them that he wanted to buy Hibs and merge them with Hearts, so that one unified Edinburgh super-team could take on Rangers and Celtic. He also planned to move the club to a new stadium on Edinburgh's western outskirts, on land owned by David Murray.

As soon as the news was announced the next morning, there were immediate angry protests outside Easter Road, with some Hearts fans who were also against Mercer's plans literally standing shoulder to shoulder with their rivals. The Hands Off Hibs campaign quickly started, led by fans' representative and former club director Kenny McLean Senior. And what a campaign it was.

Eighteen thousand fans turned up for a rally the following Saturday at Easter Road. Again, there were supportive maroon scarves among the green and white, alongside equally appalled Dundee, Dunfermline and Partick supporters. Joe Baker, Pat Stanton and Gordon Strachan spoke at the rally, and Proclaimers Craig and Charlie Reid sang 'You'll Never Walk Alone'.

Iconic Hands Off Hibs T-shirts, posters and flyers were printed. A petition received more than 60,000 signatures, and was delivered – on a Hands Off Hibs battle bus – to reportedly sympathetic Hearts officials at Tynecastle. Another copy was handed to Maggie Thatcher at Downing Street.

The campaign coincided with the World Cup, and Hibs fans who'd travelled to Italy handed out Hands Off Hibs T-shirts and got Costa Rica, Sweden and Brazil fans to sign the petition. Celebrity fan John Leslie defied telly boss orders and wore his Hands Off Hibs T-shirt on *Blue Peter*.

Meanwhile, police officers were stationed outside Mercer's Cramond home.

Another rally was held at Usher Hall on Lothian Road, where Hearts star John Robertson – in direct defiance of Mercer's orders – spoke out against the plans, and Charlie and Craig sang 'Sunshine on Leith', as it made the transition from melancholy love song to one of the greatest club anthems in the world.

The campaign was successful but the club's future still hinged on decisions that would be made by shareholders and bankers. So the fans protested at the Bank of Scotland's headquarters on The Mound. And critically, the bank confirmed that Mercer needed 76 per cent of shares, to force through a hostile takeover. Rowland's 29.9 per cent was a given, and independent business investors wouldn't be difficult. Duff had 11 per cent, which would be critical, and no one was sure whether he would sell or not.

Another key factor was the actions of Sheila Rowland, David Rowland's ex-wife. He'd installed her on the club board (as Scotland's first female football club director), but she fell for the club, joined the campaign and, reportedly, refused to sell shares that Rowland had put in her name.

And Tom Farmer, the owner of Kwik-Fit – who wasn't a big football fan but whose granddad Philip was involved with the club – played a key part in securing Hibs' future, when he bought 800,000 shares.

The bank's deadlines came and went for Mercer, and on 13 July he – sort of – admitted defeat. He'd secured 62 per cent, with Duff finally deciding not to sell his share. Mercer belligerently told the *Daily Record*, 'Because the Hibs board will not negotiate with us and because of what we believe is the perilous financial state of the club, we have decided to scrap the bid.'

If the bank had made a different decision, or if Duff had sold his share, it would probably have been a very different story. A big club could have been wiped off the map. And it seems clear that the campaign had a huge bearing on the decisions that the bank and Duff made.

As the good news was announced, Hibs fans assembled outside the stadium, as they had on 4 June, but this time they danced and sang with joy and wept with relief. The campaign had been more anger, anger, than sorrow, sorrow, but now the fans' tears were drying.

Only Mercer himself could ever know for sure what his motives were for his plans, but no one believed that he really thought that a suburban Edinburgh United would have more support than city-centre Hearts or Hibs. If he did, he was badly mistaken. Many Hibs fans think he simply wanted to kill off Hearts' rivals, which also seems unlikely. But two facts are irrefutable: Mercer was a businessman first and club chairman second; and the land that Easter Road – and Tynecastle – occupied had become extremely valuable.

The next derby was in September, at Easter Road. Mercer wisely didn't attend. There was a minor riot and 50 arrests, at least 17 people were injured, and the players had to leave the pitch for eight minutes while the trouble was sorted out. And then it was time for Hibs to move on. Tom Farmer started the big job of sorting out the financial mess.

And Hibs got back to business on the pitch, as the surprise winners of the League Cup the following year, with a side who were christened 'The Team That Wouldn't Die'.

80

Monday, 23 January 2023

Scotland's Biggest Giant-Killing: Darvel 1 Aberdeen 0

When Stenhousemuir knocked Aberdeen out of the Scottish Cup in 1995, Dons boss Roy Aitken's post-match team talk was just, 'Congratulations on being part of Aberdeen's worst result in the club's history.'

Twenty-eight years later that embarrassment was utterly eclipsed by the biggest giant-killing in the history of the cup, when sixth-tier side Darvel beat Aberdeen 1-0.

But although it was the biggest giant-killing, it wasn't the biggest shock. Darvel were playing well. They were one of a clutch of ambitious lower-league sides fully intent on taking advantage of the possibility of promotion that was eventually granted to them by the belated instigation of the league pyramid in 2015 (see iconic moment 53).

When they lined up against the Dons on their well-kept pitch in their intimate terraced ground, the East Ayrshire village side were narrowly in front at the top of the West of Scotland League. They had also already earned a remarkable result in the cup, beating a good Montrose side 5-2 away.

Meanwhile, Aberdeen were struggling in the league, their away form was terrible and they'd just lost 5-0 to Hearts, their sixth defeat in eight games.

With 2,250 home fans and 1,200 Dons – including former Scotland boss Craig Brown – packed into Recreation Park, the first half gave absolutely no indication of which team were the Premiership side (except for the fact that the Darvel players didn't have their names on their shirts).

Darvel had lots of SPFL experience, from players like Daryll Meggatt, Jordan Kirkpatrick, Ian McShane and Ross Caldwell, and it showed. They were well organised, they gave Aberdeen no time on the ball, and they passed it well themselves.

But it was one of their less-experienced players, 23-year-old forward Craig Truesdale, who was the star man on the night, full of ambition and creating opportunities.

On 20 minutes the home side got the goal that they deserved as Kirkpatrick took advantage of Aberdeen's lethargic defending, spinning inside the box to crack a deflected shot past Joe Lewis.

Aberdeen chairman Dave Cormack, sitting right behind Darvel boss Mick Kennedy, was surely considering the relative merits of each manager throughout the game. On the other side of the pitch, Dons gaffer Jim Goodwin's contingent overflowed from the modest dugout, making throw-ins a minor logistical challenge.

Aberdeen sorely lacked inspiration. They did improve slightly in the second half, but not by very much. Darvel goalie Chris Truesdale made a few good saves and there was one terrible offside decision against the visitors, but there were no hearts-in-the-mouths moments for the part-timers.

And after the home side kept the ball by the corner flag for what seemed like about ten minutes before full time, with the Aberdeen players clearly bereft of ideas to get the ball back, when the whistle went, joy erupted among the blue-and-white players and fans, who celebrated and danced together at the edge of the terrace, with Ross Caldwell draped in a 'Beefy Caldwell' spray-painted bedsheet.

And when elated Jordan Kirkpatrick and Chris Truesdale were asked after the match how they planned to celebrate, they each mentioned slightly sheepishly that they'd got work in the morning – although, apparently, quite a few of the players did head up to Glasgow to celebrate.

After the match, former Aberdeen player Frank McDougall said that if a result like that had happened when Alex Ferguson was in charge at Pittodrie, he would have made his players walk back to the Granite City.

But it was Darvel who were on the march, into the last 16.

81

Saturday, 11 August 2018

The Juniors Exodus Begins

In August 2018, the East of Scotland League kicked off with exactly three times as many clubs as the previous season, as 26 teams switched from the Junior leagues, in an exodus that would spell the end of one of the oldest football institutions in the world and inject fresh blood into Scottish lower-league football.

The Scottish Junior Football Association operated since 1886, in parallel with the senior leagues. But in 2018, 99 of the 158 Junior clubs voted to join the pyramid league setup, following the belated introduction of promotion into the SPFL from the lower leagues (see iconic moment 53).

It wasn't a step that the clubs took lightly. The Junior leagues were unfussy, cheap, popular, full of culture and heritage, and rooted in local communities.

Rather than risk losing local rivalries and leaving the Junior leagues to wither with gradually fewer and fewer clubs, the clubs acted pretty much in unison, on a region-by-region basis.

Two years after the eastern clubs made the move, a whopping 63 Junior clubs joined the brand-new West of Scotland League, in possibly the most significant change to Scotland's football league structure. The Covid lockdown badly affected that first season, but the West of Scotland League came back strong after that.

Then when promotion into the Highland League was opened up after that, the final – northern – piece of the Junior jigsaw was slotted into the pyramid structure too.

It hasn't taken long for former Juniors to make their mark in the senior leagues. Kelty Hearts and Bonnyrigg Rose have successfully progressed through the Lowland League and into the SPFL. Tranent Juniors and Linlithgow Rose are now playing in the Lowland League and Banks o' Dee in the Highland League. It's only a matter of time before the huge potential of their counterparts from the west is similarly fulfilled.

82

Saturday, 27 December 1997

Marco Negri Scores a Ridiculous Amount of Goals

When Rangers beat Dundee United a couple of days after Christmas in 1997, Marco Negri scored his 32nd and 33rd goals for the Light Blues. What's so special about that? Well, he'd amassed that tally in just 26 games, within six months of joining the club.

United may have been relieved that he bagged merely a brace that day; he'd put five past them in his second Premier Division game, after getting two against Hearts in his first. He scored 23 in his first ten league matches.

He grabbed a hat-trick in a 4-1 defeat of Kilmarnock in November, after getting four in a 7-0 hammering of Dunfermline in October. Rangers season ticket holders saw the best of the goal-hungry Italian as he bagged 23 in 15 home games.

Rangers were going for ten in a row and were four points ahead of Celtic going into the New Year derby. With their new Milanese hitman firing on all cylinders, everything was looking rosy in the Ibrox garden.

Celtic won that one but the Gers were still a point ahead. And then everything went wrong, in an unlikely location.

Negri was playing squash with his team-mate Sergio Porrini when the ball hit him in the right eye. It was so bad that the striker needed hospital treatment for a damaged retina. A couple of days later, the *Daily Record* reported that Rangers were planning to ban their players from the squash courts. Walter Smith enigmatically declared, 'Maybe the time has come to ban the players from doing everything.'

Negri's relationship with Rangers suffered a more damaging blow than his eye did. He returned from injury in February but only made sporadic appearances for the rest of the season and only scored four more goals. The *Daily Record* reported that he felt he was being treated with a lack of respect, both as a player and as a human.

And his first-team opportunities receded further when Dick Advocaat replaced Smith in the Ibrox hotseat. The Dutch gaffer sent Negri on loan to Vicenza and he eventually returned to Italy on a permanent move, playing for Bologna, Cagliari, Livorno and Perugia, but never returning to anything even remotely resembling the goal-greedy form that he'd shown in his first six months at Ibrox.

But despite his sudden travails, Negri was still the 1997/98 Premier Division top scorer, with the incredible distinction of all but two of his goals coming in the first half of the season.

83

Sunday, 28 August 2011

Scotland Win the Homeless World Cup – Again

2011, Paris – Scotland captain Robert Hare hoists the World Cup trophy into the air, and his team-mates celebrate joyfully.

But this was no run-of-the-mill World Cup. Former professional footballer Hare had been living in a Salvation Army shelter for 11 months, after losing his job and then initially spending time sleeping on the streets. But now he and his team-mates had just beaten a skilful Mexico side 4-3, by the Eiffel Tower, in the final of the 48-team Homeless World Cup.

William Hamilton, who was living in a Glasgow hostel at the time, scored a hat-trick, while William Lawrence from Rothesay made a string of good saves, and the keeper's little brother Sean scored once. Hamilton's third goal was the pick of the bunch, on the break after Lawrence had made a good save.

Scotland had narrowly defeated Kenya in the semi-final, and Ukraine in the quarters, after an impressive group stage that included beating Romania 7-0, putting 15 goals past Germany and edging a 17-goal thriller against Poland.

The triumph in Paris made Scotland the second nation ever to win the competition twice: they'd beaten Poland 9-3 in the final in 2007 in Copenhagen, after scoring hatfuls of goals in the group stages.

In the tournament, squads of eight players compete in 14-minute-long four-a-side matches, with rolling substitutions, in front of large crowds in iconic city-centre locations, which have included Princes Street Gardens in Edinburgh in 2005 and George Square in Glasgow in 2016.

Scot Mel Young and Austrian Harald Schmied came up with the concept for the competition in 2001, and Austria hosted and won the first tournament, in 2003. The competition aims – with a great deal of success – to change the players' lives and to shape attitudes towards homelessness: values that it shares with Street Soccer Scotland, a charity that works with the Scotland team and that uses football to help people who are experiencing hardship.

Taking part in the Homeless World Cup greatly boosts the players' confidence; winning it is an amazing achievement. But the real value of the competition lies in the tangible effect that the initiatives have on the players' lives.

2011 final hat-trick hero Hamilton said at the time, 'The Street Soccer programme has been amazing for me.' Street Soccer helped Lawrence find a flat before the 2011 tournament; after the final, he stated that his next step was to get home and try and get a job, while Scotland's other keeper, James Horsburgh from Edinburgh, found a flat and a job while attending Street Soccer, and said, 'Football has helped me to turn my life around.'

84

Saturday, 22 May 2021

St Johnstone Win the Double

Unless you're Rangers or Celtic, winning one major Scottish trophy is tricky enough. With the honourable exception of Sir Alex Ferguson's all-conquering Aberdeen side, winning two in one season is almost impossible. Hearts won a double in 1959/60, and the only other team to do it is by far the smallest of this select group: St Johnstone.

But that's exactly what they did, in Callum Davidson's first season as a manager, when they won the League Cup and then also the Scottish Cup.

Going into the 2020/21 League Cup semi-finals, Hibs were clear favourites, with Rangers, Celtic and Aberdeen all already out. And the men from Leith were on top against St Johnstone in the first half, but a combination of poor finishing, good defending and strong saves from Zander Clark meant it was the Perth team who went into half-time one up, through a Jason Kerr header. And the second half belonged to the underdogs – who'd been bottom of the Premiership just three months earlier – as man of the match Shaun Rooney headed home their second and Craig Conway made it three.

And in only their third League Cup Final – which wasn't a classic – they beat Livingston 1-0, with wing-back Rooney grabbing the only goal of the game. It made St Johnstone – who had won their first major honour, the Scottish Cup, in

2013/14 – the first club other than Celtic to win two domestic trophies since the start of the 2011/12 season.

But the real drama came in the Scottish Cup quarter-final, when St Johnstone lined up against a strong Rangers side, who'd already won the league and would go on to finish the Premiership season unbeaten.

Zander Clark performed heroics throughout as Rangers couldn't find a way through – until the 27th minute of extra time, when James Tavernier headed past the Saints keeper. It looked like that was that. St Johnstone had performed well but the Rangers juggernaut would roll on. But Clark had other ideas.

St Johnstone won a stoppage-time corner and Clark did what fans love to see – he joined the attack. He got his head to the corner kick, a downward header, and Chris Kane was quickest to react and turn the ball into the net for a dramatic late, late equaliser.

And then Clark capped off the ultimate man-of-the-match performance by saving two spot-kicks in the shoot-out, to send the Perth side through.

Again, Hibs – who'd just finished third in the league – were favourites going into the semi-finals but this time they were kept apart from St Johnstone, who beat St Mirren 2-1 to set up a final against the men from Leith: a chance for some Hibee revenge for that League Cup semi defeat? Not a bit of it.

This time there was no early green-and-white storm; St Johnstone created the better chances throughout and it was that man Shaun Rooney who got the only goal of the game, to cap an incredible season for his club.

When 2021 started, they'd only got their hands on any of Scotland's three major trophies once. By the summer of 2021, they'd trebled that haul.

85

Thursday, 21 May 1891

Dumbarton and Rangers Share the First Ever Scottish League Title

At Cathkin Park, on a Thursday afternoon in 1891, Dumbarton and Rangers met in a hastily-arranged play-off to determine who should be the first ever Scottish champions.

The inaugural league season had boasted goals galore and no 0-0 draws. It included short-lived so-called 'village sides' like Cowlairs, Cambuslang, Vale of Leven and Abercorn; and it featured its fair share of controversy, including when Renton – who'd been declared unofficial world champions two years earlier when they'd beaten FA Cup winners West Brom, and whose success was reputedly partly down to drinking the water that chicken had been boiled in – were thrown out of the league for playing a friendly with St Bernards, who'd been accused of professionalism, while the Scottish game was desperately clinging on to amateurism by its fingernails.

It was a season played in an era of contrasting styles: Dunbartonshire sides Dumbarton, Vale of Leven and Renton were derided in sophisticated Glaswegian circles for their long-ball 'English' approach, seen as inferior to city sides' short-passing game.

Dumbarton were top for most of the season, but lost two of their last four games, against Celtic and Rangers, as

Rangers caught up with them and they finished level on points at the top of the table.

Unfortunately, no one had decided how a tied league would be resolved, so the league committee met to work out what to do next and declared that there should be a play-off.

Rangers dominated most of the match and led 2-0 at half-time. But Dumbarton raced back into it in the last 20 minutes, scoring twice, and – long before the invention of extra time or penalty shoot-outs – the fixture resolved nothing. So the committee met again, to try to think of what to do next.

There was some confusion the next morning as the *Glasgow Herald* reported that the tie would be replayed. But it seems that the committee was split on the decision, the chairman – who represented Dumbarton – abstained from using his casting vote, the decision was adjourned for another 24 hours, and then it was finally declared that the two clubs should share the title.

In spite of the haphazard nature of that initial league finale, it was 30 years before goal average was introduced in Scotland. Far too late for Dumbarton, who were the first season's top scorers and also had the joint meanest defence.

But – despite that long wait for goal average – only one other season's top flight went to a title play-off, in 1905, and it was resolved clearly, when Celtic beat Rangers 2-1.

And Dumbarton wouldn't have long to wait for more glory – they won the second league title and didn't have to share it with anyone.

86

Friday, 14 July 1967

Aberdeen, Finalists in the United Soccer Association

The summer of love. The long, hot summer. Different people had different experiences in different parts of the US in the summer of 1967. And 18,000 spectators in Los Angeles were treated to one of the most dramatic, entertaining football finals ever played, between Aberdeen and Wolves.

But they weren't really Aberdeen and Wolverhampton Wanderers – although all of their players were present and correct. They were the Washington Whips and the LA Wolves.

I should probably explain: this was the inaugural season of the United Soccer Association, but without any American teams to play in the tournament, 12 clubs from around the world were paid $250,000 each to participate, and they were each given an American name. Hibs were Toronto City. Dundee United were Dallas Tornado. Aberdeen's 'Whips' name was chosen in a newspaper competition.

Each team played a whopping 12 group matches. Aberdeen finished top of the Eastern Division, narrowly ahead of Stoke (the Cleveland Stokers), with Hibs in third place. Dundee United finished bottom of the Western Division, on three wins and three draws from their 12 games. By the time of the final, Aberdeen had been in the States for almost two months.

The Dons/Whips lost their opening match, 2-1 to Stoke. Boss Eddie Turnbull lamented the fact that his team hit the woodwork seven times. Turnbull almost didn't make it across the Atlantic at all. He had hepatitis and had to bring his doctor with him on a brief visit before returning home for a fortnight of recuperation. While he was in DC though, with his club representing the capital city, he got to meet President Lyndon Johnson at the White House, in a special reception to celebrate the tournament.

It was first class all the way for the players. Dons centre-half Tommy McMillan was sending dispatches back to the *Press and Journal*, and happily reported, 'We are living in the Hilton hotel and what a place it is. There is TV, radio and a fridge in every room. The hotel also has tennis courts and a swimming pool and we are having a very enjoyable stay.'

The Washington Whips went to meet the NFL's Washington Redskins. Aberdeen defender Jens Petersen had a go at kicking field goals, with so much success that the Americans tried to sign him. This was before Turnbull had returned home, and he quickly put a stop to that.

On 31 May Aberdeen beat Hibs 2-1 in a game – played in front of a mostly Scottish crowd – that was considered one of the best ever in Toronto, before Dallas hosted two all-Scottish clashes: a 2-2 draw between Hibs and United, and, towards the climax of the group stage, a 2-0 win for Aberdeen over their north-east rivals, as the Dons/Whips raced with Stoke/Cleveland for the top spot.

But it wasn't all plain sailing, schmoozing, mini-bars, cheerleaders, sequins, pom poms, Andy Williams concerts, TV interviews and fun innovations like numbers on the front of shirts as well as the back, in the big fancy US tournament (although all of those things did happen).

In their game against Hibs, the Wolves team threatened to walk off en masse when it looked like the ref was about to send off Dave Wagstaffe. Glentoran's match against Brazilians

Bangu in Detroit was abandoned when players and spectators fought on the pitch. Cagliari's game against Uruguayans Cerro in New York was also abandoned when about 200 spectators chased and attacked the referee, knocking him down several times before the police arrived.

And Hibs' game against Cagliari was also halted before full time, when about 3,000 fans invaded the pitch ten minutes from the end. Hibs, who were leading at the time, were awarded the win. Cagliari players had walked off in protest when Hibs' second goal was allowed, and police had to be called to protect the referee and restore order. Three Cagliari players were suspended indefinitely from the United Soccer Association.

Dundee United also experienced the rough with the smooth in Boston for their 4-1 win over Shamrock Rovers. United goalie Sandy Davie said that the pitch 'was one of the worst I've ever seen. It was bumpy and full of holes. Some were filled with soil. The dressing rooms, too, were dreadful. So filthy, [trainer] Andy Dickson had to clean all the seats before we could use them.' And a fan threw a tomato at Tommy Neilson when he went to take a throw-in.

Tommy McMillan reported back to the *Press and Journal* that some of the refereeing had been 'atrocious'.

The group stages had been eventful, and the end result was that Aberdeen – who, along with United, joined Bangu in the top three clubs with the highest average attendances in the tournament – narrowly pipped Stoke, to set up a final against Wolves. And what a final it was.

Based on the flip of a coin, Wolves got home advantage, and the 18,000 fans scattered around inside the vast LA Coliseum were treated to a phenomenally entertaining and physical showdown, with three penalties, a red card and 11 goals, including two hat-tricks.

Wolves took the lead, before Jim Smith equalised halfway through the first half. But 12 minutes later Smith was sent off, and Aberdeen would end up playing more than 90 minutes a man down.

In four hectic second-half minutes, Aberdeen twice took the lead, first through a penalty from young Francis Munro. Wolves equalised. Jim Storrie made it 3-2 to the Scots. Wolves equalised again. And that's how it remained until ten minutes from the end, when Wolves went back into the lead for the first time in almost an hour.

But, 90 seconds from the end, Petersen launched one of his field goal-style long free kicks down the pitch, from inside his own half, and Munro nodded it home.

Wolves took the lead again in extra time, and then, in the last couple of minutes, they got a penalty when an Aberdeen player cleared a shot off the line with his hand. Bobby Clark saved the penalty, and one minute later it was Aberdeen's turn from the spot again. Munro made no mistake, levelling the game yet again, at 5-5, and impressing his English opponents so much that they bought him a year later.

So now the match went to another period of extra time, and this one was sudden death. But then, disastrously, Ally Shewan scored an own goal, and enough trophies to fill the top of a table were presented to Wolves and each of their players.

As he accepted his gong, Wolves manager Ronnie Allen called for three cheers for the Aberdeen players, and said, 'By golly, with ten men, they frightened us all to death.'

The Wolves and Aberdeen players set off on a lap of honour together. It was almost midnight by that point.

It had been a long trip for the finalists. So long that, when the Aberdeen players arrived back in Scotland, Jim Hermiston and Harry Melrose each had an extra-special welcome home, as they both met their babies that their wives had given birth to while they'd been away.

Turnbull described his players' efforts in America in general – and in the dramatic climax against Wolves in particular – as magnificent.

But the most tangible legacy of these Stateside football adventures didn't belong to Aberdeen. Dundee United had played in white before they ventured to Dallas. They returned to Texas in 1969 to represent Dallas again, finishing in third place, while Kilmarnock played as St Louis Stars. In both tournaments United/Dallas Tornado played in tangerine shirts and blue shorts.

Back home later that summer, inspired by their Tornado strip, United lined up in tangerine in a pre-season friendly against Everton. As we all know, they didn't look back.

87

Thursday, 18 June 1992

Scotland Beat the Soviets 3-0

Scotland were really quite good at Euro '92, where they played in the group of death to beat all groups of death.

Even though Andy Roxburgh's men were the bookies' least favourites at the eight-team tournament in Sweden, they played well against very strong Netherlands and Germany sides – including, for the defending European champions, Ronald Koeman, Dennis Bergkamp, Frank Rijkaard, Marco van Basten and Ruud Gullit, and, for the world champions, Andreas Brehme, Andreas Möller, Thomas Häßler, Karl-Heinz Riedle, Matthias Sammer, Stefan Effenberg and Jürgen Klinsmann – but lost those games 1-0 and 2-0.

Which meant that Scotland's final match, against the CIS, was just for glory, whereas the CIS, who'd drawn with each of the big guns, still had a chance of qualifying for a semi-final. But what's football about if it's not about glory? As Roxburgh later said, 'That last game was vital for justifying our being there.'

If you can't remember Euro '92, you might not know who the CIS were. They were the Soviet Union while the Soviet Union was breaking up. There was a fairly even split of Ukrainian and Russians players in the squad (several of the Ukrainians were playing for Rangers at the time), some Georgians and a Belorussian. The Soviet Union had qualified for the Euros, but the country had then broken up, so UEFA granted them permission to play at the tournament as the Confederation of Independent States.

It was Scotland's first time at the Euros, and they continued with the quirky shirt-numbering principle that they'd pioneered at Italia '90 – basing shirt numbers on the number of caps that each player had. The more caps, the lower the number. So Ally McCoist played up front with five on his back, right-back Stewart McKimmie wore a very centre-forward-ish number nine, centre-back big Dave McPherson strolled around with eight just below the nadir of his mullet, and, in the centre of midfield, Paul McStay and Gary McAllister played side-by-side, but wearing numbers three and eleven.

Roxburgh had created a strong collective spirit within the squad thanks to a pre-tournament tour in North America and then social events in their Swedish hotels. Hordes of Scotland fans cheered on their heroes in Gothenburg and Norrköping. And the Scotland team bus arrived at their final group game flanked by four Swedish police motorbike riders clad in Scotland shirts that the SFA had given them.

Satisfyingly, squad numbers one to eleven played for Scotland – in their idiosyncratic positions – in the first two games, but against the CIS, Roxburgh made two changes, replacing Maurice Malpas and the injured Gordon Durie with Tom Boyd and Kevin Gallacher.

Scotland had been a bit unlucky against the Netherlands and Germany – restricting the Dutch to very few opportunities and almost scoring several times against the Germans – but got the rub of the green against the CIS, when fate rewarded their quality attacking play after just seven minutes, as McStay's powerful shot from outside the box cracked back off the post, then off the back of the unfortunate diving Dmitri Kharine's head and into the net.

And nine minutes later, Brian McClair tried his luck from distance; his shot took a slight deflection off Kakhaber

Tskhadadze and ended up in the net. Remarkably, it was Choccy's first ever goal for Scotland, even though he'd played often enough to get the number six shirt. He'd recently admitted to the *Daily Record*, 'I just accept that I'm never going to score for Scotland.'

There were plenty more chances for both sides after that, but it stayed at 2-0 almost until full time. But late on, substitute Pat Nevin was chopped down in the box after some characteristic twinkle-toed twisting and turning. McAllister calmly stroked the ball past Kharine and the big crowd of Scotland fans in the stadium celebrated loudly in the rain.

Scotland finished third in their foreboding group, just one point behind eventual finalists Germany. The CIS match was probably Scotland's best ever result at the finals of a major tournament (albeit not their greatest win – we'll get to that later, of course). The CIS may be an unfamiliar name, but this was simply the re-badged Soviet Union, with players like Alexei Mikhailichenko and Andrei Kanchelskis, who'd held their own against the Dutch and Germans. But this was the disintegrating Soviet Union's last ever match, and they lost it 3-0 to Scotland – which also meant that Scotland were the only team to ever beat the CIS. And they did it with style.

88

Saturday, 12 March 1960

Eyemouth United Reach the Scottish Cup Quarter-Final

Eyemouth is a small fishing town near the English border. You can get great fish and chips there and you can often see seals in the harbour. And their local football club once went remarkably far in the Scottish Cup, just 12 years after they'd been formed.

In their early years, Eyemouth United had won the East of Scotland League three times, and in 1959/60 they were going well again, competing with local rivals Duns and Berwick Rangers reserves for the title.

Before they could compete in the Scottish Cup, the Fishermen had to qualify for it. So their cup campaign started in September, in the southern section of the Qualifying Cup. They beat St Cuthbert's Wanderers, then Vale of Leithen (6-2 away) and Glasgow University, before meeting Peebles Rovers in the final.

The *Southern Reporter* praised the 'rampaging Fishermen' as they beat their Borders rivals 2-0 in the first leg, then 4-1 the week after.

Eyemouth went straight into the second round of the Scottish Cup proper, where they were drawn at home against Division Two's Albion Rovers. A crowd of 500 turned up for the match at the Playing Fields. Unfortunately, midfielder

Dougie Martin had to go off injured and the Fishermen had to play a large part of the match with ten men, in the days before substitutes. But halfway through the first half, Eyemouth striker Wattie Burns capitalised on a defensive mix-up and smashed the ball past the Rovers keeper.

The *Southern Reporter* said that Burns's goal 'spurred the Eyemouth men on and the Rovers took a terrific grilling under their onslaught, but no more goals resulted'. At full time fans ran on to the pitch to congratulate their local heroes.

Next up was another home tie, against Cowdenbeath, who were propping up Division Two. The Borderers apparently weren't disappointed to be missing out on a glory tie. *Southern Reporter* man 'Centre-forward' said, 'The Eyemouth boys are quite sure that if they can defeat Albion Rovers they can do likewise against the not-so-far-up-the-table Cowdenbeath.'

Unfortunately Burns, after his heroics against Albion, had a stomach muscle injury and couldn't play. But his teammates managed fine without him; Norman Duff came out of retirement to fill in. And it was Duff who set up the first goal as his fellow striker Steele headed home his cross.

In the second half, two other members of the front five, Reid and Allan, made the final score 3-0. The *Southern Reporter* said 'the Fishermen were streets ahead of the Fife side in both guile and ideas' while the *Berwickshire News* was of the opinion that 'Eyemouth were superior all round and the three goals might have been four, five or even six with any degree of luck'.

So the Fishermen had reached the heady heights of the last eight.

Club vice-president Mr W. Wilson was hoping to be drawn away against Rangers, and said, 'Let the football world see how our boys can play.' The club groundsman, Mr G. Tait, would have been happy with that too, saying, 'It would take a load off my shoulders.'

But Mr Tait would have his work cut out after all, as Eyemouth were drawn at home again. It wasn't against Rangers, but not far off in terms of ability: they'd be facing high-flying Kilmarnock, who were going through their own golden period. The Ayrshiremen were unbeaten in 16 matches and in second place Division One when they made the journey to the east.

By now the British national press had picked up on Eyemouth's remarkable cup achievement, and club spokesman Dick Bruce told *Daily Mirror* reporter Jimmy Stevenson, 'We shall have to build extra turnstiles and, as we did when Celtic visited us some years ago [in the first round of the cup, in January 1953], we shall build the temporary entrances from the fish boxes. We shall need thousands, for we shall also place them all round the ground so that spectators will have a better chance to see.'

And, indeed, 3,000 fans turned up to see the overachieving Fishermen take on high-flying Killie. It was a bridge (only just) too far for the home side though. They played well but Killie edged past them 2-1. The cup run was over.

Killie made it to the final, where they lost to Rangers (the Ayrshiremen had an incredible and frustrating record of second-place finishes in those days), while Eyemouth couldn't quite add to their three East of Scotland league titles that year.

But the Fishermen will always be able to say that they were the first non-league side to reach the Scottish Cup quarter-final. Eight years later, Highland League club Elgin City did it too. But it's a trick that's unlikely to ever be repeated by any other East of Scotland League club.

89

Sunday, 27 November 1994

Raith Win the League Cup, then Take on German Giants

No one expected Division One side Raith Rovers to beat Celtic in the League Cup Final in 1994 – except for Raith manager Jimmy Nicholl and his players.

Celtic may have been going through a lean spell, but they still had Tom Boyd, Paul McStay and John Collins lining up against Raith's assortment of free transfers, veterans and youngsters.

But there were some great players among those old heads and young whippersnappers, from the almost-40-year-old Dave Narey at one end of the age range, to future Scotland regulars Stevie Crawford and Colin Cameron at the other. And Nicholl managed to get his team to play with a relaxed freedom that Tommy Burns's under-pressure Celtic side couldn't match.

Nicholl – a former Rangers player – also made the most of his connections at Ibrox, where the final was being played, while Hampden was temporarily Celtic's home ground. His team got to practise on the pitch, and the Rangers kit man left them an especially selected bag of studs.

Crawford opened the scoring but Andy Walker and Charlie Nicholas hit back and it looked like the men from Kirkcaldy would be fulfilling their expected nearly men role, until veteran captain Gordon Dalziel nipped in with five minutes left to head a rebound past Gordon Marshall.

'Out of all the goals I scored for Raith,' Dalziel later said, it was 'the most important – and probably the easiest.' And he scored 170 for them.

It went to penalties. The first 11 were scored, and then goalie Scott Thomson saved from McStay, sparking wild celebrations. It was the first major cup that Raith had ever won.

It wasn't only Raith players and fans who were happy. Ally McCoist and John Greig presented the Fifers with cases of Rangers label champagne. Pipers and thousands of happy fans welcomed the players back to Kirkcaldy. But Raith's *annus mirabilis* was only getting started.

They won Division One, an achievement made all the sweeter by finishing one point above Dunfermline, and the League Cup win catapulted them into the UEFA Cup, where they enjoyed a brief moment of surreal glory.

After getting through their first two rounds – in their first ever crack at any European competition – Raith were drawn against Bayern Munich. Those free transfers, veterans and kids would be taking on the likes of Oliver Khan, Jean-Pierre Papin and Lothar Matthäus. And in the second leg, in Munich, Danny Lennon's goal gave Raith the half-time lead on the night. The Kirkcaldy underdogs were leading one of the best teams in the world.

Unfortunately, second-half goals from Jürgen Klinsmann and Markus Babbel – combined with Klinsmann's brace from the first leg at Easter Road – gave the Bavarians a 4-1 aggregate win. Bayern went on to win the tournament, beating Benfica, PSV, Barcelona and Bordeaux, but their boss Otto Rehhagel said that the Raith games were 'the toughest we endured during the competition'.

And Raith fans can always treasure the photos of the half-time score on the huge Olympiastadion scoreboard: FC Bayern 0 Raith Rovers FC 1.

Thursday, 25 May 1922

St Mirren Win the Barcelona Cup

In 1922, Barcelona opened their new stadium, Les Corts. The special guests who they invited to play first there were St Mirren. Unfortunately, Barcelona beat the Buddies 2-1 in that historic game, but the Scots had more joy five days later.

Notts County had also been invited to Catalonia, and lined up against St Mirren at Les Corts to contest the Barcelona Cup. In front of a capacity crowd, the men from Paisley took the lead early in the second half through Dunky Walker before the venerable Englishmen equalised on the stroke of full time.

Late in extra time, Walker scored again, and the Barcelona Cup was Paisley-bound.

And the Buddies' Iberian glory didn't finish there. They headed west to Santander and then Gijón, winning two and drawing one of the four games they played there, including one match where they put seven past their Asturian hosts; five of them in the first half; six of the seven scored by Walker.

Spanish paper *El Comercio* reported that, in that multi-goal exhibition, St Mirren were the best team ever to have played in Asturias. They praised the *extranjeros'* accomplishment, cohesion, unity, speed, valour, ball control, the admirable precision with which they defended their goal, and their dangerous attacks, and reported, 'The crowd were truly enchanted by St Mirren.'

Wednesday, 2 February 2005

Vladimir Romanov Takes Over at Hearts

In Vladimir Romanov's eight years in charge of Hearts, he got through 12 or 13 managers (some had such short reigns that it was hard to be sure who counted; some were good, others weren't), they won two Scottish Cups, he invested his own money but the club accumulated tens of millions of pounds in debts, they reached the Champions League qualifying rounds, he ranted against what he saw as a corrupt Scottish football establishment where 'monkeys' told the 'mafia' what to do, they regularly beat Hibs, and he claimed that the league was fixed. Dull moments were rare.

Hearts fans had tangible on-field reasons to love him but also plenty of justification to fear the damage he was doing to their club. When he arrived they were in no doubt about how they felt.

The club was heavily in debt, and outgoing chief exec Chris Robinson was deeply unpopular because he wanted to sell their historic ground. 'This is the news we've been waiting years for,' said fans' spokesman John Borthwick. Careful what you wish for, John.

Romanov hired Phil Anderton as chief executive, Anderton appointed George Burley as manager, and money was spent on players. Including some really good players.

Burley won his first eight games in charge and Hearts were flying high in the league. Chairman George Foulkes sold his shares to Romanov and urged other fans to do the same. Everything was rosy in the Gorgie garden.

But then, suddenly, it wasn't.

Just one day after Foulkes sold his shares to Romanov, Burley left the club. It was the old 'irreconcilable differences'. Rumours that Romanov interfered in team selection refused to go away. Anderton courted some seriously big names to replace Burley. Kevin Keegan, Bobby Robson, Claudio Ranieri and Ottmar Hitzfield all politely declined.

On Halloween, nine days after Burley had left, Romanov sacked Anderton. On the same day, Foulkes left too, because of Romanov's 'unacceptable ruthlessness'. Romanov appointed his own son, Roman Romanov, to replace them both and recruited Graham Rix as manager.

Results deteriorated and the players confirmed that Romanov was picking the team. Unsurprisingly, they weren't happy about it. Romanov sacked Rix and replaced him with Valdas Ivanauskas. The players rallied to finish second in the league and beat Gretna in the Scottish Cup Final. It was only the second major honour Hearts had won in 43 years.

Despite that success, Romanov couldn't resist getting a dig in: he later said that Hearts won the cup 'despite all the referees' efforts and intrigues'. He got fined £10,000 for that.

During a disappointing run early in the next season, he turned his ire on his own players, saying he would sell them all to 'Kilmarnock or whatever club will take them' if they didn't beat Dunfermline. They drew with Dunfermline. He didn't sell them. But he was losing some of them. Key players Steven Pressley, Paul Hartley and Craig Gordon held a press conference where they confirmed that many of the players were unhappy.

Pressley and Hartley both went to Celtic in the winter transfer window. Romanov issued an angry statement lambasting hooped shirts, betrayal and the seduction of players' souls.

In the summer transfer window, Gordon was sold to Sunderland. Despite the record transfer fee, the club were simultaneously accumulating huge debts.

In the wake of Pressley and Hartley's departure, Romanov gave an interview to Russian magazine *Futbol*, where he took his criticism of assorted Scottish football targets – especially referees, Rangers and Celtic – to another level.

He said, 'If the teams are evenly matched then the referees can have a real influence on the outcome. Dodgy's not the word for it. I went there in the hope of avoiding all the sleaze we're so used to over here [in Russia]. I thought it was all clean, by the book, all gentlemen. It turns out it's much worse.'

And he claimed that Rangers and Celtic 'turned football into showbusiness with their underhand games, paying off players. What we call underhandedness, they call the norm'. Celtic chairman Brian Quinn said he would take legal advice. Romanov said he was misquoted. He was later fined £25,000.

Just a few days after the *Futbol* interview, at the press conference for Hearts' home match with St Mirren, he gave journalists – who he repeatedly described as 'monkeys' – bananas and peanuts, and a few days after that he lambasted them on Hearts' website, for expressing their sympathy for Pressley.

Under the headline 'Monkeys Go Home', he told the scribblers, 'You are one step away from becoming human beings,' and added, 'Your leader Mowgli is not taking bananas any more, now he is taking money for lies and untruthful interpretation. I beg you Mowgli, take the monkeys back to the safari park.' You would never accuse his criticism of lacking creativity.

At the club's 2008 AGM, Romanov Jr claimed that the league was fixed and that Hearts had been getting 'screwed by referees', and said, 'If a club starts to grow, they use all mechanisms to pull it down.'

Even a home crowd who were as happy as anyone to talk about getting a raw deal from refs were mostly sick and tired of the Romanovs' excuses and conspiracy theories by now. The rest of Scottish football was laughing at their paranoia.

But the club's big concerns were financial ones. The wage bill was unsustainable, debts were soaring, and players were being paid late. But Romanov Sr could still find time for a couple more particularly spectacular rants against his Scottish football demons.

First, he railed against Scottish football's 'mafia', 'maniacs' and 'criminals'. He said that in the last 12 games of the 2010/11 season, 'It was almost like someone replaced the team with a different one. Whose fault is that? Players? Managers? Or is it mafia? Each year we are forced to fight against these maniacs harder and harder.'

A few months later, he claimed that the SPL were being unduly influenced by journalists, who in turn were apparently threatened by Hearts' decent results, saying, 'As soon as Hearts moved closer to the third spot the monkeys started to squeal, lie and create conspiracy plots … the monkeys tricked the SPL, fans and themselves and showed who is in charge of the football mafia.'

This couldn't go on much longer.

Romanov revealed that he was planning to sell the club, and that he'd maybe like to go into the theatre instead. He lamented, 'I am a poor man because I invested everything in sport.'

There was still time, though, for one last intense hit of glory: the 5-1 defeat of Hibs in the Scottish Cup Final (see iconic moment 6). But key players started leaving, and buyers weren't exactly queuing up to pay for a club with massive debts.

In 2013 Hearts went into administration. At times it looked like they might not make it out the other side. But the fans rallied and invested in the club, and with investment from local business owner Ann Budge, they lived on.

That moment when Romanov stepped through the Tynecastle door in 2005 ushered in one of the most unforgettable periods of high drama at any Scottish football club. And for all the off-field controversy and/or entertainment, it should always be remembered that that era also included a good chunk of drama on the pitch.

On paper, Hearts gambled on a maverick owner and apparently lost by eventually going into administration. But it's far from a purely sad, disastrous story.

Do most Hearts fans wish that Romanov had never taken the club over back in 2005? No. They're still playing at Tynecastle, they won two Scottish Cups, they survived administration, and it was a hell of a ride.

92

Tuesday, 7 February 1922

Falkirk Break the World Transfer Record

Cockney striker Syd Puddefoot was one of the most coveted footballers of his generation. Early in his career, he scored over 100 goals for West Ham, including five in one FA Cup tie. During World War I, when English football was regionalised, he scored almost 100 goals for the London Combination team, and then was stationed at Bridge of Allan, where he played as a guest for Falkirk. After the war, he played in England's three Victory International games and scored in them all.

In early 1922, it was reported that Spurs, Chelsea and Preston all wanted to buy him. But there was another, unlikely, suitor: Falkirk fans were very keen on their wartime guest, and Puddefoot said that he wanted to move to Scotland and that the Bairns were the only Scottish club he wanted to play for. So club directors got on a train to London. Their luggage included a suitcase full of cash.

When they returned with an empty suitcase and with Syd's signature, the *Falkirk Herald* reported, 'Local football fans were agog with excitement, and the chief topic of their conversation was Falkirk's chances of lifting the national trophy.'

Falkirk had paid £5,000 for Puddefoot, which was a world record. The *Football Post* lamented the 'folly' of such eye-watering transfer fees.

Unfortunately, although his performances for the Bairns were far from disastrous and his goalscoring record in Scotland was respectable, Puddefoot didn't live up to the Falkirk fans' sky-high expectations. The team didn't make the impact on the cup that the *Falkirk Herald* said the supporters were hoping for.

Meanwhile, Puddefoot went back down south each summer, to play cricket for Essex. It was on another trip down the road, in 1924, that his relationship with Falkirk broke down.

Puddefoot was in London to play as a guest for Celtic in a charity match against West Ham – a month after Falkirk had lost to Airdrie in the Scottish Cup semi-final, by far the furthest the Bairns had got in the competition while the East End marksman was there – when he gave an interview to the *Evening Standard* criticising his treatment by Falkirk fans and complaining that his team-mates didn't pass to him enough.

The *Falkirk Herald* said, 'The statements credited to him are not calculated to increase his general popularity this side of the border, but perhaps there is more than a grain of truth to what he says.'

Either way, the writing was on the wall for Syd's time at Brockville. In February 1925 he moved to Blackburn for £4,000. The *Falkirk Herald* said, 'He is a brilliant player but with Falkirk has not been a consistently successful one.'

His last game was a disappointing draw against Raith Rovers. Puddefoot was inconsistent. When he fired a penalty straight at the keeper, reported the *Falkirk Herald*, 'many harsh things were said about him' but, in the last minute, 'To show that he can play football, he ran right through the defence and placed the ball in the net.'

That match summed up Syd's underwhelming time in Scotland, a spell that illustrates the timelessness of the risks of placing great expectations on star signings.

93

Wednesday, 18 May 1960

The Best European Cup Final Ever

Some games are so significant that they become part of a country's folklore purely for hosting the match, even without providing any of the players on the pitch.

The European Cup Final in 1960 bestrides history as one of the best games ever played, and it took place at Hampden, in front of 127,621 delighted fans – the record attendance for a final in the competition.

And the seductive quality of the match arguably inspired Scottish football to improve significantly.

Real Madrid had beaten Barcelona 6-2 on aggregate to reach the Glasgow showpiece. Eintracht Frankfurt were even more dominant in their semi, beating Rangers 12-4 over the two legs.

The final was of such a high level that the *Daily Mirror* praised Real Madrid's 'electrically charged soccer which has given them such fantastic supremacy'. The *Aberdeen Evening Express* said, 'This United Nations of football masters produced a display of soccer artistry such as Hampden has never seen and until they return is unlikely to see again,' and praised Eintracht for making the great Real Madrid side need to play so well.

The Germans scored first, as a precise Erwin Stein cross set up Richard Kress for a neat finish. Dieter Lindner had already blasted a shot that *Los Blancos'* Argentine keeper Rogelio Domínguez only just managed to turn on to the bar.

But after that it was one-way traffic in a display of skill, control and artistry that was decades ahead of its time.

It helped that Real Madrid had two of the best players in the world, Alfredo Di Stéfano and Ferenc Puskás, but their fellow forwards Luis del Sol, Francisco 'Paco' Gento and Canário were all pretty handy too.

A quick Di Stéfano double put the *Madrileños* ahead; the first was thanks to a great Canário run and cross, and for the second the Blond Arrow tucked home a rebound from a Canário shot.

Puskás hammered home the third from a tight angle then made it four from the penalty spot early in the second half. Then the Hungarian genius scored two more, first with a header from a characteristic lightning Gento run and cross and then swivelling and blasting home from just inside the box to make it 6-1.

Stein pulled one back before Di Stéfano burst through the middle and blasted a low shot past German goalie Egon Loy, and finally Stein capitalised on a defensive mistake from José María Vidal to make the final score a mind-boggling 7-3.

The Eintracht players formed a guard of honour for their dazzling opponents as they were presented with the great trophy on the Hampden turf.

The *Evening Express* reported that the Real Madrid players 'went off the Hampden pitch with the cheers ringing in their ears. It must be a long time since so few people left the famous ground before the end of a game which had become one-sided,' and added, 'Every man was a ball player with dozens of ways of beating the opposition. They had a superb understanding. They showed supreme precision in the art of passing the ball.' The newspaper also spoke well of the local support: 'The enthusiasm of the Scottish crowd proved that the support is there providing the quality is forthcoming.'

Puskás later said that the Hampden crowd 'certainly appreciated football. It was one of those blissful times when the whole team seemed to play brilliantly and we almost achieved some sort of footballing perfection.'

But the match almost hadn't gone ahead at all. The German football authorities had prohibited their teams from playing against Puskás, after he'd claimed that the German team that beat Hungary in the 1954 World Cup Final had been doped. In the end the final only went ahead after the Galloping Major sent them a formal letter of apology.

It's just as well the game did take place. It inspired the world as a demonstration of how football could be played, and among the nations determined to learn from it were Scotland. At the Scottish Football League's AGM, SFL president W.W. Terris spoke about the final, saying, 'the Scottish football public has the pleasure of witnessing club football of a standard greatly surpassing even the best that they are in the habit of seeing here, and having seen for themselves the excellence attained by these foreign exponents of the game, they have every right and reason to clamour for something better than the standard of play provided by their own Scottish clubs.'

Many of the managers and players who would be influential in shaping Scottish football for the better were in the Hampden crowd on that famous day, including Alex Ferguson (as a teenage Queen's Park player), Andy Roxburgh, Billy Bremner and Jimmy Johnstone. Willie Waddell and Jock Stein were among the Scots inspired at the time to study European coaching methods. And Stein showed a recording of the game to his Celtic team ahead of the 1967 European Cup Final. More on that soon.

Wednesday, 5 May 2010

Nuts Match 3: What a Comeback – Motherwell 6 Hibs 6

To come back from a goal down is satisfying. Cancelling out a two-goal lead is overjoying. Overturning a three-goal deficit is the stuff of dreams. But to wrestle a draw from being four goals down? That's what Motherwell did against Hibs, in one of the most dramatic, high-scoring Scottish league matches of all time.

The Steelmen were one point ahead of the Hibees, in fourth place in the table, going into this, the penultimate match of the season, on a Wednesday evening at Fir Park. And whoever finished fourth would qualify for the Europa League.

The match was 1-1 after 16 minutes, when Giles Coke cancelled out Colin Nish's opener. Early goals, for sure, but far more fantastical drama was to come.

Just 20 minutes later, Nish had a hat-trick, and the visitors were 4-1 up, with their other goal coming from Derek Riordan, who raced on to a weak Coke back-pass, rounded goalie John Ruddy and tucked the ball home from a tight angle.

It was all looking pretty desperate for the men from Lanarkshire.

John Sutton pulled one back with a header shortly before half-time, but Hibs' dominance resumed after the break as Anthony Stokes scored twice, first from a Liam

Miller cross from the right, and then from a Riordan cross from the left.

Just 25 minutes to go. Motherwell 2 Hibs 6. Home fans started to leave. Surely there was no way back now.

But then Coke scored again, tucking away the rebound from a Jim O'Brien shot that came back off the base of the post, and everything changed. Hibs seemed shocked and rattled, and they started making more and more mistakes at the back.

Five minutes after that, Hateley hit the sort of hopeful free kick from outside the box that usually leads, at best, to a weak clearance and a penalty-box scramble, but no Hibs defender rose to head it away and it somehow bounced slowly past Graeme Smith, who could only slowly prod a foot in its general direction.

But Hibs were still two goals up. Surely they would see out the win?

Just four minutes later, Sutton leapt brilliantly to meet an O'Brien corner, with Smith nowhere near getting to the ball, and the big Englishman headed it powerfully into the net. Now there was just one goal in it, all the momentum was with Motherwell and there were still 15 minutes left.

With an electric atmosphere under the lights, and the fans who'd left early either watching in the pub or listening on their car radios, the home side kept pressing, and with five minutes to go Smith gave them another gift.

Lukas Jutkiewicz, in his last home game before the end of his loan from Everton, raced on to a long ball into the box. Smith ran out to meet him, and clattered him over. Penalty. Maybe the ultimate comeback was almost complete?

Ross Forbes stepped up and blasted it towards Smith's left, but the keeper somehow got to it and parried it away (perhaps having left his line slightly early). Seemed like it wasn't to be after all. Until the third minute of stoppage time, when Sutton hooked the ball forward, from deep within his own half.

Jutkiewicz chased it, but Paul Hanlon was right with him, and shepherded him well, out away from goal. But, with his first touch, Jutkiewicz gently headed it down, then with his second, turned and blasted a left-footed shot from a tight angle, over Smith, under the bar and into the net. A great goal and a worthy climax of any 6-6 comeback.

The remaining fans went wild, and as the final whistle went just after, gaffers Craig Brown and John Hughes exchanged wry smiles, hearty handshakes and warm embraces on the touchline to cap an exhausting, unforgettable match.

Then, at the weekend, as if in an attempt to undo the pragmatic value of incredible comebacks, Motherwell drew with Rangers while Hibs beat Dundee United, and the men from Leith took fourth place after all.

But the Well fans who stayed to the end of this match will always remember the drama and excitement.

And, because third-placed United went on to win the Scottish Cup, Motherwell qualified for Europe after all.

95

Saturday, 31 March 1928

The Wembley Wizards

In 1928, Scotland beat England 5-1 at Wembley, and – if it wasn't for Scottish over-elaboration as they started to toy with their flummoxed opponents, and West Ham keeper Ted Hufton's many good saves – the wee men in dark blue shirts and baggy white shorts played so very well that the score should have been even greater.

It was probably Scotland's greatest ever performance – English ex-player Ivan Sharpe said in the *Athletic News* that Scotland's 'play was as cultured and beautiful as I ever expect to see'. The *Sunday Post*'s match headline celebrated how the 'Scots' Wee Forwards' made the 'Saxon Defence Dizzy'. And it was totally unexpected.

Scotland had already lost to Northern Ireland and drawn with Wales in their first two matches of the British Home Championship. And the press and fans weren't confident when the selectors left out regulars Jimmy McGrory, Davie Meiklejohn and Bob McPhail and chose an inexperienced 11 for the England game, with an average of seven caps each. The front five were all short; Alex Jackson was the tallest, at just 5ft 7in.

Meanwhile, in defence, Tom 'Tiny' Bradshaw (his nickname was ironic) was making his debut and would be marking Dixie Dean, in the season when the great Evertonian scored 60 league goals. And the Wembley tie would be forward

Hughie Gallacher's first game for two months after he'd been banned for pushing referee Bert Fogg into a bath.

No wonder captain Jimmy McMullan's words as he told his players to get themselves to bed, after they'd been socialising with fans in the hotel bar on the night before the match, were, 'Pray for rain.'

It did rain. And on the day, Scotland's tricky wee forwards controlled the greasy ball better than their opponents did. Much better.

Eleven trainloads of Scotland fans had travelled to London for the match; some brought their own ladders to scale the Wembley walls. But the real trauma for England came on the pitch, and among those who witnessed it in the Wembley crowd were the king and queen of Afghanistan.

'Scotland conquered the English lads in as dramatic a game as it has been my good fortune to watch,' wrote 'Captain Bob' in the *Sunday Post*. 'The Scots made football look like child's play, and set the thousands of Balmoral-bedecked chiels roaring their encouragement.'

He added, 'One of the outstanding features of the game was the amazing anticipation of Alec Jackson when Alan Morton was on the ball. From the Rangers winger came the shriekingly inviting balls that gave Alec his chances. The Huddersfield man was in position every time. One would be justified in believing that Alan and Alec had arranged some mysterious invisible channel along which the ball should travel from left wing to right. We seldom saw a ball wasted.'

It was those two who combined for the first goal, Morton setting up Jackson to score with a header after just three minutes. A minute before half-time, Alex James – a friend of Gallacher's since their childhoods in Lanarkshire – made it 2-0.

It had been a great first half for Scotland. The second was somehow even better, as the Scottish masters of possession apparently effortlessly toyed with England's big defenders, who were left chasing shadows.

Morton set up Jackson again for goal number three, James got his second, set up by Gallacher, and then, following an England corner, as the *Post* – who described Scotland's relentless attacking as almost monotonous – reported, 'Morton at once pranced with the ball to the other end. [Jimmy] Dunn dribbled on a threepenny bit and gave to McMullan, who passed on to Morton, who lobbed to Jackson, who nearly broke the roof of the net with number five.'

They added, 'Long before the finish of the game the skirl of the bagpipes was heard from all over the stadium, and not even the torrential rain and the miserable conditions could damp the enthusiasm of Scotland's sons. At the conclusion the players were mobbed by the delighted admirers, who were beside themselves with joy.'

And then, in London that evening, 'At every street corner in the West End, in every restaurant, theatre and cinema the accents of Glasgow, Aberdeen, Dundee and Edinburgh were heard proclaiming the rout of the English at the battle of Wembley.'

Sadly that great performance didn't have much of a lasting legacy – except for the Wembley authorities installing barbed wire atop their walls – although Scotland did win all three of their matches at the next year's Home Championship, with Gallacher scoring an incredible eight goals in those three games. Not bad for a 5ft 5in man who saw the red mist with Fogg. And proof perhaps that the Scotland selectors did sometimes get their decisions right.

Saturday, 24 April 1937

The World's Best-Attended Club Match Ever

On 17 April 1937, Scotland and England set a European record attendance for a football match, as 149,547 fans packed into Hampden to watch Scotland beat England 3-1; a record that still stands.

But what's probably even more impressive is that – just one week later – 147,365 watched Celtic beat Aberdeen 2-1 in the Scottish Cup Final, the most people who've ever watched a club match anywhere in the world.

And thousands more couldn't get in – the *Glasgow Herald* estimated 20,000 – with most of the gates having to be closed 15 minutes before kick-off. Hundreds of those supporters rushed a closed gate and some managed to get in, before the police quickly restored order.

Inside, some fans were as luckless as those who were locked out. *The Scotsman* reported that they had 'gained admission to the ground but found it impossible to reach a place on the terracing, and became disconsolate figures on the outside of the embankments with nothing but a view of the Mount Florida district before them'.

On the terraces, there was swaying and crushing, and ambulance men had to treat 150 people, with seven taken to the Victoria Infirmary, but thankfully there were no serious injuries.

As Don John said in the *Courier*, 'Many travelled far only to be denied admission. Greater Hampden is still too small! The authorities must guard against similar scenes in the future. The day of the all-ticket final has arrived.'

After the match, SFA secretary George Graham did, indeed, announce that, in future, the final would be all-ticket.

Celtic forward Willie Buchan later described how he remembered 'the incredible volume of the sound that greeted us as we ran on to the field. I had never heard anything like it.'

So what of the match itself? Writing in the *Dundee Evening Telegraph*, 'Pivot' called the final 'more thrilling and satisfying than any in recent years'.

Aberdeen were playing in their first ever Scottish Cup Final, and still wearing their old colours of black and gold, before they changed to red a couple of years later.

But Celtic had the best of the play, and Johnny Crum turned home a rebound from a Jimmy McGrory free kick after just 12 minutes. The *Herald* said, 'Celtic followers had a Hampden roar all to themselves.'

But Matt Armstrong equalised for Aberdeen just a minute later; a goal that was met with a 'greater roar'.

The winning goal came 18 minutes from full time, from Buchan. He later described it: 'Jimmy McGrory flicked it on, allowing me to move in on the keeper from the right-hand side of the area. The two full-backs closed in and as the keeper came out, the goal seemed to become smaller. I just managed to squeeze the ball past him and in off the post.' Celtic had won the cup for the 15th time.

According to the *Herald*, 'Many spectators lingered to have a final look at the gigantic enclosure – evidently regretting that another season had come to an end – before they were shepherded towards the exits by the police. The litter on the terracing would have done credit to Hampstead Heath after a Whitsun weekend.'

Presumably the attendance would have done, too.

97

Wednesday, 11 May 1983

Aberdeen Win the Cup Winners' Cup

The previous 96 iconic moments in this book are in no particular order; this one and the next two, on the other hand, are the three most iconic moments in Scottish football. This one has only one rival (more on that in two moments' time!) as the most remarkable achievement of any Scottish football club.

A medium-sized club with a young manager and a young, mostly homegrown team, beat Real Madrid (and Bayern Munich) to win the European Cup Winners' Cup. And then, for good measure, they also beat European Cup winners Hamburg to win the European Super Cup too.

Alex Ferguson was just 36 when he became Aberdeen boss in 1978, in his first full-time position as a manager. Before that, Aberdeen had only won six major trophies in 75 years. In Fergie's seven years at Pittodrie, they won ten.

Ferguson instilled his players with formidable self-belief – by demanding the best from them and making them believe that they were the best. He got the best out of the players who were already there – including, notably, the solid defensive triangle of Jim Leighton, Willie Miller and Alex McLeish – and they won the league in 1979/80.

But Fergie was only getting started. He recruited Archie Knox as his assistant, on the recommendation of Jim McLean, to form a bad-cop, bad-cop management team, and promoted several talented youngsters to the first team.

Playing a fast, attacking game, combined with formidable strength, they continued to develop, and when they blasted three goals past Rangers in extra time in the Scottish Cup Final in 1982 – and then met Burt Lancaster during their celebrations, at Gleneagles – they qualified to represent Scotland in the European Cup Winners' Cup.

Fergie had taught his players to walk tall against any opposition. It was just as well. The other teams in the Cup Winners' Cup that season included holders Barcelona – with Diego Maradona and Bernd Schuster – Spurs, Paris Saint-Germain (PSG), Inter, Bayern and, of course, Real Madrid.

But first up, in the preliminary round, the Dons beat Sion 11-1. The Swiss part-timers' only goal came when Gordon Strachan lost the man who he was marking because he was busy having an argument with Knox.

Next came a 1-0 aggregate victory over Dinamo Tirana, with the away leg played in mid-30s temperatures, one day after a failed five-hour-long coup there by monarchists.

In the second round, Aberdeen beat Lech Poznań 3-0. Polish national boss Antoni Piechniczek said, 'Aberdeen have some of the finest players I have seen anywhere this season. Their defence was excellent.'

Five weeks later, the quarter-final draw was made, and Aberdeen's opponents could hardly have been more formidable: Bayern Munich, whose boss, Uli Hoeneß, said he would have preferred to face Barcelona or Inter than the Scots.

But the mighty Bavarians had Paul Breitner, who'd scored in two World Cup Finals, and Karl-Heinz Rummenigge, the European Player of the Year in 1980 and '81, in their team, and they basically never lost at home.

But Aberdeen were excellent in Munich, where they secured a 0-0 draw. Striker Eric Black later said that it was the best performance he was ever involved in: 'We defended like hell at times – we had to – but it was a fantastic night.'

Dons fans queued overnight for tickets for the home leg – in the Aberdonian winter. Club chairman Dick Donald gave them soup while they waited.

The home leg is remembered as Pittodrie's greatest ever night. There was an electric atmosphere but Bayern were leading 2-1 with 15 minutes to go, when Fergie brought on subs John McMaster and John Hewitt. Two minutes later Aberdeen were leading 3-2.

Alex McLeish got the equaliser with a header from a training-ground free-kick routine, then Hewitt got the winner on the rebound after the keeper saved an Eric Black header from a 60-yard McMaster pass.

Pittodrie erupted; Bayern couldn't find a response. There was a mini pitch invasion at full time. Perfectionist Fergie had an ominous message for the other three clubs in the semis (and yet another reminder to his players of the levels he expected from them): 'I think we can play better.'

He was – as he often was – right. Aberdeen beat Belgians Waterschei Thor – who'd knocked out PSG in the quarter-finals – 5-1 at home. Fergie had asked the fire brigade to water the pitch, to make the ball move faster, and the Dons were two up in the first four minutes. And they went through 5-2 on aggregate to meet the might of Real Madrid in the final, in Gothenburg.

Sadly, defender Stuart Kennedy suffered a career-ending injury in the semi. In an act of kindness, Ferguson gave him a place on the bench in the final.

The Ullevi Stadium was packed with more than 12,000 Aberdeen fans for the final. Many of them had got there on the *St Clair* ferry, which had been diverted from its usual route to make the due-east crossing, complete with three 20ft containers full of beer. Twenty-four extra flights were laid on, and the duty free shop at Dyce airport sold more booze in one day than it usually does in a month. Some fans sailed to the game by fishing boat. Others went on specially arranged coaches, with bunk beds, that took the long way round, via Dover, Calais, Hamburg and Norway, with hovercraft and ferry crossings.

The Real Madrid manager was the great Alfredo Di Stéfano; Aberdeen had their own globally respected legend with them, as Jock Stein came along to lend his support.

Before the final, the players stayed in a hotel in the middle of a forest, with quizzes and Scrabble to help them relax, while their wives were in a five-star hotel in Gothenburg city centre.

Midfielder Neale Cooper – who was 19 at the time – later remembered a characteristic piece of Fergie pre-match motivation. Cooper was preparing to face German midfield maestro Uli Stielike, and the boss's advice was simply, 'Don't worry about him; he's rubbish.'

The rain in Gothenburg that day was torrential. The pitch was only just playable. Aberdeen responded better to the slick conditions – most of the time.

Eric Black hit the bar with a fantastic scissor kick early on, and then, from the subsequent corner, put Aberdeen one up, after just seven minutes.

The Scots were on top for most of the game, but later in the first half came the only moment when they failed to cope with the conditions, as Alex McLeish underhit a back-pass and it got stuck in the mud. Santillana – who'd already scored eight goals in the tournament – was quick to react, and Jim Leighton brought him down for a penalty, which Juanito scored.

The Aberdeen fans were briefly quiet. It was tight and it was tense. Ferguson let rip at McLeish at half-time, McLeish reacted and Archie Knox had to get between them.

But in the second half, cheered on by the crowd in what was resembling a home game, the Dons were again the better side, and created several decent chances but couldn't quite make any of them count.

And then, with just two minutes left, Black had to go off injured. John Hewitt came on and the game went to extra time.

And – in the 112th minute – it happened. The greatest goal in Aberdeen's history. Peter Weir won possession in his half, beat two men and clipped it forward to Mark McGhee on the wing.

McGhee – despite being exhausted – drove forward, went past the full-back, focussed his attention and energy on getting his cross off the sticky ground and sent in the perfect pass.

Hewitt was in the middle, unmarked. Goalie Agustín hesitated for a split second, then belatedly came out. As Hewitt later said, 'I knew he wasn't getting to it, so I just had to make sure the ball made contact with my head, which it did. I wasn't sure what I was doing, I jumped up in the air to celebrate, my hands were covered in mud. Big Dougie Rougvie wrestled me and I don't remember much after that. Just jubilation.'

All those Aberdeen fans went crazy, and their heroes kept attacking. Stielike chopped down Weir, prompting an angry Archie Knox to confront the Real Madrid boss on the touchline – before suddenly realising that the man who he was going face to face with was the venerable Di Stéfano.

But the last chance of the game, in the last minute of full time, fell to the men in white, and thousands of Scots held their breath.

The *Madrileños* won a free kick 25 yards out. To a backdrop of nervous silence, Weir, in the wall, prayed to God to not let them equalise, because they didn't deserve it. Juanito took it quickly and Leighton saved it.

But Scottish relief was short-lived: the ref, Gianfranco Menegali, ordered it to be retaken because he wasn't ready.

José Antonio Salguero's blast flew just inches wide, with Leighton at full stretch. The Aberdeen fans roared in joyous relief.

Seconds later, it was full time. Fergie ran on to the pitch to celebrate but slipped and fell in a puddle, and Knox ran straight over the top of him.

In his post-match comments, Ferguson called the victory the greatest moment of his life. And he also made time to specifically tell McLeish how proud he was of him, despite their half-time barney.

Meanwhile, Di Stéfano, clearly not bearing a grudge against Knox, said, 'Aberdeen have what money can't buy – a soul; a team spirit built in a family tradition.'

In the 40 years since that day, Real Madrid have played in ten more European finals. They've won them all. Those 12 Scots – with an average age of 23 – are still the last team to beat them in a European final.

The players continued their celebrations in their hotel in the woods, while fans partied in Gothenburg city centre, and, back home, the supporters who hadn't made it out to Sweden drove up and down Union Street waving banners and scarves and tooting their horns.

And the next day, many tens of thousands – possibly 200,000 – fans turned Union Street, King Street and Pittodrie Street into a sea of red for the open-top bus victory parade, even though quite a few fans weren't back from Sweden yet.

At those celebrations, Fergie and Mark McGhee got into a bit of a fight over a misunderstanding, and on the Friday, McGhee went into Pittodrie to apologise, where Fergie told him to come to the dock with him – with the cup – to welcome returning fans back off the *St Clair*.

And the week's celebrations were rounded off on the Saturday afternoon at a jubilant Pittodrie, where the Hibs players applauded their victorious rivals on to the pitch – and Aberdeen thanked the men from Leith by beating them 5-0.

It was one of the top two achievements ever by a Scottish side but Aberdeen's triumphs that year didn't stop there.

The next Saturday they beat Rangers in the Scottish Cup Final. It wasn't a classic, and Ferguson – apparently oblivious to the fact that his team had just won two major trophies in 11 days – lambasted, on national telly, his team's performance as a disgrace. It was only once they reached their celebration meal that he apologised and the winning players could relax and revel in their success.

Later that year, *France Football* gave Aberdeen their European Team of the Year award. Only English, Dutch and Italian clubs have won that award more often than Scottish ones (Celtic also won it, in 1970, and probably would have won it twice, if it wasn't for the fact that it was only introduced in 1968).

And finally, five days before Christmas, in the European Super Cup, the Dons had a chance to get revenge on European Cup winners Hamburg, who'd knocked them out of the UEFA Cup in December 1981.

The first leg, in Germany, was a 0-0 draw, and Pittodrie was sold out again for the second leg, which Aberdeen won 2-0, with second-half goals from Neil Simpson and Mark McGhee. The next summer, Hamburg bought McGhee.

To be honest, the Super Cup trophy was more of a sad wee plaque, and Aberdeen's victory in it was less dramatic than their Cup Winners' Cup Final or quarter-final, but it was a contest between the winners of UEFA's two top trophies, and Aberdeen won it. They'd deservedly beaten Bayern Munich, Real Madrid and Hamburg in the same year, an incredible achievement for a young team from a small city and one that fully merits the two stars on Aberdeen's shirt that commemorate it.

Sunday, 11 June 1978

Great Goals 4: Archie Gemmill Scores Against the Netherlands in 1978

He pounces on to the loose ball, wide on the right. A gentle left-foot nudge takes it past lunging Wim Jansen.

He caresses the ball again, then swivels ever so slightly on his right angle, and glides – as if through a magical realist dream – with a third neat, apparently effortless touch past flailing Dutch skipper Ruud Krol. 'Good play by Gemmill; and again!'

With his fourth touch he seems to float wraith-like into the box, past Jan Poortvliet – the Scot's presence and movement, although direct, so delicate and precise that he seems somehow only semi-tangible.

A fifth touch, with the outside of that left foot, setting himself languidly in a split second as he shapes his body, and then – with the inside of his left – strokes the ball around and over the outrushing Jan Jongbloed. 'Three-one! A brilliant individual goal by this hard little professional puts Scotland in dreamland! The miracle is beginning to happen. They need one more to qualify!'

Scotland still had 20 minutes to play against the Netherlands. Archie Gemmill's wonder goal gave them a brilliant opportunity to snatch the most unlikely glory from the jaws of previously unremitting despair.

We don't need to go into too much detail about that despair here. We don't need to talk about the unwise hubris, the misguided pre-tournament victory parade, the broken-down bus, the hotel unhappiness or the failed drug test. And let's not mention the abject performances against Peru and Iran. Or even hint at the little dog that bit boss Ally MacLeod as if to poetically encapsulate the anything-that-can-go-wrong nature of most of Scotland's 1978 World Cup campaign. And it's probably best not to think about the fact that, apart from Argentina, no other teams at the tournament were good enough to strike fear into Scotland's talented squad.

The end result of all of those misadventures was that Scotland needed to beat 1974 finalists the Netherlands by three clear goals to get into the second round. Aye, good luck with that.

But – perhaps partly because they were now in Mendoza rather than Córdoba, perhaps because MacLeod had finally seen fit to play Graeme Souness – Scotland played as if reborn. Both teams had chances early on in an end-to-end first half, and Scotland's were the best.

In the first 20 minutes, Bruce Rioch hit the bar, a Tam Forsyth goal was narrowly ruled out for offside, a Kenny Dalglish goal was harshly chalked off for a foul, and Poortvliet brought down Joe Jordan in the box, but the ref waved play on.

It was the Dutch who opened the scoring with a penalty. But Dalglish equalised on the stroke of half-time with a beautiful finish, and Gemmill gave Scotland the lead with a penalty just after the break.

And then Gemmill scored that amazing goal. And it briefly looked like it could be even more than purely a snatched moment of skill and beauty. Scotland's unlikely challenge – beating the Dutch by three clear goals – was now just a goal away, with 20 minutes to get that last key strike.

But glorious success isn't what Scotland are best known for, and that 1978 campaign, which had been elevated from such lows by the performance in Mendoza and by Gemmill's goal in particular, would be no exception to that rule. Just three minutes later, Johnny Rep pulled one back with a 30-yard strike.

Rep's goal took the wind out of Scottish sails. The great escape was off, and the match ended as the most Scottish of glorious Scottish failures.

But Gemmill's slaloming run and sweet strike stand alone, elevated to a higher plane, and burned into the Scottish consciousness.

Irvine Welsh beautifully eulogised it in one of Scotland's greatest ever books, and Danny Boyle, Ewan McGregor and Kelly Macdonald did the same in the film adaptation.

It sits among great company as one of the best individual goals ever scored at any World Cup. It was like a particularly good Messi goal. But it wasn't Messi. It was another wee trickster, a hard little professional from Paisley.

Thursday, 25 May 1967

Celtic Win the European Cup

It didn't seem fair; everywhere that Picchi, Burgnich, Facchetti or even Mazzola turned, there were two, three or even four uncompromising Scots shutting them down. For once in his life, full-back Facchetti couldn't make his famous forward runs.

Every ball out of defence seemed to stick to a man in green and white. Celtic's attacks were as relentless as the Atlantic waves on the beaches a few miles away just to the north of Cascais. And the speed they were playing at!

And while the Inter players were focussing especially on the Scots who they were most concerned about – Tarcisio Burgnich in particular was not leaving Jimmy Johnstone's side, after switching flanks with Facchetti – it was becoming clearer and clearer that almost every Celt was a goal threat.

And the Scots kept switching positions and moving all over the place, with the forwards constantly dragging their markers out of position, making room for Craig, Gemmell, Murdoch and Auld to get into dangerous areas.

Striker Renato Cappellini had another problem of his own. If Inter ever managed to win a throw-in out on the right, glowering Celtic boss Jock Stein was there near the end of the long pitchside bench, an intimidating character in his suit and shades. Whenever Cappellini tried to get the ball back, the big

Scot was always ready with some sort of angry point to make in his gruff Lanarkshire accent.

The first half had been a bit better for Inter. They'd shut up shop and started playing on the break, as planned, after taking the lead from the penalty spot in the seventh minute – expertly dispatched by the great Sandro Mazzola, poignantly on the last ground where his father Valentino ever played before tragically losing his life in the Superga air crash.

But these young Scots – who seemed to be playing with freedom and enjoyment in this, the biggest game of their lives, the first ever British club in the European Cup Final – came right at Inter's two narrow, deep defensive four-man rows, and the Italian matinee idols mustered very few counterattacks.

The Scottish full-backs Tommy Gemmell and Jim Craig played like wingers – in a team that already had two wingers and two centre-forwards. The two midfielders, Bertie Auld and Bobby Murdoch, weren't shy about getting forward either.

But Inter kept that back door bolted, albeit only just. Auld hit the bar with a looping shot. Keeper Giuliano Sarti was far and away Inter's best player, making a string of saves, the best of them from a low Gemmell shot just before half-time.

Only once did Celtic's all-out attack almost backfire, when isolated goalie Ronnie Simpson had to rush from his box to control a long ball, which, under intense pressure from Cappellini, he calmly back-heeled to John Clark.

At half-time, as Giacinto Facchetti admitted years later, despite still leading 1-0, the Inter players were shocked: 'This was not supposed to be happening.' This was Inter's third European Cup Final in four years. They'd won two of the last three, and the clubs who they'd beaten to get to this one included Real Madrid. With their defensive *catenaccio* tactics they were extremely hard to beat. Before the showpiece, *World Soccer* writer Roger MacDonald's one-sided match preview had included the line 'When Inter win the final'.

It's perhaps unsurprising that some people had written Celtic off. The first 11 European Cups had been shared by just four clubs: Real Madrid, Benfica, Milan and Inter. Celtic's team had been assembled on a shoestring; Inter's was the most expensive in Europe. And this was the first time that a British team had appeared in the final – and also Celtic's first game against any Italian side.

But in the second half the energetic Celtic players turned the tempo even higher. At half-time, Stein – still outwardly calm despite the importance of the match – had three key messages for his players. He instructed Johnstone and Bobby Lennox to play more centrally, leaving the wings to Gemmell and Craig. He told all the wide players to use more low cutbacks into the middle rather than high crosses into the box. And, most importantly, he convinced his players that their chances would come.

Four minutes after the break they thought they'd scored, but Sarti made an incredible desperate save on the line.

In the 63rd minute the Celts finally got their reward. And what a reward it was. Jim Craig slotted a pass to his left at the edge of the box, where Tommy Gemmell was sprinting in, and, without breaking his stride, he blasted a fierce, unstoppable shot into the net. It was his 16th goal of the season – his fourth in the European Cup – in his 64th appearance. Not bad for a full-back. According to *The Times*'s Geoffrey Green, Gemmell was 'a big blond cat among the Italian pigeons'.

'Three times I shouted to Jim to square it to me,' Gemmell later said, 'but he held it, and held it, and held it. Finally he drew another Inter defender to him and decided to cut it back to me diagonally. I was about 22 or 23 yards out. It was a great pass, right along the deck, and the park was like a bowling green so it was just a case of timing. I hit it with my instep, as hard as I could. When I saw the ball hit their net, I thought, "That's it, we've got them now." You could see defeat in their faces.'

And, indeed, after that, for the last half an hour Celtic's dominance was absolute, relentless and irresistible. Their incredible fitness levels – thanks to the work of trainer Neilly 'Smiler' Mochan – were unmistakable.

Mazzola later said, 'When they equalised we were running about chasing shadows.' Even Sarti was starting to get flustered, and got into an argument with photographers behind his goal when they returned the ball too quickly for his liking.

In a few frantic minutes after the goal, a long Lennox shot flew just over the bar, the German referee, Kurt Tschenscher, gave Celtic an indirect free kick in the box when he should have given a penalty, and Sarti made two more great saves, from Murdoch and Gemmell.

The ball almost never left Inter's half again. Until Gemmell scored, the Italians had been defending through choice. Now they had no choice.

The momentum was all with Celtic, who were dictating a pace that was simply too fast for flustered Inter. Another shot flew into the side netting and Gemmell hit the bar about a minute later. Then Willie Wallace had another good penalty shout waved away and Sarti somehow saved one-handed behind his back – the best of his many stops – from a close-range Murdoch header.

And then, five minutes from the end, it finally happened. Murdoch fed Gemmell on the wing, Gemmell motored into the box, selling his defender several dummies, and cut it back to Murdoch on the edge of the area, who blasted in a shot, and Chalmers nipped in front of Picchi to get a touch and turn it past Sarti.

The thousands of Celtic fans in the crowd were cock-a-hoop, with their green-and-white flags and bobble hats. Jock Stein quietly slunk from the bench back to the tunnel for a bit. Through extensive meticulous preparation he'd managed to lift all the tension off his players' shoulders, but his own emotions were becoming unbearable. Assistant boss Sean Fallon later confirmed that both he and Stein were extremely tense throughout the match – although they'd done well to hide it from the players – and that Stein didn't want the players to see him crying with pride.

In the press box, European reporters congratulated their Scottish counterparts. A Swiss scribbler told Ian Peebles, 'It's wonderful ... Celtic are a team with eight forwards!' while a smiling French writer said, 'We must all play the game your way now.'

Now it was Inter who had to try and pick up the pace, but they had a big problem: they simply couldn't retain possession, and Celtic were entirely comfortable until the full-time whistle, when their players leapt for joy and hugged each other as thousands of fans poured on to the pitch to mob their heroes.

Simpson dashed to retrieve his hat from his goal, because it had lots of players' false teeth in it. It was about as flustered as he'd been all evening. Amid the chaos, despite being pulled in opposite directions by delirious fans, man of the match Gemmell was beaming, in Picchi's shirt and a supporter's green-and-white bobble hat.

The players made it back to the dressing room but then realised that they hadn't collected the trophy yet. Getting to it through the crowd wouldn't be easy. Stein appointed Simpson and Fallon as skipper Billy McNeill's bodyguards on his tricky journey to the tree-fringed stadium's neo-classical balcony. Simpson barely made it out of the dressing room before giving up and turning back.

McNeill later said, 'I had no idea where we were going. But Sean had his wits about him and he just pushed me through. You couldn't have had a better man to muscle you through a crowd than Sean. I still don't know how he managed it.' Fallon didn't really know how they would do it either, but the two men got there eventually – 'I don't think I've ever shaken so many hands or been patted on the back so often,' Fallon said – and McNeill became the first captain to lift that famous trophy, after Real Madrid had been allowed to keep the previous one, the 27-year-old from Bellshill looking every inch the victorious gladiator, before being escorted back to the dressing room with Fallon and the cup, by police car, with policemen who insisted on being photographed with the trophy.

Characteristically, Bill Shankly summed up Celtic's achievement more succinctly than anyone when he told his friend Stein in the dressing room, 'John, you're immortal.' Stein just laughed.

Before the match, Stein had said, 'We don't just want to win this cup. We want to win it playing good football, to make neutrals glad we've done it, glad to remember how we did it.' And, indeed, an elderly Portuguese official told him, after the game, 'This attacking play, this is the real meaning of football. This is the true game.' Stein placed a hand on his shoulder, smiled and simply said, 'Go on, I could listen to you all night.'

McNeill handed out the winners' medals – from a shoe box – to his team-mates at the post-match reception in a Lisbon restaurant later that night, where the Inter players applauded them; that was when they eventually arrived, after getting a lengthy post-match lambasting from manager Helenio Herrera.

Lisbon didn't have much love for Inter, especially since they'd narrowly beaten Benfica in the final two years earlier – in Milan. Few neutrals – and only a minority of Italians – were keen on Herrera's defensive tactics. Celtic's attacking style went down a storm, with many tens of millions watching on telly around Europe.

A Lisbon newspaper reported, 'Celtic won the match, the cup and the hearts of the public.' French magazine *Miroir du Football* said, 'Surely, never in the history of world sport has a team created as many new fans as Celtic, never has a victory been more warmly welcomed, nor a winning goal been greeted with such an explosion of joy throughout the continent.'

UEFA general secretary Hans Bangerter said, 'Celtic showed everyone that attacking football is successful and I hope their method of play will revolutionise the game.'

Herrera himself simply said, 'It was impossible to stop the onslaught of Celtic.'

Many years later, Inter defender Burgnich went further, saying, 'We just knew, even after 15 minutes, that we were not going to keep them out. It was a miracle that we were still 1-0 up at half-time.' And, like Facchetti, he admitted, 'Even in the dressing room at half-time we looked at each other and we knew we were doomed.'

On the day after the final, when the victorious Celtic travelling party got off their plane in Glasgow, Rangers chairman John Lawrence was at the airport to congratulate them.

Fallon later said, 'I actually think the part of the European Cup win I enjoyed the most wasn't Lisbon, but bringing the cup home to Glasgow and seeing the joy it had brought to so many people. That journey back to Celtic Park, with the streets packed and the stadium overflowing, will stay with me for ever.'

Steve Chalmers said, 'When we turned into London Road, we were greeted with the colourful sight of hundreds of people hanging out of their tenement windows and there were flags everywhere.'

Then it was into a packed Celtic Park, where the players clambered on to a lorry that had been hastily borrowed from local maintenance man Mr Stewart, for a joyous victory parade. You can be sure that Inter wouldn't have conducted their parade on a similar vehicle.

While fans who hadn't made it to Lisbon were celebrating in Glasgow, some Celtic supporters in Lisbon were having trouble finding their way back to Scotland, having made plans for getting there without too much thought about how to get home. The British Embassy had to help more than 200 people get back.

Those stranded fans might have been better hitch-hiking east to Madrid rather than north to Scotland, because, at the Bernabéu, two weeks after Lisbon, their heroes turned in another world-class performance.

Before the final, while the quietly confident Celts were relaxing at the opulent Palacio Hotel in Estoril, Stein had been given an invite to face Real Madrid in Alfredo Di Stéfano's testimonial. There was a strong suspicion that the Spanish giants wanted an opportunity to beat the team who they thought would win the European Cup, and consequently claim that they instead were the de-facto European champions.

Stein asked his players if they were up for it, and they jumped at the chance to prove themselves against another great team.

More than 100,000 fans showed up, and Celtic played so well that they won the Madrid locals over, just like they'd wowed the neutrals in Lisbon.

In a keenly contested match, reserve goalie John Fallon was excellent, but Di Stéfano's night undoubtedly belonged to Jimmy Johnstone, who gave one of his best ever performances, full of his best tricks and turns, earning the hearty applause of the home fans.

Bobby Lennox got the only goal of the game, set up by – who else? – Johnstone.

It was a fitting epilogue to an excellent season when Celtic won every competition they entered, with their incredible performance in Lisbon the undoubted jewel on that glittering crown: a European Cup Final performance that, 50 years later, Sir Alex Ferguson described as 'the greatest feat in football'.

Bibliography

Bannerman, C., *Against All Odds: The Birth of Inverness Caledonian Thistle FC* (Inverness: Inverness Caledonian Thistle FC, 1997)

Brack, T., *The Game on New Year's Day: Hearts 0 Hibs 7* (Edinburgh: Black & White Publishing, 2012)

Burns, P. & Woods, P., *Oh, Hampden in the Sun* (Edinburgh: Mainstream Publishing, 1997)

Chalmers, S. & McColl, G., *The Winning Touch* (London: Hachette Scotland, 2012)

Crampsey, B., *The First 100 Years: Scottish Football League* (Glasgow: The Scottish Football League, 1990)

Dalglish, K. & Winter, H., *Dalglish: My Autobiography* (London: Coronet Books, 1996)

Davies, J., *The Making of the FIFA World Cup* (Chichester: Pitch Publishing, 2022)

Gordon, R., *Glory in Gothenburg* (Edinburgh: Black & White Publishing, 2012)

Gordon, R., *Scotland 74: A World Cup Story* (Edinburgh: Black & White Publishing, 2014)

Hesse-Lichtenberger, U., *Tor! The Story of German Football* (London: WSC Books, 2002)

Hodge, I., *In Black and White: The Rise, Fall and Rebirth of Gretna Football* (Sheffield: Chequered Flag, 2015)

Macpherson, A., *Jock Stein: The Definitive Biography* (Newbury: Highdown, 2007)

McLean, J. & Gallacher, K., *Jousting with Giants: The Jim McLean Story* (Edinburgh: Mainstream Publishing, 1987)

McNeill, B. & Black, J., *Hail Cesar: The Autobiography* (London: Headline, 2004)

Morgan, J., *In Search of Alan Gilzean* (Glasgow: BackPage Press, 2010)

Peebles, I., *Celtic Triumphant* (London: The Sportsmans Book Club, 1968)

Rafferty, J., *One Hundred Years of Scottish Football* (London: Pan, 1973)

Reilly, L. & Brack, T., *The Life and Times of Last Minute Reilly* (Edinburgh: Black & White Publishing, 2010)

Rough, A. & Drysdale, N., *The Rough & the Smooth: My Story* (London: Headline, 2006)

Smith, T., *Gordon Smith: Prince of Wingers* (Edinburgh: Black & White Publishing, 2011)

Sullivan, S., *Sean Fallon: Celtic's Iron Man* (Glasgow: BackPage Press, 2013)

Turnbull, E. & Hannan, M., *Eddie Turnbull: Having a Ball* (Edinburgh: Mainstream Publishing, 2006)

Watson, M., *Rags to Riches: The Official History of Dundee United* (Dundee: David Winter & Son, 1992)

Wilkie, J., *Across the Great Divide: A History of Professional Football in Dundee* (Edinburgh, Mainstream Publishing, 1984)

Wilson, J., *Angels with Dirty Faces: The Footballing History of Argentina* (London: Weidenfeld & Nicolson, 2016)

Winner, D., *Brilliant Orange: The Neurotic Genius of Dutch Football* (London: Bloomsbury, 2000)

Index